COSMOPOLITAN MINDS

COGNITIVE APPROACHES TO LITERATURE AND CULTURE SERIES
EDITED BY FREDERICK LUIS ALDAMA, ARTURO J. ALDAMA,
AND PATRICK COLM HOGAN

Cognitive Approaches to Literature and Culture includes monographs and edited volumes that incorporate cutting-edge research in cognitive science, neuroscience, psychology, linguistics, narrative theory, and related fields, exploring how this research bears on and illuminates cultural phenomena such as, but not limited to, literature, film, drama, music, dance, visual art, digital media, and comics. The volumes published in this series represent both specialized scholarship and interdisciplinary investigations that are deeply sensitive to cultural specifics and grounded in a cross-cultural understanding of shared emotive and cognitive principles.

COSMOPOLITAN MINDS

*Literature, Emotion, and the
Transnational Imagination*

BY ALEXA WEIK VON MOSSNER

UNIVERSITY OF TEXAS PRESS *Austin*

First paperback edition, 2015

Requests for permission to reproduce material from this work should be sent to:
    Permissions
    University of Texas Press
    P.O. Box 7819
    Austin, TX 78713-7819
    http://utpress.utexas.edu/index.php/rp-form

♾ The paper used in this book meets the minimum requirements of ANSI/NISO
Z39.48-1992 (R1997) (Permanence of Paper).

LIBRARY OF CONGRESS CATALOGING-IN-PUBLICATION DATA

Weik von Mossner, Alexa.
    Cosmopolitan minds : literature, emotion, and the transnational imagination /
Alexa Weik von Mossner.
        pages   cm. — (Cognitive approaches to literature and culture series)
    ISBN 978-0-292-73908-6 (hardback)
    ISBN 978-1-4773-0765-6 (paperback)
    1. American fiction—20th century—History and criticism.   2. Cosmopolitan-
ism in literature.   3. Empathy in literature.   4. Cognition in literature.
5. Human rights in literature.   6. Transnationalism in literature.   7. Expatriate
authors—Psychology.   8. Expatriate authors—Criticism and interpretation.
9. Authors, American—20th century—Political and social views.   I. Title.
II. Title: Literature, emotion, and the transnational imagination.
    PS374.C65W45   2014
    810.9′0052—dc23

                                                                    2013046020

doi:10.7560/739086

FOR MICHAEL

CONTENTS

ACKNOWLEDGMENTS

THIS PROJECT WOULD NOT HAVE BEEN POSSIBLE at all without the generous help of a great number of people inside and outside of academia. I would like to thank Ira Allen, Thomas Austenfeld, Frank Biess, Boris Bugla, Ursula Heise, Marcel Hénaff, Nicole King, Lisa Lowe, Anne Reynes-Delobel, Bruce Robbins, and Don Wayne for their valuable feedback at various stages of the project's evolution. Michael Davidson was the one who first gave me the idea to concern myself with cosmopolitanism, and I will be forever grateful for his extraordinary support and excellent guidance. It was through Bruce Dick that I was able to make contact with a number of important scholars of African American literature who, himself included, gave me valuable input on the chapters on both Richard Wright and William Gardner Smith. Of those, I am particularly grateful to Michel Fabre, who welcomed me into his house in Paris and generously opened up his extensive private archive for me. Like all scholars in the field, I deeply appreciate Michel's seminal work on black American expatriates in general and Richard Wright in particular. We all will continue to profit from it.

I also want to thank Amritjit Singh, David Bakish, Edward Margolies, and Richard Gibson, who all have helped me greatly in tracking down information on William Gardner Smith. Richard Gibson was especially helpful because he put me in contact with Smith's family. My great thanks here go to Smith's sister Phyllis M. Ford, who gave me a warm welcome in her house in Philadelphia, and who provided me with a wealth of valuable information about her late brother. She was also the one who helped me to establish contact with Ira Gardner-Smith, who has become a wonderfully supportive friend over the past few years. Without these people, much of the information included in my chapter on Smith would not have been unearthed, and I am especially indebted to Ira for permitting me to quote from her late husband's letters and unpublished manuscripts. Part of my research was conducted at the New York Public Library, which generously gave me access to the Farrar, Straus and Company Files, and at the Beinecke Rare Book and Manuscript Library at Yale University, where the Richard Wright Papers and some of William Gardner Smith's papers are archived. I very much want to thank both institutions for their generous open-door policy and helpful staff.

My special thanks go out to Jim Burr at the University of Texas Press and to Patrick Colm Hogan, who has supported my project enthusiastically from the moment I first contacted him. I am also deeply indebted to Patrick's pioneering work on literature and emotion. Without it, this book would not have been possible. Mark Bracher was kind enough to share with me the page proofs of his own chapter on Richard Wright before it was published in his book *Literature and Social Justice* (University of Texas Press, 2013). My thanks also go to Leslie Tingle and Paul Spragens for their work in preparing the book for publication, and to Ryan Schneider, whose astute comments helped me to rethink some passages of the manuscript. In a different way, my understanding of the emotional dimensions of cosmopolitanism has greatly benefited from the extremely rich and lively discussions with that particularly bright group of graduate students at the University of Fribourg who enthusiastically took up the challenge of spending a whole semester on the exploration of the cosmopolitan imagination. And I certainly owe a deep debt of gratitude to my wonderful friends and family in the United States and Europe, who all supported my project wholeheartedly over the past years. Finally, I want to thank my husband, Michael von Mossner, for his unwavering emotional and intellectual support.

In its early stages, my project was supported by several generous grants and fellowships from the University of California, San Diego, including a UCSD Center for the University Pre-Doctoral Humanities Fellowship, a Humanities Dissertation Research Fellowship, and a Dissertation Fellowship from the UCSD Literature Department. On the other side of the Atlantic, a research grant from the Swiss National Science Foundation made it possible for me to return to the United States at a later time to conduct additional research for the book.

An earlier and substantially different draft of a portion of chapter 3 appeared as "Confronting *The Stone Face*: The Critical Cosmopolitanism of William Gardner Smith" in the *African American Review* (Spring/Summer 2012). Chapter 4 includes some material that first appeared in the *African American Review* (Fall 2007) as "'The Uses and Hazards of Expatriation': Richard Wright's Cosmopolitanism in Process."

COSMOPOLITAN MINDS

LITERATURE, EMOTION, AND
THE COSMOPOLITAN IMAGINATION

ON MAY 25, 1948, FORMER BROADWAY ACTOR and war veteran
Garry Davis walked into the United States embassy in Paris and handed
the authorities his American passport. He no longer had any use for identification papers, he declared to the perplexed officials, because from now
on he would live without his U.S. or any other citizenship—a free and
independent man. While dropping bombs on German civilians during
World War II, Davis explains in his 1961 autobiography *The World Is My
Country*, he had come to understand that the roots of war were inherent
within the nation-state system, built as it was on "division, aggressiveness,
fear and the terrible consequences" of those traits (24). As a result of this
recognition, he decided to reject henceforth all exclusive loyalties and, as a
citizen of the world, to give his primary allegiance to mankind as a whole.
This is what Davis explained to the rather puzzled American consul, who,
after some debate, followed the young man's wishes and administered the
Oath of Renunciation, thereby declaring him stateless. Determined not to
break any laws, Davis promptly went to the French Bureau d'Étrangers,
asking for a legitimization of his cosmopolitan presence in France. The
French officials, for their part, now showed considerable confusion. For
the time being, they gave him a ninety-day visa, which they stamped—for
want of better alternatives—on the very same paper slip that said Davis
no longer had an American passport or citizenship.

When, three months later, his French visa ran out, Davis took up residence on the grounds of the Palais de Chaillot, which had been temporarily declared international territory for the meeting of the United Nations
General Assembly. Camping out on the steps of the old palace, he became
an instant celebrity, and his claim to world citizenship, which he related
directly to hopes for perpetual peace and the prevention of World War III,
was the topic of many public debates. In France, prominent writers and

public intellectuals like André Gide, Albert Camus, Jean-Paul Sartre, and André Breton supported Davis's call for a world government. Even on the other side of the Atlantic, in those early days of the Cold War, his gesture had not gone unnoticed. The *New Yorker* acknowledged his project, writing, "Mr. Davis, whether he acted wisely or foolishly, is in step with the universe. The rest of us march to a broken drum," and *Life* noted that Davis had "aroused a deep longing for peace" (quoted in Davis, 55). Soon enough, Davis was showered with mail from all over the world, addressed to *"Garry Davis, Steps of the Palais de Chaillot"* and to *"Garry Davis, World Citizen, Paris"* (43).

These addresses, as well as many of Davis's deliberations, are strongly reminiscent of another, much earlier, world citizen: Diogenes of Sinope, the Cynic philosopher who famously declared himself a *kosmopolitês*— a "citizen of the cosmos"—and who chose to spend his life in a tub belonging to the temple of Cybele, a Greek deification of the Earth Mother.[1] Like Diogenes, Davis came to reject all patriotic ties and duties. His radical claim to world citizenship and the enthusiastic reactions it generated around the world are interesting in the context of this study because of the conditions of their emergence. Recent sociological approaches to cosmopolitanism rightly insist on the social and emotional nature of the development of cosmopolitan worldviews. Gavin Kendall, Ian Woodward, and Zlatko Skrbis suggest in *The Sociology of Cosmopolitanism* (2009) that critical and reflexive modes of cosmopolitanism emerge "from bonds of solidaristic sentiments and the imagination," while at the same time insisting on "the hard, real and socially-spatially located origins of such cosmopolitan bonds" (152). Davis's claim to world citizenship seems to have been the result of exactly this combination: on the one hand, it originated in the historical and political context of his time that made him a bomber pilot in World War II. On the other hand, it grew out of the waves of empathy and compassion he felt as an individual when imagining what the bombs he dropped did to the civilians below—regardless of the fact that the civilians in question were declared enemies of the American people. Allegiance to a worldwide community, as Elaine Scarry has noted, in part depends on people's individual ability to *imagine* other people, whose injuries they must conceive of as their own ("The Difficulty," 99). In the case of Garry Davis, the result of such imagining was an empathetic emotional response and, ultimately, the rejection of parochialism and a search for new and broader attachments, based on different communalities.

While the question of how much we can feel for distant others has been a concern of theoretical debates about cosmopolitanism since its inception in ancient Greece, philosophers disagree about the exact relationship between emotion and the cosmopolitan imagination. Stoic philosophers like Cicero and Hierocles famously developed *oikeiōsis*—a concept that maps our affections concentrically, putting our strongest affections at the center where they are closest and most familiar to the self, and placing progressively weaker affections toward objects or persons further and further away from the center. Seeing the natural parochialism of human affection as the central obstacle to a good and cosmopolitan life, the Stoics argued that rational agents must cultivate apathy toward the near and dear, that they must learn to resist *oikeiōsis* in order to collapse the circles and become true "citizens of the world." Indeed, as Graham Long has pointed out, it is not difficult to see "that emotions of anger or contempt toward those beyond our borders, or feelings of love or care toward more particular communities—our families, nations, or states," can potentially "undermine the force of cosmopolitan moral duties" (327). These good arguments notwithstanding, we must be careful to not jump to the conclusion that a cosmopolitan worldview is necessarily devoid of affect. After all, Garry Davis's move toward radical cosmopolitan ethics seems to have been prompted not by detachment and apathy, but by empathetic imagining and emotional engagement.

That he was thus motivated would probably not surprise Martha Nussbaum. Over the past two decades, this American philosopher has been the most vocal advocate of what Long has termed "sentimental cosmopolitanism": a version of ethical world citizenship that stresses our imaginative and emotional attachment to distant others (see Long, 317). In *For Love of Country* (1996) Nussbaum insists, with reference to the Stoic concept of *oikeiōsis*, that "Our task as citizens of the world will be to 'draw the circles somehow toward the center' . . . making all human beings more like our fellow city-dwellers" (9). This is a *task* rather than a natural process because it is much easier for us to feel for and with the members of our in-groups, a tendency that psychologist Martin Hoffman calls "empathy's familiarity bias" (22). Cultivating the imagination, both Hoffman and Nussbaum believe, allows us to have empathic emotions also for the members of an out-group, people who do not resemble us closely but with whom we nevertheless share many traits, not least the capacity to love and to suffer. The literary scholar Bruce Robbins, although critical of Nussbaum's universalism, at least partially agrees with this notion in *Feeling Global* (1999), arguing that "people can get . . . emotional," too, "with those who are not fellow nationals" (70). These positions stand opposite those of scholars such as Benedict Anderson, David Miller, Michael Walzer, and Benjamin Barber, who insist that one of the inevitable fallacies of cosmopolitanism is that we are biologically equipped to care *only* for those who are near and dear to us, which makes caring for distant others difficult if not humanly impossible.[2]

In the following pages, I will side with Nussbaum, Hoffman, and Robbins in this dispute, but look more closely at both the crucial role played by the imagination in the development of cosmopolitan emotions and the role played by emotions in the development of cosmopolitan imaginations. Furthermore, I will be centrally concerned with the ways in which not only direct experience, but also literary texts, can offer such engagements. As Susan James has observed, "it is not always enough to offer people good reasons for changing their beliefs, expecting their emotions to fall in line" (234); often, it takes strong emotional experiences—real or imagined—to move people to adopt a more cosmopolitan stance and to act on behalf of distant others. Since it relies centrally on our ability to empathize with fictional characters, in turn also cultivating our ability to empathize more generally, literature emerges as a particularly fruitful site for the creation of such emotionally powerful experiences.

Nussbaum has famously made the claim that literary texts are central to cultivating the cosmopolitan imagination and to developing moral feelings for others. In her view, such cultivation is bound to have significant effects on people's real-life choices and actions. "[T]he great contribution" of literature to the life of the citizen, she explains in *Cultivating Humanity* (1997), "is its ability to wrest from our frequently obtuse and blunted imaginations an acknowledgement of those who are other than ourselves, both in concrete circumstances and even in thought and emotion" (111–112). Scholars such as Suzanne Keen have problematized Nussbaum's belief in a direct link between the cultivation of readers' empathy and altruistic *behavior*, insisting that more empirical evidence is needed before we can make such claims (see *Empathy*, 92). We must indeed be careful not to overestimate the ability of literary texts to influence their readers' actions in the real world. At the same time, however, we should keep in mind that cognitive psychologists have already begun to produce empirical evidence of such influence (a point I will return to) and that there are also historical examples, such as the considerable effect of Harriet Beecher Stowe's sentimental novel *Uncle Tom's Cabin* (1852) on the American public.

There is also the fact that most politically engaged writers are convinced that their texts *do* have tangible effects on their readers. This was the case, at least, for the diverse set of American expatriate writers who will be considered in this book: Kay Boyle, Pearl S. Buck, William Gardner Smith, Richard Wright, and Paul Bowles. Each of these writers relied on what Keen has called *"authorial strategic empathizing"* ("Narrative," 83) in order to move their American readers to adopt less parochial worldviews. In their fiction and nonfiction produced during World War II and the early Cold War period, these writers explored the uses and hazards of physical dislocation and the sometimes violent shifts in understanding that result from an affective encounter with previously unknown people and places—shifts that lead to a troubled sense of belonging and often to new, cosmopolitan solidarities. Boyle, Buck, and Smith all demonstrably believed in the link between their readers' sympathy for fictional protagonists and their actions in the real world, and wrote their texts accordingly. Wright and Bowles employed a different strategy, manipulating their readers' empathy in ways that provoke feelings of fear, guilt, shame, and disgust, and thus a cognitive recognition of their own parochialism and morally questionable behavior. Reading the literary texts of these authors gives us a better understanding of how emotions can further as well as hinder the development of cosmopolitan imaginations.

One of the central observations in this book is that the relationship between emotion and the cosmopolitan imagination in fact extends in both directions. Strong emotions, whether they are triggered by experience, memories, or the imagination, tend to inform our "rational" judgments, and they in turn feed our imagination. If that imagination is shared, as a literary writer would do, it can in turn trigger the emotions of readers, feeding their imaginations and informing their judgments and decision-making. The theoretical foundation of this argument is provided by cognitive science, specifically by the work of neuroscientists such as Antonio Damasio and Joseph LeDoux, who have been telling us since the early 1990s that their clinical research suggests that we should see emotions not as irrational outbursts of feeling (and thus the opposite of reason), but as an integral part of our rational thinking and decision-making processes. As Damasio explains in his path-breaking *Descartes' Error* (1994), "emotion, feeling, and biological regulation all play a role in human reason" (xxiii). LeDoux similarly argues, in *The Emotional Brain* (1996), that "the struggle between thought and emotion may ultimately be resolved, not simply by the dominance of neocortical cognitions over emotional systems, but by a more harmonious integration of reason and passion in the brain" (21). These neuroscientific accounts also insist on the importance of both the human body and the environment in the generation of emotions. One of the concerns of this study will therefore be with the physical journeys to Europe, Asia, and Africa of the American writers it considers, and with the resulting emotional engagements that led them to reflect critically on American parochialism and their own obligations to others.

Most centrally, however, it will be concerned with the *emplotment of cosmopolitanism* and the way in which emotions form the very basis of such emplotment in these writers' novels, short stories, and nonfiction texts. Narrative, as Patrick Colm Hogan has convincingly argued, "is intimately bound up with emotion" and "even real life emotion is bound up with narrative" (*Mind*, 5). For this reason, it is important to investigate the ways in which literary texts are structured and animated by emotions, and I have found that cognitive approaches to emotion, which build on the insights of neuroscience and cognitive psychology, are particularly helpful for such investigations. This book will therefore employ a cognitive approach to explore the role of basic emotions such as attachment, lust, anger, fear, hatred, guilt, shame, and disgust in the development of the cosmopolitan imagination and its emplotment in literary texts.

My investigations into the relationship between literature and cosmopolitanism are perhaps somewhat less affirmative than Nussbaum's, and they also rest on a different theory of emotion. While Nussbaum, too, relies on cognitive research in her exploration of the relationship between emotion and literary texts, she embraces what is called an "appraisal account" of emotion.[3] Appraisal theorists understand emotions as the outcome of goal-related judgments elicited by conscious or unconscious inferences about changes in the likelihood of goal achievement rather than being directly elicited by perceptual experiences. In this account, we experience an emotion because we believe that a certain occurrence changes our prospects for achieving a certain goal, be it our own physical survival or the avoidance of pain. While this study will occasionally draw on appraisal accounts of emotion not only by Nussbaum, but other philosophers, including Robert Solomon, and by cognitive psychologists such as Nico Frijda and Keith Oatley, it will mostly follow Hogan's *perceptual* account of emotion, which is indebted to the work of Damasio and LeDoux.[4]

This approach, to which we will return in the second section of this introduction, aims to reconcile neuroscientific perception theories with appraisal theory, offering, in my view, the most convincing account of our emotional engagements with the imaginary worlds of literary texts. In studies such as *The Mind and Its Stories* (2003), *Affective Narratology* (2011), and *What Literature Teaches Us about Emotion* (2011), Hogan argues that because the literary imagination is bound up with emotion, it is useful to consider the two of them together. In *Understanding Nationalism* (2009), he argues that such consideration also allows us to get a better understanding of the narrative emplotment of nationalism. As the following chapters will demonstrate, the same is true for the narrative emplotment of cosmopolitanism. By investigating the role of universal emotive principles in such emplotment, *Cosmopolitan Minds* aims to offer a contribution to the growing body of cognitive approaches to literature and culture, while at the same time acknowledging the importance of specific cultural ties and particular attachments. Reading cosmopolitan literary texts from a cognitive perspective allows for a better understanding of how these texts use emotional appeals to resist the dominant ideologies of their time. Perhaps even more important, such a reading also leads us to better appreciate the crucial and complex role imaginative and emotional engagements play in the development of solidarities that stretch beyond self, family, community, and nation.

Cosmopolitan Minds is therefore also related to recent efforts to conceptualize and analyze "cosmopolitan" literatures of various origins, efforts led by scholars such as Timothy Brennan, Amanda Anderson, Jessica Berman, Rebecca Walkowitz, Berthold Schoene, and Robert Spencer.[5] Many of these scholars have turned their critical eyes to literatures other than American, and I am certainly not suggesting here that my selection of texts is in any way comprehensive or complete. But I do take seriously the claim made by Kendall, Woodward, and Skrbis, as well as by countless other scholars, that we must pay attention to "the hard, real and socially-spatially located origins" (152) of cosmopolitan imaginations and projects. Robbins insists on the multiplicity of such projects, defining individual cosmopolitanism(s) as "habits of thought and feeling that have already shaped and been shaped by particular collectivities, that are socially and geographically situated" ("Actually Existing," 2). Brennan has even argued that cosmopolitan imaginations can only be properly understood in the context of "specific national-cultural mood[s]" ("Cosmo-Theory," 661). For these reasons, this study focuses on American literature specifically, and on authors whose cosmopolitan imaginations seem particularly interesting. Given that such imaginations inevitably oppose what Paul Gilroy has called "the continuing dangers of race-thinking" (*Against*, 8), as well as essentialist gender constructs, it would not have made sense to limit the selection to a specific ethnic group or gender. As Ryan Schneider has demonstrated in his study *The Public Intellectualism of Ralph Waldo Emerson and W. E. B. Du Bois* (2010), a cognitive analysis of the cultural work performed by American writers who conceived of both race-thinking and race reform as emotive processes must almost necessarily cross color lines. In a similar vein, *Cosmopolitan Minds* explores both the important differences and the very interesting similarities between the ways in which American writers of different backgrounds go about the emplotment of cosmopolitanism.

As we shall see, American cultural formation played as large a role in the development of these writers' transnational imaginations as the cultures of the various host countries in which they lived. Like Garry Davis, they were all born as American citizens, even though not all of them kept their U.S. citizenship at all times. For reasons related to issues of class, race, gender, sexuality, and, not to forget, politics, they were all to a certain degree marginalized, and therefore "othered," in American society. Partly as a result of this internal marginalization, they all spent significant periods of their lives outside of their native country. They were all deeply affected by the events of World War II and the early Cold War period, and some of them, like Richard Wright, even felt prompted to support Davis's call for a cosmopolitan world government. In the face of war, genocide, and struggles for postcolonial liberation, they grappled symbolically with their American heritage as well as the emotional and intellectual challenges inherent in the development of a reflexive and critical cosmopolitan stance. Despite their transnational experiences and intentions, however, they—with very few exceptions—continued to write in English and for an American audience, even after decades of expatriation.

I have chosen to focus specifically on the cosmopolitan imaginations of *transnational* writers because I agree with Gerard Delanty that while transnationalization is not to be equated with cosmopolitanism—since transnationalism can exist without cosmopolitanism and vice versa—it "can be a significant precondition of cosmopolitanism" (83).[6] In the case of the five authors selected here, dislocation, and the resulting change of their physical environment, *were* central to the emergence of the cosmopolitan imaginations that we find in their work. In its focus on the work of American writers who lived and worked outside the nation, *Cosmopolitan Minds* also contributes to recent work in literary studies that reconceptualizes U.S. cultural production in its global context. As Wai Chee Dimock writes in *Through Other Continents* (2006), "Rather than being a discrete entity," American literature "is better seen as a crisscrossing set of pathways, open-ended and ever multiplying, weaving in and out of other geographies, other languages and cultures" (3). Different routes of transit, Dimock maintains, constitute "connective tissues" that "thread

American texts into topical events of other cultures" (3). The American texts under consideration in this book are a case in point. Not only did they emerge within the force fields of geographies, cultures, and politics of countries other than the United States, their cosmopolitan imaginations were the result of emotional engagements that were complexly transnational in nature, rather than parochial or simply imperial, as American engagements so often are.

The most pertinent argument, however, for understanding these American texts as part of world literature is that their story structures are built on what Hogan has called "literary universals" and thus on universals in human emotion. As Hogan explains in *Affective Narratology*, "the particularity of an individual work is at least in certain respects comprehensible only by reference to the ways in which it relates to a more general pattern. . . . patterns that recur across works in different traditions and different historical periods" (9). By paying attention to such cross-cultural and transhistorical narrative patterns, as well as to the ways in which they have been used by Boyle, Buck, Smith, Wright, and Bowles for the emplotment of cosmopolitanism, we are able to arrive at an understanding of these writers' works as cosmopolitan on the level of content, as well as on the level of narrative structure. After all, cosmopolitanism is often defined as a stance that affirms principles that are universal in their scope while also recognizing and even celebrating difference and particularities. Before turning to the narrative emplotment of cosmopolitanism, however, we should first give some more thought to the ways in which emotion has been theorized in the context of cosmopolitanism and intercultural understanding.

PAROCHIALISM, COSMOPOLITANISM, AND OUR FEELINGS FOR OTHERS

Although there seems to be general agreement that emotional attachments play a major role both in our parochialism and in our ability or *in*ability to develop cosmopolitan worldviews, a detailed study has not yet been dedicated to the subject. This is all the more remarkable given that the issue can hardly be avoided. Emotions—including pleasurable emotions such as love, pride, and sympathy, but also some less comfortable ones like fear, anger, and guilt—play a major role in both nationalist and cosmopolitan deliberations. Whether we consider political, moral, or "sentimental" cosmopolitanism, each of these conceptual approaches has to deal with questions of how much we *must* care for our "compatriots" and for our nation, and how much we *can* care for noncitizens and other others.[7] As Hogan has pointed out, "societies such as the United States are pervaded by practices that enhance the motivational force of national identifications" (*Understanding*, 9), and U.S. nationalist ideology historically has indeed tended to cast a particularly strong spell over its subjects. Being an American, as political sociologist Seymour Martin Lipset reminds us, has always been "an ideological commitment. . . . Those who reject American values are un-American" (31) and thus unpatriotic. While all nations tend to generate ethnocentrism and a certain notion of collective uniqueness—and as a result, have some sort of built-in resistance to cosmopolitanism—the United States has been, in Yi-Fu Tuan's words, "outstandingly ethnocentric, full of confidence in its own superiority" (73). To be cosmopolitan in the sense of building transnational solidarities—and in the sense of valuing other emotional attachments as highly as (or perhaps more than) one's Americanness—tended to be understood, especially during the mid-twentieth century, as an unpatriotic lack of appreciation for one's fortune of having been born an American. The question then arises whether U.S.—or any—national feelings can be compatible with a cosmopolitan outlook.

The ex-American world citizen Garry Davis would probably argue that they cannot. His brand of cosmopolitanism, after all, is predicated on the total rejection of any affiliation with a nation-state, and so he sees "only division, aggressiveness, fear, and the terrible consequences" when looking at the American flag (24). Contemporary cosmopolitan philosophers, however, are generally much less radical with regard to patriotic feelings. They often emphasize, as, for example, does Kwame Anthony Appiah in an essay entitled "Cosmopolitan Patriots" (1998), that "the cosmopolitan patriot can entertain the possibility of a world in which *everyone* is a rooted cosmopolitan, attached to a home of his or her own . . . but taking pleasure from the presence of other, different, places that are home to other, different, people" (91).[8] While Appiah's attitude here seems to speak largely to a cultural cosmopolitanism—an attitude that is difficult to distinguish from many versions of multiculturalism—he expresses a notion that is widely shared by those theorists who advocate what they call, like Appiah, a "rooted cosmopolitanism."[9] There is nothing wrong, they say, with loving and being proud of the place we are from, as long as we are also able to enjoy other places and people on their own terms, and are willing to accept that they love their home countries as much as we love ours. Rooted cosmopolitans—who "accept the citizens' responsibility to nurture the culture and politics of their homes" (Appiah, "Cosmopolitan," 92)—are often set in opposition to the specter of the *root-less* cosmopolitan, a radically independent being who has no home, no attachments, and no sense of responsibility.[10] Advocates of rooted cosmopolitanism often point to the "sociopathic" quality of its rootless variant, arguing that it is natural and healthy for human beings to be emotionally attached to their homes, their families, and their friends. They often assert that we cannot, and in fact should not, feel for foreign places or strangers in the same ways. It is indeed quite remarkable that recognition of the human need for emotional attachment and commitment to those attachments so often and so easily get translated into the double claim that "love of country" and a feeling of pride for one's fatherland are social necessities. This leads to the idea that empathy and solidarity that extend beyond that fatherland are against human nature and potentially dangerous for human conviviality.

Bruce Robbins has challenged this notion repeatedly and, I believe, successfully. In *Feeling Global* he takes up Benedict Anderson's famous claim that nations are "imagined communities" that develop a "deep, horizontal comradeship" (Anderson, 7), explaining that "If [national] culture is the domain of feeling, then for Anderson there is no culture of cosmopolitanism, only an elegant, decorous absence of feeling" (*Feeling*, 69). This, however, Robbins continues,

> does not, in fact, follow from Anderson's premises. Feelings are produced within a bounded administrative unit on a national scale, but it is not the bounds themselves that do the affective producing; the same sorts of feeling are also produced . . . by the sorts of connections now increasingly common on a transnational scale. If people can get as emotional as Anderson says they do about relations with fellow nationals they never see face to face, then why not with those who are not fellow nationals, people bound by some other sort of fellowship? . . . Why is it that Martha Nussbaum is forced to affirm so energetically that "the life of the cosmopolitan . . . need not be boring, flat, or lacking in love"? (*Feeling*, 69–70)

These crucial questions point in two important directions. First, it is more than doubtful that our emotional engagements have to be, or indeed ever are, bounded by national borders. Second, we should question what exactly keeps our emotional concerns confined within all kinds of boundaries or, conversely, allows them to extend beyond those boundaries. Before we address either of these issues, however, we must first ask a more fundamental question: what exactly *is* an emotion?

PERCEPTIONS, JUDGMENTS, AND EMOTIONS

As mentioned earlier, a number of contemporary philosophers have integrated the insights of cognitive science into their work on emotions, the appraisal theorists among them going so far as to claim that emotions should be regarded as cognitive *judgments* about the world.[11] Nussbaum, for example, takes what she calls a "cognitive-evaluative" view (23) of the emotions in *Upheavals of Thought* (2001), arguing that emotions evaluate as good or bad, beneficial or threatening, those occurrences and people we perceive to have importance for our own well-being. Emotion is closely related to belief and evaluation in this approach, which posits that once we change our evaluation of an object, we will change our emotions toward it.[12] Scholars like Peter Goldie and Ronald de Sousa have challenged the understanding of emotions as judgments, arguing that emotional rationality is not reducible to the rationality of beliefs.[13] In addition, Nussbaum has been criticized for relying too heavily on the Enlightenment notion of an autonomous subject when she asserts that individuals can change their emotions—even those that are socially induced—once they can no longer stand up to the (rational) criticisms leveled at them as a result of a changed understanding. While this critique is justified to a degree, most psychologists would assert that cognitive processes *do* play a role in the way we feel about things. Rather than rejecting Nussbaum's account entirely, we should therefore acknowledge that things are in fact more complex than she makes them out to be.

Robert Solomon, for years one of the most eloquent advocates of understanding emotions as judgments, admitted in a more recent piece that the appraisal account "lacks the keen sense of *engagement*" he now sees as essential to emotions ("Emotions," 77). This sense of engagement is explained more easily by what Hogan calls perceptual accounts, because they can encompass not only emotional episodes guided by our cognitive judgments but also more spontaneous and automatic emotional incidents and events. The perception theory that Hogan himself has developed is particularly helpful for my purposes here, because it aims to reconcile appraisal and perception theories and because it seeks to explain why we react emotionally not only to what we perceive directly, but also to things we remember or imagine. Given that both the nation and any transnational or cosmopolitan formation are by definition imagined communities, such an explanation is very much needed.

Hogan acknowledges the obvious advantages of viewing emotions as judgments. It indeed makes a lot of sense to claim that we do not react emotionally to things we perceive unless we have put them in relation to ourselves. Our emotions, Nussbaum claims, are not so much related to the identity of an object, but to "the way in which the object is seen" (*Upheavals*, 28). The sight of a stranger might not affect us in any way emotionally unless we make a judgment about whether or not he can endanger us, or whether he is in any other way related to the goals we have at that particular moment. However, it is not that simple. Hogan reminds us, with recourse to the work of LeDoux, that our emotional responses are not always governed by such judgments or appraisals. Meeting the stranger unexpectedly in a dark alley may make us jump even before we have made any judgment about the potential danger he represents. In fact, we might feel embarrassed once we realize that the man is our perfectly harmless next-door neighbor.[14]

Such instances of "delayed decoding" are of course central to our enjoyment of all kinds of literary and film genres, most importantly the psycho-thriller and horror film. But they do pose some problems for appraisal accounts of emotions, since strong emotional reactions occur before any specific cognitive goal-achievement-based judgments have been made.[15] On the other hand, it is clear that cognitive processes play an important role in the *experience* of an emotion, and that they may also *bring about* an emotion, especially when we consider emotional triggers that are not actually present, as in the case of memories and one's imagination. Hogan acknowledges that appraisal "is a crucial part of most emotional experiences," but he insists that it is "not the cause of emotion" (*Affective*, 51). Rather, emotions are triggered by what Damasio has called "images" (*Self*, 111), and these may either be images of something that is present, or memories of something that happened in the past, or the vivid imagination of something that may happen or is presented to us as fiction. "Whether 'live,' reconstructed from memory, or created from scratch in one's imagination," explains Damasio, "the images initiate a chain of events" as the "[s]ignals from the processed images are made available to several regions of the brain" (*Self*, 112). Appraisals can provide what Hogan calls "an occasion for emotion-generating (or emotion-inhibiting) imagination, perception, and memory" (*Affective*, 51), but they cannot produce the emotion itself. The most important point here is the explanation offered by this account of why we respond emotionally not only to directly perceived situations and people, but also to *imagined* plots and characters.

Appraisal theorists are likely to explain our emotional reactions to fiction in terms of simulation. Keith Oatley, for example, suggests that "*In understanding narrative a subject may identify with the protagonist of a plan, and the simulation can have many of the properties of real plans, including the property of eliciting emotions appropriately to the junctures that the plan reaches"* (*Best*, 108; emphasis in original). However, Hogan argues that this scheme does not really explain our engagement with narrative fiction, because our emotional response is in fact "not a matter of the probability calculations that go along with that simulation" (*Affective*, 55). Rather, it is "some version of an empathic response" (55–56) that is triggered by perceptual factors. That we respond to *fiction* is irrelevant in Hogan's account. Instead, it is a question of *vivacity*. Images that are in greater detail and that are more concrete lead to more forceful emotional reactions, while more abstract renderings lead to a weaker response, regardless of whether these images are remembered, imagined, or "real." I will further elaborate the consequences of this account for our engagement with literary texts in the section after next; for now, I want to consider its significance based on whether or not we are capable of feeling with and for distant others.

FEELING WITH AND FOR OTHERS

Robbins argues that if we can feel with distant others within the boundaries of a nation—which clearly seems to be the case—there is no good reason why we should not be able to do so in relation to others with whom we are bounded in different ways. Once we realize that emotions are the result of things we perceive, remember, or imagine, as well as of our cognitive appraisals of these things, we must assume that these processes play a central role in *all* our interactions with the world, regardless of national or other boundaries. A number of psychological studies concerned with intercultural understanding and solidarity have given thought to the role of emotion in such processes, and it is quite interesting to consider them in relation to Hogan's perceptual account.

Carol Gould, for example, maintains that a mode of solidarity that transcends parochial boundaries "centrally involves an *affective* element, combined with an effort to understand the specifics of others' concrete situations, and to imaginatively construct for oneself their feelings and needs" (156). Given Hogan's claim that our emotional responses to nonpresent and nonfamiliar situations or people are generated by our imagination (and that these emotional responses can in fact be elaborated by our emotional memories), we must assume that the affective element is in fact the *result* of the imaginative construction.[16] The more vivid the imaginative construction, the stronger will be the emotional response. The fact that Gould writes about an *effort* to understand the specifics of others' concrete situations suggests that there is a deliberate cognitive process involved in such constructions. Jean Harvey, too, argues that we should conceptualize "moral solidarity around the relationship of empathetic understanding" (27), while reminding us that such a relationship "does not 'just happen'" (35). Rather, "it requires active involvement with the other undertaken with a willingness to learn and to try to feel another's pains and joys" (35).

Cognitive processes thus play an important role in our emotional responses to distant others. We need to be *willing* to imagine their concrete situations and to subject ourselves to the perhaps painful process of feeling some of their feelings. If that willingness is lacking, we can avoid empathic pain by simply not making the effort. As Elaine Scarry has noted, imagined objects tend to lack vivacity in comparison with perceptual objects (see *Dreaming*, 4), and we are therefore less *compelled* to respond emotionally to them. However, as Martin Hoffman has shown—and as I will discuss in more detail in chapter 3—even when the object is present, an empathic response can be partially or fully inhibited by cognitive factors (see Hoffman, 34). This is why the German philosopher Hans-Georg Gadamer is correct when he argues, in *Truth and Method* (1960), that a certain amount of goodwill is essential for *any* successful interaction, *any* hermeneutic "conversation," between ourselves and others. Such interactions are important because, in Gadamer's view, they enable us to better comprehend not only our interlocutors, but also the prejudicial nature of our own understanding. Only the challenge posed by a text or another person, he claims, enables us to see as constructed what we have learned to see as natural, because it is "impossible to make ourselves aware of a prejudice while it is constantly operating unnoticed" (298). The problem, however, is that, as cognitive judgments, those same prejudices tend to make us somewhat or very unwilling to engage in challenging conversations in the first place.

Worse still, negative cognitive judgments are often supported by powerful emotions. As Karsten Stueber reminds us in *Rediscovering Empathy* (2006), we must consider "the whole range of . . . our reactive attitudes towards others, such as being angry, being insulted, feeling ashamed, or being proud" (209), which may further diminish our willingness to let our prejudices be challenged in a hermeneutic conversation. At the same time, these reactive attitudes also tend to interfere with our empathic abilities. There is often a deeply ingrained resistance to empathizing with another person—present or not—if the person in question belongs to another gender, race, religion, or nation. As Hogan has pointed out, such identity categories codify in-group/out-group divisions that tend to inhibit empathy toward the members of the out-group by developing negative prejudices about that group (see *Affective*, 248). Feeling empathy with a member of the out-group therefore requires a considerable amount of cognitive and imaginative effort, and the effort further increases with spatial distance.

These insights, I believe, can help us answer the question, posed by the work of Bruce Robbins and others, of how exactly humans can learn to stretch their solidarities beyond the parochial.[17] Part of the answer to this question is political, as addressed by scholars like Seyla Benhabib and David Held, who, focusing on issues of cosmopolitan justice, tend to overlook emotional ties.[18] The other part of the answer, however, lies in a better understanding of the role played by empathy and other emotional engagements in the development of cosmopolitan and transnational imaginations. This is at the center of what Graham Long calls "sentimental cosmopolitanism."[19] Long's central thesis is that emotions are needed as *motivation* for people to act upon the cosmopolitan moral principles they have already accepted. He believes that "sentimental" cosmopolitanism plays an important role because it "aims to reshape [emotional] attachments—to reshape *people*, if you like, so they are more responsive to cosmopolitan demands" (327). Long admits that such reshaping is a complex and difficult process, and he looks to Martha Nussbaum to answer the question of how it can be achieved.

Nussbaum suggests that humans can get some "outside help" to boost the vivacity of their imagination of others, and thus their emotional responses to them. In "Compassion and Terror" (2007), she calls for the cultivation of a "culture of respectful compassion" that educates children "through stories and dramas . . . to decode the suffering of others," which "should deliberately lead them into lives both near and far" (32). This implies a direct link between the kind of empathy we use in our engagement with literary texts and the kind of empathy we employ in our interaction with actually existing others. It also corresponds in interesting ways with Scarry's assertion that the "ordinary enfeeblement of images has a striking exception in the verbal arts, where images somehow *do* acquire the vivacity of perceptual objects" (*Dreaming*, 4–5). If literary texts can help readers create imagined objects that are as vivid and forceful as perceptual objects, then a perceptual account of emotion will lead us to expect an emotional response to the narrative that is similar to the one that would ensue in case of direct perception of the object. As Hogan has explained, whether an image is directly perceived, remembered, or imagined is irrelevant for an emotional response. What counts is the degree of its vivacity. The vivacity of the image alone, however, does not determine the *kind* of emotion we will experience. It also cannot change the fact that the reader may intuitively resist empathetic engagement with members of an out-group, real or imagined. For a story to reach beyond the boundaries of an in-group, it would need an element that reshapes human attachments in ways that would lead to an empathic engagement with the (imagined) members of an out-group.

Given the enormous diversity of literary texts, we should expect that such cosmopolitan stories come in all shapes and forms, and to some degree they do. It is interesting to note, however, that the example offered by Bruce Robbins in *Feeling Global* is an intercultural and transnational *love story*: Michael Ondaatje's Booker Prize–winning novel *The English Patient* (1992), in which a male-female romance is "being set against the stupidity of national belonging and national hatred"—an authorial choice that, in Robbins's view, is "specifically and self-consciously, if also temporarily and ambivalently, cosmopolitan" (Robbins, *Feeling*, 165). Robbins considers Ondaatje's novel in the context of his response to Benedict Anderson's notion of an "eroticized nationalism" that is characterized by "imaginings of fraternity" across racial divides (Anderson, 203). *The English Patient*, Robbins argues, is one of many literary texts that mark "the hesitant and equivocal emergence of an internationalist parallel: an eroticizing of bonds not just across different races within one nation but across different nations" (164). While Robbins makes an important point here, he neither pays much attention to the general narrative patterns that may underlie the specific plot of Ondaatje's novel, nor looks more closely at the ways in which the text appeals to readers' emotions in order to engage them affectively, as well as cognitively, in a narrative that opposes parochial claims. However, in doing so, we will better understand what *kinds* of stories encourage readers to stretch their imaginations and empathic attachments beyond the parochial, and what narrative strategies they employ. Hogan's work on literary universals and the emplotment of nationalism, I believe, gives us some valuable tools for such an analysis.

THE ROMANTIC EMPLOTMENT OF COSMOPOLITANISM

Much of Hogan's work over the past decade has been dedicated to the isolation of three cross-cultural prototype narratives—the heroic, the sacrificial, and the romantic tragicomedy—which are "literary universals" in the sense that they are "generated from the prototypical structure of our emotion concepts" and therefore bound up with universals in human emotion (*The Mind*, 11).[20] In *Understanding Nationalism* (2009), Hogan links these prototypes to the phenomenon of nationalism, arguing that, like metaphor, narrative "guides the way we understand and respond to the nation" (12). The heroic and the sacrificial tragicomedy, he demonstrates, are both well suited for the emplotment of nationalism and often have been used in its service. The romantic structure, however, is a special case. While, as Doris Sommer has observed with reference to Latin American writers, the romantic plot has also been used by writers to bolster nationalist projects (see 75), Hogan argues that such uses are in some measure undermined by the prototype's "antidivisive or incorporative tendency that tends to repeat itself with increasingly large groups all the way up to humanity as a whole" (*Understanding*, 20–21). The logic behind this assertion is as simple as it is convincing: Romantic love stories tend to pit two desperate lovers against a social system that opposes their love—Shakespeare's *Romeo and Juliet* being a prime example—and they usually invite us to empathize and sympathize with the lovers, not with the system that threatens to destroy their love. On the national level, such stories may call for the overcoming of subnational differences for the lovers' sake, but, as Hogan points out, "if romantic emplotment offers us an argument against regional subnationalism, then it must equally offer us an argument against nationalism. If it works against the oppositions among different racial groups in the United States, then it must work against the oppositions among different national groups globally" (21). For this reason, he detects in the romantic plot an intrinsic tendency toward internationalism, or, in the terminology I use here, toward cosmopolitanism. In fact, I believe that the term cosmopolitanism is more accurate than the term internationalism in describing the "antidivisive or incorporative tendency" that Hogan sees at the heart of the romantic prototype.

Given these observations, it should not surprise us that all of the literary works I will consider in the following chapters involve a romantic emplotment of cosmopolitanism, even if not all of the writers use the prototype's unique combination of emotional attachment and sexual desire as blatantly as Pearl S. Buck does in her intercultural love stories. As I will show in chapter 2, Buck was a master in what we could call the *sentimental* emplotment of cosmopolitanism, and it was this unabashed sentimentalism that made the Nobel Prize winner both one of the most successful American authors of all time and a persona non grata among literary scholars. However, we will see that Boyle, Smith, Wright, and

Bowles offer their own versions of romantic emplotment, pitting individual emotional attachments and affections against misguided social systems, thus opposing the racial, religious, ethnic, national, and other ideologies that work toward reinforcing in-group/out-group divisions. Boyle's engaged novels about the uncertain destiny of stateless refugees during World War II and Smith's sensitive account of the complicated relationship of the African American community in Paris with the Algerian War all rely on the emotional power of the romantic tragicomedy to articulate affect-driven forms of cosmopolitan ethics that value transnational solidarity and cooperation.

Even though we would not immediately connect the work of Richard Wright or Paul Bowles with the notion of the romantic love story, some of the prototype's central features are prominent in their narratives as well. Wright's angry professions of radical independence and detachment tend to collapse on themselves because of an existential need for love and attachment. Bowles's gruesome tales of Western encounters with North Africa dramatize the confusing maze of curiosity, attachment, lust, fear, and disgust that often marks romantic engagements with "exotic" others, alerting American readers to the fatal consequences of their naïve parochialism. Despite their great differences in other terms, these American writers are united not only by their literary engagements with the members of one or several out-groups; a further point of connection is a focus on individual relationships of attachment and an explicit resistance to American nationalist ideology.

These, of course, are exactly the elements mentioned by Robbins when he writes about the cosmopolitan aspect of Ondaatje's *The English Patient*. He thus indirectly affirms Hogan's claim about the "antidivisive or incorporative tendency" of the romance plot and his assertion that "the tacit romantic emplotment of politics tends, not toward nationalism but toward internationalism" (*Understanding*, 21). Indeed, Robbins himself notes that, in *The English Patient*, we find "Small signs, perhaps, that cynicism about the nation and its representatives is lurching unsteadily toward some alternative moral code, in which love and internationalism will at last be coupled" (*Feeling*, 168). Robbins takes pains to stress the "unsteady" nature of such an "alternative moral code," which unites emotions of attachment and affection with the openness of internationalism. But this code nevertheless roughly corresponds to what Nussbaum has called "ethical cosmopolitanism": "an overall ethical doctrine about how people should organize their loyalties in a world where we have many types of local attachment, and in which strangers at a distance also seem to demand our ethical concern" ("Capabilities," 403). In Nussbaum's view, reading novels such as *The English Patient* will not only help "to wrest from our frequently obtuse and blunted imaginations an acknowledgement of those who are other than ourselves" (*Cultivating*, 111–112); it will also help us become moral actors in the real world. Since there is a good deal of disagreement about this particular quality of literary texts, as mentioned earlier, I want to dedicate the final section of this introduction to a brief discussion of the debate, primarily because the issue has a high degree of relevance to all the writers who will be discussed in later chapters.

COSMOPOLITAN LITERATURE AND MORAL ACTION

For a philosopher, Nussbaum has a remarkably steadfast belief in the positive social impact of literary texts. In her view, "narrative imagination is an essential preparation for moral interaction" (*Cultivating*, 90), and a cultivation of literary empathy quasi-automatically leads to the cultivation of social empathy. Nussbaum even considers it "impossible to care about the characters" imagined by realist writers like Charles Dickens and George Eliot "in the way the text invites, without having some very definite political and moral interests awakened in oneself" (104). Not only is reading literary texts envisioned as a beneficial activity for those who want to cultivate their understanding of various others, but literature also becomes a central element in the education of the responsible citizen within and beyond the nation. Nussbaum's great trust in the vital role of literature in "cultivating powers of imagination that are essential to citizenship" (85) is bound to discomfit scholars in literary studies. Narrative description has been understood, at least since Foucault, as a potential means of control and domination, and Marxist scholars like Fredric Jameson have argued that literary texts have a "political unconscious" that is the product of successive layers of political repression.[21] Many poststructuralists, moreover, would simply doubt that literature can "cultivate" anything in such foreseeable ways. The most interesting aspect in the given context, however, is the critique of Nussbaum's claims by cognitive literary scholars who have engaged directly with their psychological and narratological dimensions.

Suzanne Keen's *Empathy and the Novel* (2007) is particularly interesting in this regard, because it concerns itself in great detail with the novel's potential ability to stir readers to social and political action in the real world. Keen in fact agrees with Nussbaum that readers feel both empathy with and sympathy (or compassion) for fictional characters, as well as with and for other aspects of fictional worlds. Empathy, she demonstrates, is central to our understanding of narrative *in general*, be it the narrative of a sentimental, popular novel or a highly experimental, modernist text. Keen thus happily affirms "the robustness of narrative empathy, as an affective transaction accomplished through the writing and reading of fiction" (xv). The problem she sees with Nussbaum's argument is that only "scant evidence exists for active connections among novel reading, experiences of narrative empathy, and altruistic action on behalf of real people" (xiv).[22] Having experienced strong emotions while reading a novel about the fate of another human being, readers may simply search for the next immersive reading experience rather than acting on behalf of similar humans in the real world.

These are not the only potential problems involved in the claim that empathetic reading leads to more cosmopolitan attitudes and behaviors in the real world. As Keen explains, critiques of empathy by feminist, postcolonial, and critical-race scholars point to the potential danger of "the empathetic individual's erasure of suffering others in a self-regarding emotional response that affronts others' separate personhood" (xxiv). In this reading, which corresponds to the warning from Karsten Stueber mentioned above, empathy is regarded as a typical manifestation of Western arrogance, which in fact "occludes the other's true feelings by imposing Western ideas about what ought to be felt" (Keen, *Empathy*, 142). This is related to the general suspicion toward ethical readings of literature that has pervaded literary criticism throughout much of the past century. As Marjorie Garber, Beatrice Hanssen, and Rebecca Walkowitz remind us in *The Turn to Ethics* (2000), ethical approaches in fact form a long tradition in literary criticism, dating back to at least the eighteenth century. With the rise of poststructuralism in the 1970s, however, such approaches were seen as part of a problematic Western "master discourse" that "presumed a universal humanism and an ideal, autonomous and sovereign subject" (viii). This was especially true for concepts of cosmopolitan conviviality and intercultural understanding, which were considered Western and imperialist in their "ethics" rather than truly cosmopolitan.[23]

Over the past two decades, however, literary scholars have begun to reconsider the potential value of ethics, partially as a result of the ideas and influence of Emmanuel Lévinas. In Lévinas's understanding, ethics becomes an existential, dialogical process, with the obligation toward the "Other" holding the highest possible value.[24] New approaches to ethics thus tend to foreground plurality, diversity, and difference instead of unified systems of knowledge and belief. While the universalist and naïvely subject-centered bias of ethics has thus been partially transformed, contemporary scholars have not simply done away with the subject. In a 2008 article, Hubert Zapf explains that one of the issues that has found attention in interdisciplinary debates on ethics involves "the ways in which literature, as a form of knowledge that is always mediated through personal perspectives, reflects the indissoluble connection between ethics and the human subject, a subject, however, not understood as a mere cognitive ego but a concrete, bodily self implicated in multiple interrelationships" (853).

This notion of an embodied self that is caught up in various and complex relationships with the world is central to my understanding, in *Cosmopolitan Minds*, of the cosmopolitan literary imagination. Ethics, as Garber, Hanssen, and Walkowitz point out, "is a process of formulation and self-questioning that continually rearticulates boundaries, norms, selves, and 'others'" (viii), and some of this self-questioning and rearticulation may take place within and with the help of literary texts. Scholars such as Nussbaum and Wayne Booth have asserted that such imaginative reworking may also resonate in the social world in which these texts are produced, and while the objections I have mentioned above must be kept in mind, there is also some evidence in favor of this assertion.[25] Despite her skeptical stance in *Empathy and the Novel*, Keen acknowledges that there are certain factors that "give pause to the skeptic who would argue that literature makes nothing happen" (xxv). For example, what Keen calls "empathetic fiction" tends to reach a much wider audience because many readers prefer emotionally engaging stories. There is also "the perseverance of novelists" (xxv), such as those under consideration in this book, who believe that their emotionally engaging literary texts can have an effect on the real world.

To these two factors, we must add a third: that empirical evidence for connections between novel reading and real-world action is growing. The recent work of Keith Oatley is of particular interest here. Oatley agrees with Keen that the impact of fiction "is largely emotional" ("Emotions," 41), but he also asserts, as Booth had already claimed in the late 1980s, that reading fiction can give us the sense that we are entering into a new relationship with an author, a narrator, and/or any number of characters. Like other relationships, these literary relationships "can potentially transform us" (42). In another recent piece, Oatley goes so far as to propose that "emotion recognition, in ourselves and others, is a skill," further suggesting "that by reading literary fiction, we can practice and improve it" ("Communications," 206). Empirical studies conducted by Oatley and various collaborators support this proposition.[26] Writers may thus not be entirely mistaken when they hope that their literary texts will have some effect on their readers' attitudes and behaviors in the real, social world. The cognitive literary scholar Mark Bracher has even argued that "literature emerges as a privileged site for promoting social justice" because it can help correct "the faulty cognitive structures that are ultimately responsible for injustice" (xiii). Bracher argues that (some) literary texts are particularly well suited to foster such corrections because "they engage readers in repeatedly performing more adequate routines for processing information about other people" (xiii).[27] Of course, empathy and emotion play an important role in the performance of such "routines," as they do in our willingness—or even desire—to engage with literary texts in the first place.

We are therefore looking at a complex interaction among sociocultural conditions, individual authorial engagements, literary texts, and readers, and such complexity demands an interdisciplinary approach. Sociologists Shai Dromi and Eva Illouz have recently suggested that a dialogue among sociological, psychological, and literary approaches is helpful for studying the complex role of texts in the social articulation of ethical and moral standpoints. In their view, "A novel which exposes the reader to a sense of injustice or to a dilemma and which imbues these dilemmas and injustices with emotional value is not only a work of fiction but what we may call a *critique*" (352). The role of a literary text in civil society, they explain, is twofold. First, a text can itself serve as a critique of the social world in which it is produced. Second, individual members of the reading public, which include "common readers, popular reviewers, and high-brow critics" (353), voice their own critiques of such literary texts and, by extension, of their own social world. These multiple critiques, whether they are voiced by authors or by readers and reviewers who have processed these texts, express the concern of various speakers with what they perceive "to be the greater good of society" (353). Dromi and Illouz's interdisciplinary approach is particularly useful because they include the *authors* of literary texts in their exploration of how moral and ethical standards are formed and transformed through the production and consumption of literature. Understanding literary texts as "critiques" allows us to conceptualize them as modes of communication among various actors within a transnational public sphere.

EMPLOTTING COSMOPOLITANISM IN COLD WAR LITERATURE

There is something very helpful about understanding cultural products as one of many modes of critique that are always mediated by previously held attitudes and attachments.[28] If we want to better understand certain

forms of American literary cosmopolitanism of the early Cold War period, we should thus pay close attention to the sociocultural conditions in
which these forms emerged. Kendall, Woodward, and Skrbis rightly insist
that cosmopolitanism as a social and cultural condition exists in a complex relationship with the cosmopolitan individual; however, I would argue that this relationship does not necessarily have to be "mutually nour-
ishing" (7), as the authors suggest. The American ideological climate in
the mid-twentieth century was in fact actively *discouraging* of individual cosmopolitan projects bound to transcend the physical and ideological boundaries of the American nation. At the same time, however, the
stark inequalities and social tensions within American society seem to
have opened up possibilities for individual cosmopolitan development for
those who were not fully incorporated into the American national project.

Prominent among these inequalities and tensions have been racial, gender, and sexual discrimination, and, during the mid-twentieth century, the
discrimination against communists.[29] As I shall argue, these decidedly *un-*
cosmopolitan conditions in the United States furthered the development
of cosmopolitan imaginations, and not least because they produced strong
emotional reactions *against* the prevailing order and a certain openness to
alternative points of view and cultural practices. This was at least the case
for Boyle, Buck, Smith, Wright, and Bowles, all of whom, for various reasons, felt marginalized in American society and thus developed an incom-
plete and troubled sense of belonging that prompted them to seek experiences outside of their home country, experiences that profoundly changed
their self-understanding and creative imagination.

For an understanding of the emotional dimensions of cosmopolitanism, and the role of literature in it, it is imperative to pay close attention
to the cosmopolitan critiques that these writers voiced in individual texts.
The narratives I have selected for this study seek to engage their readers'
emotions through a romantic emplotment of cosmopolitanism. As literary imaginings, they are expressions of their authors' strategic empathizing, and by necessity, they also bear traces of these authors' own emotional entanglements. Keen notes that empathetic fiction is often "written
by women, racial and ethnic minorities, and postcolonial citizens" (*Empathy*, xxiv), so it is perhaps no coincidence that empathetic fiction was
the "weapon of choice" for all of the writers I will consider in the following chapters. Whether they concerned themselves with transnational
love and compassion or with more negative emotions, such as fear, anger,
guilt, shame, and disgust, which can complicate, prevent, or even further
cosmopolitan solidarities, they all foreground the importance of emotion

in their characters' engagements beyond the American nation. In one way or another, they all suggest that the communication with, understanding of, and feelings for others rely on a complex dialectic, one in which historically situated emotional developments interact constantly with rational deliberations and the imagination to produce deeper insights and new commitments. For this reason, these narratives enact aspects of imaginative and emotional engagement that are relevant to contemporary theories of cosmopolitanism.

Each of the following chapters examines a different American writer and a different aspect of emotional literary engagements across borders. Examining the work of Kay Boyle, the first chapter explores in more depth the role of empathy and sympathy in not only the reading but also the writing of literary texts. It pays particular attention to Keen's concept of *authorial strategic empathizing*, which explains well the way in which not only Boyle but all authors under consideration in this book consciously crafted their texts in order to stretch their readers' empathy beyond parochial borders. Boyle's personal experiences in war-torn Europe and her deep emotional entanglement with stateless refugees led her to imaginatively engage with questions of citizenship and human rights. In novels like *Primer for Combat* (1942) and *1939* (1948), Boyle demonstrates her thorough understanding of the legal and humanitarian consequences that spring from the binding of the "Rights of Man" to citizenship in a nation-state. I suggest that these novels offer readers imaginative and emotionalizing engagement with an issue that was at the center of cosmopolitan philosophical and political debates after World War II. Boyle's trenchant critique of a human-rights concept that treats a human being as a citizen *first*, and only then as a person, powerfully resonates not only with Hannah Arendt's *The Origins of Totalitarianism* (1951), but also with the work of contemporary political theorists like Seyla Benhabib, Giorgio Agamben, and Jacques Rancière, who consider the legal consequences attendant upon forced displacement today. Boyle's literary imagination powerfully demonstrates that caring for the rights of others necessarily involves empathic and emotional engagement.

The second chapter uses the literary work of Pearl S. Buck for an exploration of the question of whether there can be a successful *sentimental* emplotment of cosmopolitanism. It considers the alleged "gratuitousness" of sentimental emotions, drawing on the work of cognitive film scholars and psychologists such as Ed Tan, Nico Frijda, and Carl Plantinga to explore the suitability or unsuitability of such "excessive" emotions for a romantic emplotment of cosmopolitanism. Buck's sentimental novels about interracial love and intercultural understanding provide a particularly interesting ground for such exploration. Though she won the 1938 Nobel Prize for Literature, literary scholars still tend to dismiss Buck as a mediocre writer of popular fiction. I argue that such a dismissal overlooks not only her interesting cultural position, but also the complex cosmopolitan engagement displayed in much of her work. Growing up as a child of Southern Presbyterian ministers in rural China, Buck became what David Pollock and Ruth Van Reken have termed a Third Culture Kid: a person whose childhood is spent navigating different cultural worlds and who builds emotional relationships with all of them, while not having full ownership of any. As I will demonstrate, her transcultural upbringing and her emotional engagement with what she called her "several worlds" shaped Buck's sentimental cosmopolitanism as well as her highly successful literary style.

Chapter 3 considers the importance of *sensitivity* and *empathic guilt* in the cosmopolitan novels of William Gardner Smith. Exploring the complex relationship between an increased empathic responsiveness and the development of what psychologist Martin Hoffman calls "bystander guilt over inaction" (102), it argues that this relationship is crucial for the processes of self-reflection that scholars in sociology and political theory have put at the heart of concepts of critical, reflexive, and "thick" cosmopolitanism. Smith's 1963 novel *The Stone Face* is interesting in this context, because it demonstrates that empathic guilt can arise in response to direct perceptions as well as to memories and imaginations, and that it is a vital component in the emergence of the critical cosmopolitan imagination. A relatively little-known African American writer, Smith belonged to the black expatriate community in Paris during the 1950s and 1960s, and also spent some time in Kwame Nkrumah's Ghana. Another example for the romantic emplotment of cosmopolitanism, *The Stone Face* deals openly with both the debilitating effects of American racist ideology and the complicated relationship the African American expatriate community in Paris had to the Algerian War. Linking black, Jewish, and Algerian histories of oppression, Smith's novel is a powerful reminder that cosmopolitan solidarities across national, ethnic, and religious boundaries must be motivated by an empathic engagement with others.

The fourth chapter looks at the powerful emotions that led another African American writer, Richard Wright, to abandon his country, arguing that his repeated professions of radical independence and (racial) rootlessness must be seen in relationship to the anger he felt toward the American "home" he both passionately loved and despised. The chapter explores the negative and often debilitating emotions that tend to dominate Wright's novels—*fear*, *anger*, and *shame*—and looks at his reflective essay "How 'Bigger' Was Born" (1940) to demonstrate the centrality of such emotions in the creation of his influential first novel, *Native Son* (1940). It then turns to Wright's second novel, *The Outsider* (1953), as another intriguing example of the romantic emplotment of cosmopolitanism. Like *Native Son*, *The Outsider* features a protagonist who is driven by fear and anger, but unlike *Native Son*'s Bigger Thomas, Cross Damon is also tormented by *transgression guilt* and remorse. The latter emotions, which are a direct result of the novel's love story, are what allow Cross to move away from radical and murderous solipsism toward an understanding of the importance of human community. Both novels force readers into an uneasy alliance with black protagonists who, as a result of American racial politics, have become insensate and ruthless "monsters" with no regard for human life. In his final and unpublished novel "Island of Hallucination," Wright uses a different rhetorical strategy. Here, the black monster is even more "monstrous" as a result of its life in the United States, but it is no longer the protagonist and thus no longer invites readers' empathic alignment. My focus in the discussion of all three novels is on the ways in which Wright aligns readers with morally transgressive protagonists and their negative emotions in order to promote cosmopolitan ethics.

Chapter 5 investigates the role of *disgust*, *horror*, and *fascination* in the literary imagination of Paul Bowles and the meaning of disgust, specifically, for the narrative emplotment of cosmopolitanism. It considers both the physical disgust we experience in response to inanimate objects that we perceive as threatening, and the sociomoral disgust we sometimes feel in relation to the members of ethnic, national, or religious out-groups. In this context, I explore what Noël Carroll has called the "paradox of horror" (10): the seeming contradiction that we can actually enjoy literary passages or film scenes that induce strong negative emotions such as fear, disgust, and horror. Bowles was a master of horror. A longtime expatriate in Morocco, he used his fiction to explore various Orientalisms, confronting his naïve American protagonists with environments that are alien and threatening to them. I will look at Bowles's short story "A Distant Episode" (1947) and his first novel, *The Sheltering Sky* (1949), as pertinent examples of his strategic use of readers' disgust for a shocking revelation of the possibly horrific consequences of cultural ignorance and supremacist arrogance. *The Sheltering Sky*, I will argue, is yet another example of the romantic emplotment of cosmopolitanism, but one that produces highly uncomfortable emotions in readers as they mentally simulate the divergent fates of its three American travelers in the Sahara desert. In his exploration of the complex relationships between imagined and physical interactions with foreign environments and cultural others, Bowles suggests that the emotional knowledge acquired by the traveling body of the would-be cosmopolitan can be both enlightening and fatal. In its intensive engagement with North African culture, his work offers a complex perspective on cosmopolitan engagement—and its limits.

I intend this book, then, as a contribution to cognitive literary and cultural studies in two ways. It puts cognitive approaches to emotion and narrative emplotment in communication with recent theories of cosmopolitanism, in an attempt to explore how American literary works have served as affective modes of cosmopolitan critique. Given that a number of scholars have made the claim that literary texts are central to cultivating the cosmopolitan imagination, and further given that strong emotional experiences are often needed to move people to act on behalf of distant others, this book suggests that cognitive theories of emotion can help us greatly in the analysis of the narrative strategies of literary texts that invite readers to stretch their imaginations beyond parochial boundaries. Investigating empathic narrative strategies that work across such boundaries, while at the same time acknowledging the importance of particular attachments and cultural ties, it demonstrates that literary cosmopolitanism is a matter of both universal principles and relational constraints. At the same time, this literary analysis can make a significant contribution to the larger field of cosmopolitanism studies by foregrounding how empathic engagement and powerful emotions like love, compassion, curiosity, anger, fear, shame, and disgust can promote or hinder the emergence of critical cosmopolitan imaginations. It is my hope that this study will contribute to an understanding of how cognitive approaches more generally might facilitate a better understanding of the complex emotional processes that inform both parochial identities and cosmopolitan commitments that go beyond self, community, and nation.

CHAPTER 1

EMPATHETIC COSMOPOLITANISM: KAY BOYLE
AND THE PRECARIOUSNESS OF HUMAN RIGHTS

THE YEAR 1939 WAS AN IMPORTANT POINT in the history of Europe and the world. It was the year in which Germany and the Soviet Union concluded a nonaggression pact, the year in which Hitler's armies invaded Czechoslovakia and Poland, and the year in which France, Britain, and the countries of the Commonwealth declared war on Germany: the year in which World War II officially began. For the American expatriate writer Kay Boyle, who at the time lived in Mégève in the French Haute-Savoie, 1939 was an important year personally as well. It was the year in which she met Baron Joseph von Franckenstein, a political refugee from Austria who would, four years later, become her third husband. The outbreak of the war, of course, worried Boyle, but in the long interim between the initial declaration of war and the first German attack on France, very little was to be felt of it in the remote ski regions of the Haute-Savoie. So little, in fact, that in February 1940, Boyle complained in a letter to Caresse Crosby that "half the world is skiing while the other half dies" (quoted in Spanier, 146). Only a few months later, however, leisurely skiing was no longer an option. Those who still skied in the Haute-Savoie often did so in order to hide from the new authorities. With the German invasion of France on May 10, 1940, the situation in Boyle's host country had changed drastically, and her personal feelings for Joseph von Franckenstein soon turned her attention toward the uncertain fates of those who, as a result of German aggression, had become stateless refugees and thus lost all citizenship rights. As she had always done in her life, the writer began to transform her personal experiences and emotions into letters, essays, short stories, poems, and novels.

In this chapter, I will use two of Boyle's novels of the time—*Primer for Combat* (1942) and *1939* (1948)—to examine in greater detail the role of emotion in the production and structuring of literary texts, and the ways in which these narratives allow (or even encourage) readers to empathize with protagonists who are members of an out-group. Boyle's personal experiences in war-torn Europe and her deep emotional entanglement with stateless refugees led her to imaginatively engage with questions of citizenship and human rights. In *Primer for Combat* and *1939*, she demonstrates her thorough understanding of the legal and humanitarian consequences that spring from the binding of the "Rights of Man" to citizenship in a nation-state. Although both novels are informed by modernist literary strategies, they are, at heart, love stories, and it is through the prototypical romance plot that Boyle offers readers the opportunity to emotionally engage with an issue that was central to cosmopolitan, philosophical, and political debates after World War II. Her trenchant critique of a human-rights concept that treats a human being as a citizen *first* and only then as a person powerfully resonates not only with Hannah Arendt's *The Origins of Totalitarianism* (1951), but also with more recent scholarship on cosmopolitanism, human rights, and forced displacement. Considering Boyle's novels in this context reminds us that caring for the rights of others involves moral and ethical appraisal, as well as the underlying *motivation* that comes from an emotional engagement with others.

In the first section of the chapter, I will explore in depth exactly how novels engage audiences, and what role empathy plays in both the creation and the understanding of literary texts. I argue that Suzanne Keen's notion of "strategic empathy" offers a good explanation for the deliberate use of romantic prototypes in the political fiction of Kay Boyle, as well as in the literary work of the transnational American authors that I discuss in subsequent chapters. At the same time, I insist that a writer's own emotional experiences, which underpin her deliberate artistic and political choices, inevitably must leave traces in the literary text. The writers I discuss offer good examples for how this plays out in individual novels and nonfiction writings. By way of example, the second section considers Boyle's experiences as a "rootless" cosmopolitan in interwar Europe, demonstrating how her personal experience often translated into highly autobiographical but nevertheless discrete pieces of fiction. The third section will then turn to Boyle's novel *1939*, demonstrating how her increasing politicization led the writer to move away from a more solipsistic concern with her own condition as an uprooted expatriate in her earlier fiction to the deliberate use of strategic empathy in a story about the fates of disenfranchised others. In the fourth and final section of the chapter, I examine Boyle's romantic emplotment of moral cosmopolitanism in *Primer for Combat* before finally tracing her increasing political and artistic radicalism to her potboiler novels of the mid-1940s, which exemplify her most drastic use of strategic empathy.

STRATEGIC EMPATHY AND THE LITERARY IMAGINATION

Empathy is the key element in our understanding of others. Defined by psychologist Martin Hoffman as "an affective response more appropriate to another's situation than one's own" (4), empathy is what allows us to slip into another person's shoes and to feel some of her feelings. Recent research in the field of neuroscience suggests that the *mirror neuron system* plays a key role in our ability to empathize and socialize with others. Some of the same neurons that fire when we watch another person do something also fire when we carry out the same action ourselves. As the Italian neurologist Marco Iacoboni points out, mirror neurons provide, "for the first time in history, a plausible neurophysiological explanation for complex forms of social cognition and interaction" (5–6). Not only does the mirror system help us recognize the *actions* of others, it is also centrally involved in our response to their *emotional* expressions. "Emotions, like actions, are immediately shared," explain Giacomo Rizzolatti and Corrado Sinigaglia in *Mirrors in the Brain* (2008). "The perception of pain or grief, or of disgust experienced by others, activates the same areas of the cerebral cortex that are involved when we experience these emotions ourselves" (xii). The notion of perception is crucial here, since it explains why the same neurons also fire when we watch an actor in a film. "We have empathy for the fictional character," writes Iacoboni, "because we literally experience [some of] the same feelings ourselves" (4). In the context of film, the close-up is particularly relevant because it focuses our attention on the facial expressions of a character. In what Carl Plantinga has called "the scene of empathy" ("Scene," 239), the human face on film not only communicates information about the emotions of the character that the viewer can use for cognitive mind-reading, but it also allows for *emotional contagion*, "the phenomenon of 'catching' others' emotions or affective states" (243).[1] In this way, responding to people on film is very similar to responding to people in the real world—with the difference that the filmmakers focus our attention in ways that tend to intensify emotional responses.

What seems fairly obvious in the case of film is also true for literary texts, despite the fact that the only things we directly perceive with our eyes are the famous black dots on a white page. This suggests that we can also empathize with the actions and emotions of *imagined* people whom we do not perceive directly. Philosopher Eva Dadlez even maintains that "Imagination is involved in empathetic emotion both when one empathizes with fictional entities and when one empathizes with actual persons" (7). Her use of the word "imagination" stresses the cognitive component of such processes and is thus related to the notion of "simulation" that we find in the work of psychologist Keith Oatley. In *Such Stuff as Dreams* (2011), Oatley builds on the appraisal account of emotion he developed in his earlier *Best Laid Schemes* (1992), arguing that writers "offer us appraisal patterns for certain emotions" (122) and that "fiction is a kind of simulation, one that runs not on computers but on minds" (x). Referring to the work of Alvin Goldman (2009), Oatley speculates that what we use in novel reading is not so much what Goldman calls the "mirroring route" (44) to empathy—the process of emotional contagion that allows us to automatically "catch" the actions and emotions of others. Rather, it is the "reconstructive route" (Goldman, 44), or what Oatley calls "imaginative empathy," which relies on a combination of cognitive simulation and emotions that occur "because of the simulation" (*Stuff*, 114).[2] Martin Hoffman similarly assumes that more elaborate, "effortful" cognitive processes are involved in our empathic response to literary characters and situations. Hoffman argues that processes of *mediated association*, involving the decoding of "semantic meaning" (49), and *role taking*, involving either "imagin[ing] oneself in the other's place" or "focus[ing] directly on the other's feeling" (54), play important roles in this cognitively elaborated version of empathy. Such "cognitively advanced modes" of empathy (61), Hoffman suggests, are particularly important in situations in which the eliciting object cannot be directly perceived, as it is in the case of our engagement with literature.

The question, then, is what exactly triggers our empathic response to a literary character. For appraisal theorists such as Oatley, it is our *cognitive simulation* of the character's goals and our assessment of the likelihood of the achievement of these goals. Patrick Colm Hogan's perceptual account of emotion, which is the one I will be following here, posits that it is the imagination itself that triggers the emotional response. The fictional nature of a literary work, in this account, is irrelevant; it is the "sensory vivacity" of directly perceived, imagined, or remembered images that triggers the emotional response (Hogan, *Affective*, 56). If what we perceive is a person (or animal), and if that person (or animal) expresses a strong emotion, we are likely to experience a strong empathic response. However, our neocortical system—what Goldman calls the "reconstructive route"—allows us to simulate and evaluate the eliciting conditions cognitively and thus to interfere with that automatic mirror response in ways that may be more or less accurate. To use Hogan's example, we may experience strong empathic emotions when perceiving a person with a relatively neutral facial expression if we vividly imagine that person to be in profound grief. Hogan calls this the "elaborated version" of empathy. "Elaborative empathy," he explains, "generally involves a self-conscious attempt to imagine the condition of the other person"—and thus cognitive processes of role taking that rely "largely on concrete imagination" (*What Literature*, 65). In addition, it relies on emotional memories that are empathic in nature, as well as "memories that are egoistic" (65). Elaborative empathy, which is related to Oatley's "imaginative empathy," is central to our enjoyment of literary fiction. It allows us to respond with strong empathic emotions when vividly imagining the situation and emotion of a fictional character who is important to us.

How important fictional characters are to us is at least in part determined by the narrative itself. As Suzanne Keen describes in "Narrative Empathy" (2010), "Narratives in prose and film infamously manipulate our feelings and call upon our built-in capacity to feel with others" (64). Interestingly, readers (and viewers) tend to enjoy such manipulation, and, knowing that what they experience is "only fiction," they are much less guarded than usual in their empathetic responses. According to Keen, "fiction . . . disarm[s] readers of some of the protective layers of cautious reasoning that may inhibit empathy in the real world" ("Narrative," 69), and so they might end up empathizing with and caring for a fictional character of a different nationality, ethnicity, race, or class whom they never would have befriended in real life. Such empathizing with one or several members of an out-group may of course just happen, but it may also be the result of what Keen calls *authorial strategic empathizing*. Evoking Gayatri Chakravorty Spivak's notion of "strategic essentialism," Keen explains that "strategic empathizing occurs when an author employs empathy in the crafting of fictional texts, in the service of 'a scrupulously visible political interest'" (83).[3] Since Boyle and all of the other writers I consider in this study deliberately used strategic empathy to make their readers feel with various others, it is worth looking more closely at this important rhetorical tool and its relationship to the romance plot.

Keen builds her concept on Hogan's earlier distinction between "categorical empathy" and "situational empathy." In *The Mind and Its Stories* (2003), Hogan reminds us that empathy tends to be based on some sort of similarity, because "to empathize with someone is to put oneself in his/her place, and that substitution presupposes something that is shared" (140).

While categorical empathy grows out of the collective self-definition of an in-group, situational empathy involves a shifting or "fusing" of perspectives in a process in which one draws on memories (and associated feelings) that are similar to what the other person (real or fictitious) goes through. By empathizing with the *situation* of people, we can approximate and understand some of their feelings and concerns. Situational empathy, therefore, can lead us to feel with members of an out-group, with whom we do not share a great number of group-defining features. In his more recent work, Hogan has suggested that rather than "a form of empathy per se" (*Affective*, 248), categorical identification makes emotional contagion *more likely* with members of the in-group and *less likely* with members of an out-group. In this view, there is "only one sort of empathy with a number of variables governing its initiation, development, and final intensity" (248). Among the most important variables are in-group/out-group division and categorical identification.

Literary works may both foster and weaken such categorical identification, and, as I have pointed out in the Introduction, Hogan stresses the "special value of romantic narratives" (*Affective*, 250) for the cultivation of attachment-enhanced empathy across group boundaries. He argues that the three major cross-culturally recurring genres of sacrificial, heroic, and romantic tragicomedy have all been employed to bolster categorical identifications, but that the narrative structure of the romantic tragicomedy in the final analysis works against in-group/out-group division because of its prototypical structure, which involves "two emotions (attachment and sexual desire) but a single object (the beloved)" (129). One of the reasons for the continuing attractiveness of romantic love stories is that they involve a particularly intense happiness goal, namely, the combination of attachment and desire, and that they invite the reader to simulate and empathically relate to that happiness goal. Here is Hogan's account of the typical love story:

> Two people fall in love. They encounter an obstacle to their union, commonly in the form of some superior social authority. That authority is most often parental. However, it may also be religious or political. The opposition frequently results from the lovers belonging to identity groups that do not intermarry—different classes, castes, societies, and so on. There is often a rival (belonging to a group that is seen as appropriate for intermarriage) who is preferred by the blocking social authority. This leads to the physical separation of the lovers. . . . During this separation, there may be death (in tragic versions) or imagery of death. There is also

often some form of indirect communication that serves to sustain both the hope and the suffering of the lovers. . . . The reunion often includes a reconciliation with family, though the rival often dies or is exiled. (*What Literature*, 33–34)

Because it invites readers to develop attachment-enhanced empathetic emotions for two individual lovers who struggle against a hostile social authority that aims to prevent their union, the romantic plot is inherently antidivisive, which makes it a wonderful tool in the hands of writers who want to use strategic empathy to encourage the overcoming of some kind of in-group/out-group division. Such writers, however, must think carefully about which audience(s) they are planning to address.

Keen suggests a tripartite distinction that focuses on the rhetorical strategies available to the author, consisting of "bounded strategic empathy," "ambassadorial strategic empathy," and "broadcast strategic empathy" ("Narrative," 71). Although all three of these are *rhetorically employed* forms of narrative empathy, Keen explains that they address different target audiences. Bounded strategic empathy is primarily addressed to readers of an in-group (71); ambassadorial strategic empathy "addresses chosen others with the aim of cultivating their empathy for the in-group" (71); broadcast strategic empathy, finally, "calls upon every reader to feel with members of a group, by emphasizing common vulnerabilities and hopes through universalizing representations" (71–72). At first glance, we would assume that the third of these strategies, "broadcast strategic empathy," is most conducive to cosmopolitan projects, but as we will see, there aren't always clear boundaries between the three modes. In all cases, however, strategic empathizing is a variety of *author's empathy* and a function of his or her political aims. In Keen's words, it "describes how authors attempt to direct an emotional transaction through a fictional work aimed at a particular audience, not necessarily including every reader who happens upon the text" ("Narrative," 83).

This brings up the question of the role of the emotional engagements of authors—as well as their individual capacity for empathy—in the creation of literary texts and in their choices of particular forms of prototypical narratives and strategic empathy. Countless studies have demonstrated that fiction writers score particularly high on empathy tests, which explains their supreme abilities to imagine the feelings and motives of fictional people.[4] However, not all of the manifested authorial feelings in stories can be reduced to strategic (and thus deliberate) empathizing, since human beings are rarely ever conscious of all of their affective engagements. As sociologist Jeffrey Alexander puts it, politically engaged fiction writers respond "not only to actual situations outside of themselves but to their own inner desires to speak on behalf of oppressed groups to society at large" (77). This certainly does not exhaust the scope of an author's desires, however. As we will see in the following sections on Boyle, as well as in later chapters, *personal* experiences and related emotions play an important role in what authors are prone to imagine and choose to write, and these more individual engagements inevitably merge and mingle with their political desires. Authors may or may not be conscious of these desires and related emotional engagements, but in all cases their emotions play a central role in the development of their literary imaginations.

In the case of transnational authors, the emotional engagements and desires manifested in their stories must be expected to include some of the transnational experiences and emotions that have shaped their lives and outlooks. As Hogan reminds us, "leaving home and normalcy is always a matter of risk—specifically, emotional risk" (*Affective*, 30), and some of the effects of this emotional risk-taking are likely to be found on the pages of cosmopolitan literature. Boyle's transnational life experiences and her engaged fiction writing are an excellent example of this complex process. She was only twenty-one years old when she left the United States in 1923, and although she planned to stay only for the summer, sixteen years went by before she set foot again on American soil. Over these many years in Europe, Boyle developed not only into a successful novelist, short story writer, and poet, but also into a critical cosmopolitan who was deeply involved in the political and social crises of her various host countries.

KAY BOYLE AND THE AFFECT OF HUMAN RIGHTS

Although she was, in her way, part of the modernist "Lost Generation" from the outset, Boyle's experiences were very different from most of her compatriots. While she shared the general spatio-temporal location and the discontent with American realities that we associate with the Lost Generation, she had no war experience—as had Hemingway, Dos Passos, cummings, Stein, and many others, as volunteers for the ambulance corps in World War I—and she did not choose Paris as her destination.[5] Having fallen in love with the French exchange student Richard Brault in her hometown of Cincinnati, Boyle became a French citizen through marriage in 1923 and spent the first years of her expatriation in a shabby flat in Le Havre and elsewhere in France and England, moving to Paris only in the late twenties. "These two facts," she later wrote in *Being Geniuses To-*

gether (1968), "would seem to disqualify me as a member of the lost generation or as an expatriate" (Boyle in McAlmon, 11), and indeed, her engagement with her various host cultures was quite different in nature. In a 1924 letter to her friend Lola Ridge, Boyle expresses her impatience with the attitudes of her fellow American expatriates, who she writes seemed "mortally afraid of getting away from the center of action, from their cliques" (quoted in Spanier, 16).[6] Boyle certainly did not have that fear. Instead of clinging to the modernist cliques in Paris, she spent most of her years abroad trying to find a sense of belonging within complicated love relationships and even more complicated marriages. When her marital union with Brault began to crumble in 1925, she left him for the terminally ill Irish-American expatriate Ernest Walsh, with whom she spent an exciting, exhausting, and devastating six months in the south of France. After Walsh's death, she gave birth to their daughter and then moved to Paris, to London, and back to Paris again. In 1932, upon her official divorce from Brault, she married the French-born American Laurence Vail, whom she later left for the Austrian-turned-stateless-turned-American Joseph von Franckenstein, who became her third and last husband. Over the course of twenty years, she lived with her ever-growing family—Boyle had eight children with her various partners—first in France, then in England, in France again, Austria, England, France, the United States, Germany, and, finally, the United States again.

Boyle's multiple displacements and what Thomas Austenfeld has called her "deep expatriatism" (*American Women*, 44)—the fact that she became intensely involved with her host cultures at a cultural, social, political, and personal level—had lasting effects on her outlook and self-understanding.[7] Unlike many members of the Lost Generation, she developed over the years the critical and reflexive style of cosmopolitanism that Gavin Kendall, Ian Woodward, and Zlatko Skrbis single out as the most genuine mode of world citizenship.[8] In *The Sociology of Cosmopolitanism* (2009), the authors differentiate among three "fundamental types" of cosmopolitan engagement: the "sampling style of cosmopolitanism" (115), the "immersive style of cosmopolitanism" (119), and the "reflexive style of cosmopolitanism" (121). The first type involves only superficial engagement with cultural otherness, usually "on the terms of the user, frequently as consumer" (116). It is the vantage point of many tourists and class-conscious "frequent travelers," who, as Craig Calhoun so succinctly puts it, are "easily entering and exiting polities and social relations around the world, armed with visa-friendly passports and credit cards" (90). Engagement of the second type is, according to Kendall, Woodward, and Skrbis, "deeper, more strategic and desiring," involving a cosmopolitan who actively seeks immersion in foreign cultures (119). In Boyle's time, this was the vantage point of many members of the Lost Generation, who spent several years or even decades in foreign cultures. Such cultural "immersion" can be quite limited, which becomes clear when we take seriously Caren Kaplan's observation that because of their lack of commitment to and engagement with their host societies, the modernist "exiles" in Paris were really nothing more than "bands of permanently displaced tourists" (47). The third, reflexive type of cosmopolitan, finally, "shows a genuine commitment to living and thinking beyond the local or nation and is more likely to *act* in cosmopolitan ways that are ethically directed" (Kendall, Woodward, and Skrbis, 121). It is the mode of cosmopolitanism that was embraced by the writers whom I consider in this study, and the fact that Boyle tended to chronicle her own development in her fiction makes her texts a suitable starting point for the exploration of the emplotment of such reflexive modes of cosmopolitanism in literary texts.

Cosmopolitan literature, according to Martha Nussbaum, features "people who, by virtue of their outsider status, can tell truths about the political community, its justice and injustice, its embracings and its failures to embrace" (*For Love*, 140). The overwhelming majority of Boyle's fiction does take such an outsider's perspective on the achievements and failures of specific political communities. This particular combination of outsider perspective and empathetic engagement was also of crucial importance for Boyle's own cosmopolitan development, and it perhaps also explains her often uneasy shifting between a more experimental, modernist style and a more realist, sometimes even sentimental, style that valued the easy conveyance of story over formal experiments. Over time, Boyle went from publicly demanding that "the plain reader be damned" to embracing a style that was deliberately targeted at the (female) masses.[9] Although this can partially be explained by material needs (Boyle had to feed her eight children after all), her stylistic ambivalence was also the result of her increasing concern about political developments in Europe and her desire to make American readers *care* about the related dangers to human rights.

In the 1920s and 1930s, Boyle had already begun to concern herself with the problem of physical and emotional displacement. With their concentration on the painful existence of the rootless, indeed homeless, cosmopolitan, her highly autobiographical early novels are an example of Nussbaum's claim that "Becoming a citizen of the world is often a lonely business" (*For Love*, 15). While Boyle's first novel *Process* (1928/2001)[10] is set in the United States and retrospectively concerned with the social and personal situation that drives its heroine out of the country and into the world to "start a new life,"[11] most of her other novels of the time—*Plagued by the Nightingale* (1931), *Year before Last* (1932), and *My Next Bride* (1934)—concentrate on the experiences and problems of an American abroad. These narratives may be read as a sort of fugue on psychic homelessness, offering irregular but progressive repetitions on a pattern. Presenting heroines who are drifting, wandering, and utterly displaced, Boyle asks her readers to empathize with these women's pain and fears and to understand and *feel* the emotional price the cosmopolitan woman, especially, pays for her abandonment of the comforts of family and nation.

Over time, however, Boyle's concern increasingly moved toward what we could loosely consider a more Stoic brand of cosmopolitanism, one that emphasizes a multiplicity of connections. Roughly speaking, the development we observe when considering Boyle's first four novels contextually and consecutively is that of (1) disillusionment with home country and family, (2) disillusionment with host country, (3) recognition of the futility or impossibility of return, (4) a resulting spiritual and emotional homelessness, (5) an emerging desire for a new attachment, and (6) the attempt to develop a new rootedness outside of nation and family—often through the almost desperate attachment to another individual. This attachment, the attachment to and passionate sexual desire for another person, is nearly always the attempted remedy in Boyle's early fiction, but alone it never cures the emotional ailment. The only remedy for spiritual homelessness, as it emerges in Boyle's early fiction and then becomes a dominant feature in her later work, is not just interpersonal love and connectedness, but love on a greater scale: a more universal love that reaches out and goes beyond, embracing humankind as such.

I have chronicled this development elsewhere and will therefore not engage with Boyle's early novels in more detail here.[12] What should be clear, however, is that already in this first stage of her artistic career, Boyle relied on a romantic emplotment of cosmopolitanism, taking advantage, consciously or unconsciously, of what Hogan calls the prototype's "antidivisive or incorporative tendency that tends to repeat itself with increasingly large groups all the way up to humanity as a whole" (*Understanding*, 20–21). Whether her novelistic celebration of love and connectedness necessarily equals the "rooted cosmopolitanism" that Kwame Anthony Appiah and others have embraced—which would be firmly rooted in (and patriotically inclined toward) one's original culture—is questionable. Boyle seems to advocate in these novels a more fluctuating and multifaceted practice, relying on intersubjective understanding and on planting and transplanting one's roots as one goes along. In addition, she reminds readers that unchanging rootedness in a single community and naïve forms of patriotism can be a dangerous illusion in a world that is changing swiftly. Thoroughly informed by her firsthand experiences with the growing impact of National Socialism in Austria, her novel *Death of a Man* (1936) confronts readers not only with yet another deracinated American heroine, but also with an Austrian doctor who, as a result of his misguided and blind enthusiasm for the emerging National Socialist movement, loses his lover, his community, and his home.[13] Boyle's increasing politicization during this period is also mirrored in other literary projects of the time, most prominently in the remarkable anthology *365 Days* (1936) and in "The White Horses of Vienna," a short story about Austrian anti-Semitism, which won her the O. Henry Award in 1935.[14]

From the late 1930s on, Boyle continued to concern herself in her fiction with problems of roots and of rootlessness; however, she did so now in the context of human rights in a Europe torn apart by World War II, focusing on the emotional, physical, and moral consequences of forced displacement and on the victims of the Nazi politics of expansion. The year 1939 was, as I pointed out earlier, a particularly important year for Boyle, as later evidenced by the title of one of her most intriguing novels. Via a detour to England, she and Vail had moved their family back to France in 1937, and it was there, in the Haute-Savoie, that she met Baron Joseph von Franckenstein. Von Franckenstein had been an Austrian citizen, but he had left his country only days before the so-called Anschluss, the German annexation of Austria in March 1938. Since his Austrian citizenship had become nonexistent with the Anschluss, and since he refused to become a German citizen, von Franckenstein lived as a stateless refugee in the French mountains, teaching classical languages in a boarding school there. The French declaration of war on Germany on September 3, 1939, made his position even more precarious, since it automatically made him an "enemy alien" in France because he belonged formally to a country to which he, in fact, refused to belong. As a result, the French authorities offered him two options: either he could join the French Foreign Legion or he would be incarcerated in an internment camp. His own preferred choice—to join the French army and fight against the Nazis—was out of the question, and so he eventually chose internment.

Boyle was deeply affected by von Franckenstein's dilemma. "Long before we fell in love," she later explained to her biographer Sandra Spanier, "he was a metaphor to me for all the European persecuted millions" (quoted in Spanier, 147). She began drafting a novel that featured an Austrian protagonist who was in the same situation as von Franckenstein, naming it after the year in which everything changed: *1939*. However, the ever more unstable situation in France soon forced her to interrupt her work on the book, as her priority shifted toward saving her family as well as her lover. Only after everybody—including von Franckenstein—had been safely moved to the United States, was she able to return to writing.[15] The next years remained tumultuous, with Boyle trying to arrange a new life for herself and her children in a country that she had left sixteen years before while at the same time seeking a divorce from Vail so that she could marry von Franckenstein. In addition, she could not forget those "persecuted millions" for whom von Franckenstein had become a metaphor, and so she made up her mind "to raise money for the French cause by writing 'day and night' and giving lectures" (Spanier, 149). As part of that effort, she wrote three other novels—one of them *Primer for Combat*, to which I will turn in the final section of this chapter—and so it would take almost a decade until she finally completed and published *1939* in 1948.

Despite the belatedness, Boyle could not have chosen a better and more befitting publication year for the novel. Not only was 1948 the year in which Garry Davis decided to become voluntarily stateless in protest against the inhumane aggression of World War II, but the place Davis chose for his protest—the Palais de Chaillot in Paris—is also where the United Nations General Assembly adopted the Universal Declaration of Human Rights (UDHR) on December 10, 1948.[16] Like Davis's act of protest and Boyle's fiction, the Declaration arose directly from the experience of the war, representing the first global expression of rights to which all human beings are inherently entitled regardless of their national citizenship or other aspects of identity or status. Like the earlier League of Nations, the United Nations itself, and the Declaration of Human Rights that it had adopted, were deeply indebted to Immanuel Kant's seminal essay "Toward Perpetual Peace" (1795), in which he discusses the importance of republicanism and the "right to universal hospitality" (*Gastrecht*), or what he calls "cosmopolitan right" (*Weltbürgerrecht*), for a world in which all human beings live in lawful association with one another and participate in a global civil order.

Contemporary scholars of cosmopolitanism have criticized Kant's cosmopolitan project for its inherent Eurocentrism.[17] Nevertheless, he remains one of the most important thinkers in the field of political cosmopolitanism.[18] After the humanitarian catastrophes of World Wars I and II, his moral universalism and the concept of a global civic order were particularly attractive not only for war veterans such as Garry Davis, but also for leading world politicians and for intellectuals such as Hannah Arendt and Karl Jaspers, who both had personal experience of what it meant to be(come) racialized and stateless individuals.[19] The "cosmopolitan intellectual" championed by Jaspers and Arendt in their postwar writings is, as Ned Curthoys points out, "a persona fashioned in response to their experience of the horrors of nationalism, racism, and totalitarianism." Arendt and Jaspers's understanding of the world citizen, Curthoys explains, "shares in a moment of cosmopolitan idealism that shaped legal vocabularies in and after the Second World War."[20] Given these historical factors, it is hardly surprising that Boyle's imaginative work of the 1940s shares many concerns with that of Arendt and Jaspers. As I will show in the next section, Boyle's trenchant critique in *1939* powerfully resonates with Arendt's *The Origins of Totalitarianism* in particular, even as it engages the reader in totally different ways, namely, in the form of a love story. By inviting contemporary readers to empathize with *the situation* of a decent and innocent man who has been stripped of his rights, *1939* allowed them to understand and to *care about* one of the most important humanitarian and political problems of their times.

EMPATHIZING WITH BARE LIVES: *1939*

1939 is a short but complex novel that follows separately the lives of its two main protagonists—a married French-American woman and her Austrian lover—over the course of just one day. Unlike most of Boyle's novels of the 1940s, the book is characterized by a relatively dense style and formal experimentation, and it was, as Spanier puts it, "certainly . . . not crafted with an eye to commercial appeal" (164). However, despite the frequent shifts in time and narrative voice, the almost entirely interior and psychological action of *1939* offers readers intriguing insights into what it meant to become a victim of the bizarre logic of World War II and how individuals had to make moral choices from within that logic. Jessica Berman explains in *Modernist Commitments* (2011) that, "by creating an imaginative version of characters, relationships, stories, and events within the realm of human affairs," even a complex experimental text "becomes a laboratory for action in the world, committed not to mirroring reality, but to redescribing and reworking it" (21). In *1939*, Boyle attempts such redescribing and reworking of a reality that horrified her. While "the flavor of the syntax . . . is decidedly Faulkner," writes Spanier, "the sentiments expressed in the novel are vintage Boyle" (164), concerned as they are with interpersonal love, as well as with complex ethical and moral dilemmas. And so it is hardly surprising that she is relying on the prototype of the romantic tragicomedy for the structure of her story, modernist experimentation notwithstanding. Using third-person narration to convey her story, she also grants direct access to her protagonists' thoughts and feelings through stream of consciousness writing and internal monologues. She thus invites readers to see things through her fictional lovers' eyes, to empathize with both their difficult situations in wartime Europe and their thoughts and emotional upheavals in response to those situations.

At the beginning of the novel, Corinne Audal, who has left her French husband to live with the Austrian ski instructor Ferdl in the French mountains, goes over the routines of her first day without her lover. Following the French declaration of war on Germany, Ferdl has gone to enlist as a volunteer in the French army. Corinne, who is deeply in love with the young man, is left behind and filled with the fear that she might lose him forever, realizing as she does that he is "scarcely a man now but a designation of war" (16). She does not want Ferdl to fight on the side of the French, because, in her view at least, he belongs no more to France than he belongs to Austria or Germany. The only place he really belongs to is the place next to her. We learn that Ferdl is a labor migrant, who came to France "to make his living" (86). Despite his decision to go away, however, his mother insists on Ferdl's close emotional attachment to Austria, asserting that "he love[s] his country. He love[s] his people; he always wanted to come back to us" (86). In her eyes, Ferdl "subverted" the honor of his Austrian family by falling in love with a foreigner, a married Frenchwoman at that, and abandoning his native country for her. Although Ferdl has done his best to explain that "He'd been away to other countries and he knew about other customs and the way things might happen without family or church or anything else coming into it" (99), nobody in his family is willing to understand his "bizarre" choice to love and live outside of the nation.

As a long-term expatriate, Ferdl is a transnational subject, a person who permanently lives in a foreign nation-state without completely giving up his original cultural, social, or emotional allegiances. Having left the familiar certainties of his original community behind, and being well-versed in the language and culture of another country, he seems to practice what Kendall, Woodward, and Skrbis call the "immersive style of cosmopolitanism" (119); but he is a cosmopolitan who is torn apart by his conflicting attachments and loyalties to both individual people and to countries. He literally stands between two women, his French lover Corinne and his possessive mother, and between the two countries that they represent for him—France and Austria. This difficult situation becomes even more complicated when he loses his Austrian citizenship as a result of the German annexation, which confronts him with two choices: either become a German citizen and be able to be with his mother or become a French citizen and continue living with Corinne. Boyle thus personalizes the moral dilemma of Ferdl's national belonging by linking it to his feelings for individual people, a move that makes it easier for her readers to empathize with the young man's struggle to make the "right" choice. Since Corinne is the other main protagonist of the story, offering insights into her own deep emotions for Ferdl, the reader is likely to side with her rather than with Ferdl's more distant mother, who, as is quite typical for the romance prototype, personifies the blocking parental authority that seeks to hinder the lovers' union. As a result of this romantic modeling, the reader is inclined to hope that Ferdl will choose to become French and stay with his lover rather than agreeing to become part of the Third Reich in order to fulfill the wishes of his mother.

We learn that Ferdl, rather opportunistically, tries to do both. He applies for French naturalization, as well as for a German passport, in order to be able to meet his mother in Italy. He regrets the latter decision at the French–Italian border, however, where he understands that he is "an Austrian still; in spite of the *Anschluss*," but that this will change as soon as he lets the border officials "touch the passport of Germany and put their validation on it" (145). After a moment of hesitation, he tears his new German passport into pieces, thus making his choice not only against Germany, but also against his mother. This spontaneous gesture of rebellion and refusal—which is, as Austenfeld points out, a "fundamental choice" in a "classic ethical dilemma" (*American Women*, 54)—invites readers to sympathize with Ferdl: confronted with a difficult ethical dilemma, he, after some initial wavering, ends up making the "right" choice in favor of both antifascist France and his lover. This choice, however, has severe consequences for Ferdl. His refusal to affirm Nazi Germany as his new country turns him into "a man without a country" (Boyle, *1939*, 137), because, at the same time and regardless of his personal decision, the French declaration of war on Germany makes him—as an ex-Austrian— also unacceptable as a French citizen. Ferdl's ethical stance against Nazi Germany is thus, as Austenfeld points out, in no way rewarded by France (see *American Women*, 55), and he certainly is not allowed to fight in the French army. As Ferdl's friend Tarboux explains to him, as a simple result of historical developments, his very personhood is in the process of disappearing:

> There are probably several shapes and forms of disappearance, Ferdl. Whatever you were before has disappeared now with your civil status and the currency of your country. You are not an Austrian; you are a foreigner with foreign papers committed to France now, asking France for a legal identity because your identity, like Austria's, has been wiped off the slate. (*1939*, 131)

With the disappearance of Austria, Tarboux explains matter-of-factly, Ferdl as a person has disappeared as well, at least as far as his position as a bearer of rights is concerned. From now on, there is no one and nothing that can protect him.

The cynical observation that Boyle puts into the mouth of one of her characters is bound to trigger in readers what Hoffman calls "empathic distress" (30) and "sympathetic distress" (95): understanding the inhumanity and callousness of the forces that cause Ferdl's "disappearance" as a human being, and imagining how he must feel in response to it, they are likely to feel some form of attachment-enhanced empathic response such as compassion or pity for Ferdl and some vague kind of what Hoffman terms "empathic anger" (96) at the French authorities. I will return to the notion of empathic anger in chapter 3, when I discuss the value of negative moral emotions with reference to the cosmopolitan fiction of William Gardner Smith; for now, I want to concentrate on the reader's feelings of attachment-enhanced empathy and compassion for the member of a disenfranchised out-group, and on the way in which Boyle's novel confronts readers in an imaginary and highly emotionalizing way with the moral dilemma that also prompted Hannah Arendt's call for "the right to have rights" as a result of her own experiences under Nazi rule.[21]

In her 1951 *The Origins of Totalitarianism*, originally written in English and first published in the United States, Arendt dedicates a whole chapter to the decline of the nation-state and the end of the Rights of Man. There, she concerns herself with the problems inherent in a set of "universal" rights that can be claimed and enforced only by individuals who hold "proper" citizenship of a nation-state. "The first World War," she writes, "exploded the European comity of nations beyond repair," and the civil wars that followed caused "migrations of groups who . . . were welcomed nowhere and could be assimilated nowhere. Once they had left their homeland they remained homeless, once they had left their state they became stateless; once they had been deprived of their human rights they were rightless, the scum of the earth" (267). In a climate of mutual hatred and "conflicting national claims," Arendt goes on, "two victim groups emerged whose sufferings were different from those of all others . . . [because] they had lost those rights which had been thought of and even defined as unalienable, namely the Rights of Man" (268). These two groups, according to Arendt, were "[t]he stateless and the minorities," who "had no governments to represent and to protect them and therefore were forced to live either under the law of exception of the Minority Treaties . . . or under conditions of absolute lawlessness" (268–269).

The plight of people who become stateless under such conditions, Arendt explains, "is not that they are not equal before the law, but that no law exists for them; not that they are oppressed but that nobody wants even to oppress them" (295–296). However, as the French philosopher Jacques Rancière points out in his essay "Who Is the Subject of the Rights of Man?" (2004), Arendt's formulation is somewhat bizarre, if not misleading, since "As a matter of fact, there were people who wanted to oppress them and laws to do this. The conceptualization of a 'state beyond oppression' is much more a consequence of Arendt's rigid opposition between the realm of the political and the realm of private life" (299). Boyle's novel suggests that such a rigid opposition does not in fact exist. Mentally simulating Ferdl's situation in *1939*, readers cannot help but realize that his position as a stateless person encompasses both the political and the private realms of his life and that the fact that no law exists to *protect* him does not mean that nobody wants to oppress him. On the contrary, French law insists that stateless subjects must be sent to internment camps if they do not join the Foreign Legion. There is, then, a law *governing* but not *assisting* Ferdl, since there are neither laws nor rights that he could claim for himself; with the loss of his state, he has lost all the rights of a citizen, but he has not ceased to be subject to external legal formations.

Boyle's novel thus offers a trenchant moral critique of a humanitarian catastrophe, a critique that was fueled by her own observations during the late 1930s, as well as her personal outrage about the insufferable situation of von Franckenstein. In Corinne, Boyle creates a female protagonist who is as powerless about the fate of her stateless lover as she was herself, despite the fact that she is—as Boyle was at the time—a naturalized French citizen. A vastly more powerful social authority than Ferdl's absent mother, the French government blocks the achievement of the lovers' happiness goal in the most radical way possible. If Tarboux earlier told Ferdl that "whatever he was before" is now in the process of disappearing, he later tells Corinne that, as "an enemy alien of military age," Ferdl "doesn't count as a man any more" (64). As Tarboux explains, people such as Ferdl are categorized solely as "suspects . . . not men any more, but suspects" (67). What happens to such "suspects" in the French internment camps, Tarboux professes not to know, but he asserts that "in any Fascist country they'd have been shot the first week to save the food" (67). Whether or not this will happen to Ferdl depends on many factors, but none involves his human rights, which he lost precisely at the moment when he lost his citizenship and became a "mere" human.

In his theoretical exploration of this paradoxical situation, Rancière points to Italian philosopher Giorgio Agamben's notion of *homo sacer* as offering an interesting alternative conceptualization to that of Arendt— one that draws on the work of Arendt itself and on Carl Schmitt's notion of the "state of exception."[22] Agamben, Rancière explains, "identifies the state of exception with the power of decision over life" (300), in that it can reduce life to what Agamben calls "bare life," namely, one excluded from the law, but nevertheless included under it at the same time.[23] From Agamben's perspective, "bare life" is human life that is "included in the juridical order . . . solely in the form of its exclusion (that is, of its capacity to be killed)" (*Homo Sacer*, 8), and the prime example of *homo sacer* and bare life, he contends, is the concentration camp prisoner. At the moment at which a sovereign state takes away all legal rights from a person and condemns him or her to an existence in a concentration camp, the prisoner has become *homo sacer*, namely someone who is still alive but who can be killed with impunity at any time. The "human" rights of this prisoner disappear with all his or her other rights. The tragic irony is that in the instant one is reduced to one's basic humanity, one loses the capacity to lay effective claim to human rights.[24]

The terrible consequences of this tragic irony—with different degrees of proximity and personal affectedness—Arendt and Boyle experienced and witnessed during the early 1940s. Boyle shows in her novel how the individual is affected by these consequences, offering thus an alternative mode of social critique that Arendt probably would have appreciated. As Berman reminds us, "for Arendt, action and the process of creating stories, including those stories found in artworks, are not only irretrievably linked but also crucial for the human sphere of politics" (*Modernist Commitments*, 20). In Berman's view, such "human stories . . . also have the constitutive power to generate an ethical relation within the web of human interaction" (20). Like Arendt, she suggests that we should understand imaginative narrative "as a form of action whose power is predicated on its very distinction from life" (21). In this view, Boyle's *1939* is a form of political action that aims to constitute an empathic and ultimately ethical relation not only between her readers and the fictional character of Ferdl, but also between those who are safe in their citizenship and those who are reduced to the state of bare life. As Hogan points out, "attachment-enhanced empathy is extremely important in our general emotional lives and in ethical response as well" (*What Literature*, 44n4). The romantic prototype, which is particularly well suited to produce such attachment-enhanced empathy, can have both happy and tragic endings, but Boyle chooses to leave her agonized reader without any kind of closure or resolve. At the end of *1939*, we do not find out Ferdl's fate; as we leave him walking in the company of a gendarme toward an internment camp in the Isère Valley, his final thoughts resonate with the plight of interned suspects everywhere: "How long is it going to take me to get out?" (152).[25] In 1939, no one in the world could have answered that.

As a deeply committed political writer, Boyle left little doubt about the motives that prompted her to write *1939*. "There is a responsibility to the present and the future which each of us must accept," she wrote on the dust jacket of the novel,

> and that responsibility can best be learned by an understanding of the immediate past. There is a choice which each of us must make in his own personal life before a world order of which we may be proud can come into being. The more I write, the more I find my protagonists faced with that personal choice; and in *1939* I have put into fiction form a portion of what I believe.[26]

This statement reflects the complex relationship between the author's cognitive beliefs and her use of strategic empathy in the creation of fictional characters who, in the end, seem to have a life of their own—a phenomenon often observed in literary writers. It also suggests that *1939* can justifiably be considered, in the terms used by Shai Dromi and Eva Illouz, to be part of "a social practice" that "enacts and performs moral evaluation" (352). Dramatizing the fate of a man who becomes stateless, the novel asks readers to put themselves in his place, and, as Hogan points out, "that substitution presupposes something that is shared" (*The Mind*, 140). Boyle makes use of Keen's "broadcast strategic empathy" in order to remind readers that our common humanity should be prevented from disappearing with parochial forms of citizenship. "Forming a relationship of moral solidarity with the victims of oppression," argues the Canadian philosopher Jean Harvey, "can involve various kinds of 'learning,' empathetic understanding of their grim experiences, and action toward lessening or ending their oppression" (33–34). *1939* invites readers to feel with Ferdl and his powerless lover, to then make the appropriate moral choice, and to stand in solidarity with similar real-world people who have been deprived of their human rights.

EMPATHY AND MORAL SOLIDARITY: *PRIMER FOR COMBAT*

Although it was published six years before *1939* in 1942, Boyle's *Primer for Combat* concentrates on a later historical moment—the German occupation of France—as well as on a later stage in the life of the stateless refugee and enemy alien. Set in the summer of 1940, the novel is presented as the "armistice diary" of Phyl, an American expatriate living with her husband Benchley and their children in the French mountains. It features not one but two Austrian refugees, one being Phyl's lover Wolfgang and the other her friend Sepp von Horneck.[27] As Spanier remarks, in Phyl we again have a heroine who shares many traits with Boyle and whose life resembles Boyle's at the time. Not only does Phyl have the same historical correspondence partners as did Boyle, many of them quite prominent personages, but she is also similar to the author in that her first husband was French, her current one is a cool-headed American, and her lover is an Austrian skier (see Spanier, 159). What is different, however, is that Wolfgang has chosen to join the French Foreign Legion over incarceration at the internment camp (von Franckenstein chose the internment camp). Sepp, by contrast, who is a teacher of Latin and shares with Wolfgang not only an ex-nationality but also the resulting fate of statelessness, is at the beginning of the novel still hiding from French officials in the mountains, trying to avoid either of the options handed down to enemy aliens.

Primer for Combat is characterized by an oppressive and gloomy atmosphere, and, as Austenfeld reminds us, it is important to keep in mind that the novel was published in the early 1940s and that Boyle, at the time of writing, "was not aware of the events that would lead up to 1945, she did not yet know the extent of the persecution of Jews, she did not know about D-Day and the eventual Allied victory. For all she knew, fascist Germany was there to stay for the next thousand years" (*American Women*, 56). Recording France's tragic and bitter defeat by the "Thousand Year Reich," Boyle uses the diary format of her novel to convey the stream of consciousness of her heroine, as well as her own shrewd political and historical observations. Although she is interested in the differing lives of all those that history and fate have rounded up in a small village in the Haute-Savoie, the dissimilar destinies of the two stateless Austrians are Phyl's (and Boyle's) most passionate concern. Phyl's heart trembles when she reads, in a French paper, about "the rapidity with which the Fascist methods are being put into effect. First no Jews in the French army, navy, or government services; no men to be employed in any official service whose fathers were not French; and now, no doctors, pharmacists, or dentists may practice in France unless their fathers were Frenchmen" (237).

Phyl—and in turn, the reader—know that no one is really safe in France anymore. As her friend Hans Arp tells her, it is "a vital necessity to read every newspaper in unoccupied France every day to be certain that one ha[s] not become overnight one of the category which no longer enjoys legal standing" (238). The apparent arbitrariness—guided by Nazi ideology—with which Vichy France exercises its power over the lives of people living in its territory frightens all foreigners around Phyl. She is well aware that as a "foreign-born" woman who has "acquired French nationality through marriage," she might "be declared by Vichy to be no longer French" and that her passport might be revoked (238). The state of exception that prevails in France makes it impossible to determine who will lose their citizenship rights next and why, and as a result, a profound sense of risk is tangible in Phyl's narrative. In addition, the blocking social authority of the Vichy regime—which is as powerful here as it was in 1939—threatens to destroy the lovers' hopes for a happy future, a risk that is immediately grasped by the empathic reader, who is invited to simulate Phyl's situation and concerns and, as a result, feel some of her feelings. The rhetorical strategy employed by Boyle, then, is that she invites readers to feel with a member of their in-group who thinks highly of and feels strongly for individual members of an out-group. The intimate first-person narration makes this an easy task, because it closely aligns readers with the heroine, offering absolutely no information that could counter or qualify her account.

Phyl decides to act on behalf of those she loves, as long as she is still able to do so. On one hand, she ponders what to do with her own family at this dangerous time.[28] On the other, she engages herself passionately, accepting increasing amounts of risk on behalf of Wolfgang and Sepp in order to get them the necessary paperwork to escape to the United States. With Wolfgang—who has already left France with the Foreign Legion and thus is put at a spatial distance from her—Phyl can communicate only through letters, whereas with Sepp she can talk personally whenever he comes down to the village or she hikes up to his chalet in the mountains. In both cases, however, Phyl faces a race against time: in Sepp's case because the likelihood that he will be found and arrested increases every day and in Wolfgang's case because it is clear from his letters that after being transferred from Portugal to the Sahara, he is disintegrating, both mentally and physically. As in *1939*, the separation of the lovers is linked to imagery of possible or impending death. This raises the stakes for both the heroine and the reader, who not only feels empathy with Phyl but is also likely to hope independently that the two lovers may be reunited, thus attaining their happiness goal.

Primer for Combat therefore invites readers to experience the plight of the stateless through the eyes of a woman who is desperately trying to save them. Phyl travels across the French–Swiss border—by bike, by bus, and on foot—to institutions that might be able to help her get the passports and visas that would transform her charges into rightful citizens again. Her motivation for helping Wolfgang is a combination of attachment and sexual desire; after all, the two lovers are planning a new life together in the United States. Her engagement on behalf of Sepp, by contrast, springs in part from her moral principles, but since, as Graham Long reminds us, emotions are in fact needed as a *motivation* for people to act upon the cosmopolitan moral principles they have already accepted (see 327), it is also built on attachment, in this case personal friendship and her deep admiration for Sepp's stubborn integrity. His refusal "to admit that Austria is anything but Austria" (*Primer for Combat*, 270) and the fact that he is willing to face the internment camp rather than become a collaborator of any stripe impress Phyl profoundly. When she explains this to the Spanish consul who comes to Sepp's aid, however, he shows little interest in her passionate plea. Coldly, he hands her the papers necessary for Sepp's escape from France, telling her that she "must not tell [him] these things" (270).

Others in the novel are more impressed by Phyl's personal engagement and her willingness to stand in solidarity with disenfranchised others. When Phyl is searched by a female French official at her reentry into France and the woman finds Sepp's Austrian passport and the accompanying letter from the Spanish consul, she gives Phyl a look. "Those are for a friend," Phyl confides, and

> without a word, but as though I had suddenly and for the first time spoken a language that was familiar to her, she put them back into the rucksack's outer pocket.

"Then they are sacred," she said. . . .

When we got outside, the officials asked her what she had found, and she said she had found nothing at all. (304)

An instance of moral solidarity between complete strangers, this brief encounter points to the cosmopolitan undertone that informs Boyle's novel, despite all the talk of nations and patriotic feelings that pervades *Primer for Combat* as much as *1939*. The two women both understand at this moment that someone's life is at stake, someone who no longer has any rights to claim for himself, and that someone else is risking her own imprisonment to help that someone stay alive and become a person again. In a sense, then, we might say that the official recognizes Sepp as *homo sacer*, but with the polarity reversed. His papers are "sacred" because he is someone's friend. The even deeper recognition here is that of personal emotional ties, even when they run contrary to national imperatives. A true cosmopolitan at this particular moment, the official forgets her patriotic duties to Vichy France and thus saves two lives. The reader, who up to this moment has been anxiously awaiting the border official's reaction, is likely to experience a sense of relief and even gratefulness.

Political scientist Thomas Pogge addresses almost precisely this issue in a 1992 article, "Cosmopolitanism and Sovereignty," when he writes that "from the standpoint of a cosmopolitan morality—which centers on the fundamental needs and interests of individual human beings . . . [the] concentration of sovereignty at [the nation-state] level is no longer defensible" (58). While Pogge goes on to argue for a different organization of state sovereignty—the *political* and *legal* lessons to draw from the proven negative effects of total nation-state sovereignty—Boyle focuses in her novels on the lessons of an emotionally motivated cosmopolitan morality that the *individual* must learn from the catastrophe of World War II. Phyl inhabits this standpoint and so does the unnamed woman at the French border. The same is the case for Sepp, who is, after Phyl, the true if somewhat hidden hero of the novel. Wolfgang, by contrast, proves to be a bitter disappointment. In a letter to Phyl, he writes finally that he is going to trust his French wife's connections to Vichy France more than Phyl's efforts. His opportunistic stance contrasts sharply with Sepp's stubborn integrity, and it is clear that not only Phyl's but also the author's sympathies are with the latter.

This is, in fact, quite an interesting variation on the prototypical romance plot, which tends to focus on two lovers, usually adding a "rival" who embodies yet another threat to the lovers' happiness because he or she is presented as the "wrong choice" for the hero or heroine. *Primer for Combat*, however, does not know any rivals in this sense, although Phyl is positioned not just between two, but three, men—Wolfgang, Sepp, and her own husband. While we know that such complicated constellations were not unusual in Boyle's own turbulent life, they can easily cause problems for readers' empathy if not properly handled. Boyle, however, makes sure that her readers do not empathize very much with Phyl's husband, who is nice but bland. Wolfgang, too, remains, in part because of his absence, an abstract entity in the reader's mind, and so it is really Sepp whose vitality and integrity invite empathetic engagement, making the story one of disappointed love and rewarding friendship.

The question of individual moral integrity in the face of catastrophe looms large in *Primer for Combat*, as do personal and national honor. Both Spanier and Austenfeld point to Boyle's remarkable appeal—on the back of the original dust cover of her novel—to Americans to buy war bonds. At first glance, this seems a decidedly *un*cosmopolitan gesture. Supporting such a reading, we see Boyle using her firsthand knowledge of the situation in Europe as a marker of expertise to explain that "I have seen what can happen to the lives of men and women in defeated countries. It is our responsibility to see that this does not happen here [meaning the United States]. But it is not enough merely to believe this, however profoundly, or to make statements about it, or to write books attempting to make it clear. There are actual things to be done" (Boyle quoted in Austenfeld, *American Women*, 58). The "actual thing to be done" is the *individual* (financial) engagement of Americans in the war against the fascist European war parties. Here, Boyle not only affirms the cosmopolitan morality of American involvement in the war (the book was published after the entry of U.S. forces into World War II), but also emphasizes the importance of personal engagement beyond mere talking, reading, or indeed writing. The political purpose of Boyle's use of strategic empathy in *Primer for Combat* could hardly be more obvious. And while Austenfeld certainly has a point when he speculates that Boyle's "deep expatriatism in Europe brought with it a fresh awareness of the real-life implications of national identity" (*American Women*, 59), it is worth pointing out that Boyle's cosmopolitan imagination, her reaching beyond national constraints on selfhood, by and large, was not based on the application of a particular universal principle. Rather, it was often a direct result of personal considerations, of her absolute implication in the emotional messiness of a life lived across national boundaries. As Spanier has repeatedly noted, Boyle's highest value was the emotional connection between human beings, a fact that supports Long's claim that abstract moral cosmopolitan principles can only be sustained on the basis of affective concerns (see Long, 327). We see this fruitful intersection of the emotional, the moral, and the political in a particularly interesting fashion in Boyle's other two novels of the mid-forties: *Avalanche* (1944) and *A Frenchman Must Die* (1946).

Both of these books—for which she postponed the completion of her more experimental *1939*—are sentimental "potboiler" novels that Boyle wrote about the French resistance. *Avalanche* is marked by the dual (and perhaps equally dubious) distinction of being, at the same time, both Boyle's greatest commercial success and the book that ruined her reputation as a serious writer of literature.[29] Set in the early 1940s, *Avalanche* is a romantic spy thriller that does not shy away from formulaic plot devices that combine the heroic and the romance prototype, or from crude characterization and rally-to-the-cause patriotism. Nobody could summarize the novel more pointedly than did Edmund Wilson in a 1962 review:

> A blond heroine, half French, half American, who fled France when the Germans came, returns to work with a relief committee and becomes involved in the underground movement in the mountains in the Haute-Savoie. The villain is a Gestapo agent masquerading as a Swiss clock manufacturer, who sneers at the French so openly . . . that the reader is at first led to think that this character must himself be a French patriot masquerading as a German spy, and is later impelled to wonder how he has ever held down his job. The hero, Bastineau, leader of the mountain resistance, combines the glamour of Charles Boyer with the locomotive proficiency of Superman. (128)

Wilson here offers an almost cognitive reading that emphasizes the reader's likely inferences about the characters of the narrative. But even if we overlook some of his witty spite, we do not get a sense that this is a novel pervaded by a cosmopolitan spirit. Readers of the book may understand Wilson's indignation at Boyle's style, as well as wonder whether her reflexive cosmopolitanism perhaps suffered a temporary breakdown as a result of the stressful war years. As clearly as the characters are divided into heroes and villains, they are attached to national labels: France and America for the heroes and Germany for the bad guys. This is quite clearly an emplotment of nationalistic patriotism. Boyle, however, defended both *Avalanche* and her second potboiler book, *A Frenchman Must Die*, rather eloquently, and the nature of her defense is important in our context: "I wanted those two books," she writes in a personal letter to Spanier, "far more than any of my others . . . to reach as great a number of Americans as possible, and so I wrote them, and without apology, for the *Saturday Evening Post*" (quoted in Spanier, 163).

Boyle made it very clear that reaching out to Americans in order to convey her political message was more important to her than the effects that a deeply sentimental spy thriller might have on her reputation as a "serious" writer. In 1928 Boyle signed a manifesto that declared, "the plain reader be damned," so we can hardly assume that she did not know in what trouble she might get herself as an artist writing a romantic thriller that tried to *warm the hearts* of its readers about the heroic struggle of French resistance fighters against Nazi Germany. If Wilson's derogatory critique upset and annoyed her—and it did—that was most of all because he obviously did not understand what she was trying to do *politically*. Like Pearl S. Buck, who faced similar allegations throughout her career, Boyle was a highly political writer, not in spite of, but in part because of, her repeated use of romantic and sentimental elements in her novels.[30]

One might thus forgive her the outrageously stereotypical Germans, Frenchmen, and Americans who populate *Avalanche*. Her attempt to *somehow* get the American public emotionally involved in what was happening in Europe was, like the note on the back of *Primer for Combat*, one of her ways of *doing* something about the catastrophe she was witnessing. The fact that in *Primer for Combat* Phyl breaks her adopted country's laws in order to help a friend points to an important tension between Boyle's belief in the moral authority of (good) nation-states and her equally strong belief in the need for individuals to be reflexive and critical, and to act against the laws of sovereign nation-states when the latter act immorally.[31] Thus, on one hand, Boyle advocates supporting nation-states (for example, in her appeal to buy war bonds) in order to strengthen their abilities to act in the name of cosmopolitan morality. On the other, when the nation-state fails to act morally, as it inevitably will, it is the duty of the individual to act from an emotionally motivated personal moral sense—often *against* the dictates of both the nation-state and the national sense of morality. This notion is expressed not only in Boyle's admiration of resistance fighters, but also in her later political activism against social and political evils in American domestic and foreign policy.

We can thus draw a straight line between the spirit that pervades Boyle's novels of the 1940s and the fact that twenty-five years later—at the age of sixty-two—she was confined in a California detention center for protesting against the Vietnam War.[32] Having developed a cosmopolitan imagination as a result of her experiences and emotional engagements in wartime Europe, Boyle was concerned with the needs, duties, and potential of the individual in her relations with other people. Despite—or perhaps because of—her often bitter feelings toward her home country, Boyle spent the remaining forty years of her life as an engaged American citizen, and a committed and politically active cosmopolitan. The door of her house in San Francisco, Spanier points out, "was always open to those whose struggles she supported: blacks, American Indians, students in dissent, pacifists, and 'those who work for the liberation of all groups and peoples'" (198). Throughout her career, her efforts as an activist and an artist were aimed at fostering critical engagement, as well as a spirit of responsibility—throughout and beyond the nation—on behalf of others, whether they were conationals or otherwise.

CONCLUSION

Authorial strategic empathizing, I have shown in this chapter, is the result of complex emotional engagements, which, in the case of Kay Boyle, were profoundly transnational in nature. An author's literary imagination, which crucially relies on her capacity for empathy, is informed by emotions that arise in response to her direct perceptions, memories, and imaginings, and in some cases, these emotions may lead the author to the deliberate emplotment of a critical cosmopolitan ethics. Since it is shared, this imagination can in turn trigger empathic emotions in readers (e.g., compassion for the disenfranchised members of an out-group), and potentially lead to moral and ethical reflection and, in some cases, prosocial action. In Boyle's case, at least, it led to her active involvement in American and international politics, and her always full house suggests that she also inspired others to get engaged. Unlike Arendt, who, as Volker Heins reminds us, sharply distinguished "between the affective and cognitive capacities of humans" and who believed that "public affairs cannot be truly democratic if governed by 'sentiment'" (723), Boyle seems to have shared with many contemporary feminists the view that "affective relations of solidarity are in fact an essential complement to the recognition of . . . human rights" (Gould, 148).[33] Furthermore, she clearly believed that inviting readers to build emotional relations of solidarity with *fictional* characters would lead to similar recognitions, hoping that her imaginative narratives, so closely modeled on real-world experiences, would help build cosmopolitan solidarities. We must thus understand her as one of those political novelists who, as Jane Tompkins has put it, "have designs upon their audiences, in the sense of wanting to make people think and act in a particular way" (xi), and who make deliberate use of strategic empathy for rhetorical and political purposes.

No one, of course, can guarantee that the use of strategic empathy will lead to the desired results. Keen reminds us that while "the research on empathic accuracy records the remarkable degree of correctness in human mind-reading abilities, . . . [n]o one narrative technique assures readers that our empathic reaction precisely catches the feelings embedded in the fictional characters" ("Narrative," 80). For writers such as Boyle, who hope to reach readers with emotionally resonant representations, there is always the risk of what Keen calls "empathetic inaccuracy" (81). According to Keen, such inaccuracy can manifest itself in two ways: as *failure* or as *falsity*. In the first case, the author's empathetic imagining of a fictional world does not *"transmit to readers without interference,"* resulting in elements of the story that evoke empathy in readers in ways that are against the author's "apparent or proclaimed representational goals" (81). In the second case, "narrative empathy short-circuits the impulse to act compassionately or to respond with political engagement" (81). This latter form of inaccuracy has been the concern of a number of literary scholars who fear that emotionalizing narratives are in fact *depoliticizing* in their effects on audiences and *amoral* in their intentions because they exploit the feelings of imagined others for careless and callous consumption by readers.[34] The main target of this kind of critique has been the sentimental novel, and Pearl S. Buck—to whom I now turn—is among the group of novelists that have been hailed by commentators as influential as Oprah Winfrey for writing books that take "root in your heart,"[35] while she has also been chastised by literary critics for her reliance on cheap sentimentality and an "excess" of feeling in her mass-marketed novels about cosmopolitan solidarity and interracial love. Given Tompkins's argument that some sentimental novels are written "in order to win the belief and influence the behavior of the widest possible audience" (xi), it is worth looking more closely at the way in which a sentimental literary style can be a function of cosmopolitanism.

CHAPTER 2

SENTIMENTAL COSMOPOLITANISM: THE TRANSCULTURAL FEELINGS OF PEARL S. BUCK

WHEN PEARL SYDENSTRICKER BUCK received the Nobel Prize for Literature in 1938 for her evocative books about China, the majority of the American literary establishment was vaguely shocked. Given the fact that Buck was only the third American writer and the first American woman to be honored with the prize in the thirty-seven years of its existence, one might have expected a little more patriotic solidarity and pride from Buck's peers. However, not only was the general consensus among U.S. literati at the time that no American woman writer produced work that was significant enough to deserve the important award, but many also felt that Pearl Buck was a particularly poor choice. Robert Frost unflatteringly declared, "If she can get it, anybody can," and William Faulkner famously got so upset that he declared the prestige of the Nobel Prize to be ruined, vowing that he had no desire to ever end up "in the company of . . . S. Lewis and Mrs. China-hand Buck" (both quoted in Sherk, 106).[1] Of course, Faulkner did not hesitate to accept the Nobel Prize when he was later selected for it, but his brusque reaction was symptomatic of the discontent and hostility that Buck's nomination evoked in American literary circles.

The general dissatisfaction resulted from a combination of several factors. Many felt that, because of her peculiar biography, Buck was not a real American writer. What made things worse, however, was that her peers were less than enthusiastic about her literary achievements. When the permanent secretary of the Swedish Academy, Per Hallström, emphasized in his award presentation speech the "remarkable trend" in Buck's books toward "opening a faraway and foreign world to deeper human insight and sympathy within our Western sphere," calling that "a grand and difficult task, requiring all [her] idealism and greatheartedness" (312), he unwittingly named the exact points that so concerned Buck's critics. In highlighting her ability to evoke *sympathy* in her reader, and in praising her *idealism* and *greatheartedness*, Hallström came close to presenting a laundry list of what for modernists were the unforgivable sins of sentimental—read *bad*—literature. After all, the oft-attested sentimentality of Buck's novels marked her as a writer for the (female) masses, and, as Suzanne Clark reminds us in *Sentimental Modernism* (1991), a sentimental writing style and the addressing of a female mass readership were especially fatal for women writers in the twentieth century if they wanted to be respected as serious artists (see 2). This is a lesson that Kay Boyle had to learn, and it also marked the career of Pearl Buck. Together with her extremely prolific output—Buck wrote over eighty books, about seventy of them novels—and her tremendous commercial success, the sentimentalist tone of much of her fiction all but assured that this particular Nobel Prize winner would be disparaged by literati and reviewers alike, and for the most part ignored by literary scholars.

However, given Buck's passionate cosmopolitan agenda and the immense influence she had on the American public, particularly in the 1940s and 1950s, a more intensive academic engagement with her literary work seems imperative.[2] It was through her novels—in conjunction with her wide-ranging nonfiction work and her political activism—that Buck managed to influence the American public to a degree that few other American authors have reached. Her biographer Peter Conn even goes so far as to say that "Never before or since has one writer so personally shaped the imaginative terms in which America addresses a foreign culture" (xiv).

In this chapter, I will use Buck's work for an exploration of the question of whether there can be a successful *sentimental* emplotment of cosmopolitanism. I define this as the sentimentalist version of the romantic emplotment of cosmopolitanism that I have considered in chapter 1. Since, as Patrick Colm Hogan has so aptly shown in *Understanding Nationalism* (2009), the romantic plot "has an antidivisive or incorporative tendency" that tends toward a transnational inclusion of others (20), we must ask ourselves whether this also holds true for plots that are built on the romance prototype, but confront their readers with the problematic "excess" of emotion that is considered so typical for the sentimental novel. In the first section of this chapter, I draw on the work of cognitive film scholars in my investigation of the nature of sentimental emotions, giving special attention to the phenomenon that sentimental narratives are ultimately pleasurable and rewarding, despite their repeated elicitation of negative or painful emotions, such as sorrow, compassion, pity, and grief. In this context, I also consider the alleged "gratuitousness" of sentimental emotions and explore their suitability or unsuitability for literary texts that aim to stretch their readers' empathic engagements beyond parochial boundaries.

The second section will then look more closely at the idiosyncratic mode of sentimentalism in Buck's fiction. Growing up as daughter of Presbyterian missionaries in China, Buck spoke vernacular Chinese before she learned English, and her cross-cultural upbringing led not only to complex emotional attachments, but also to a literary imagination that was deeply influenced by Chinese storytelling traditions. While Chinese and American critics have deplored a certain lack of Chinese—or American—authenticity in Buck, I suggest that we get a much better understanding of her peculiar cosmopolitan outlook and literary style if we view her as neither Chinese nor American, but as what David Pollock and Ruth Van Reken have called a Third Culture Kid: a person whose childhood is spent navigating worlds that are significantly different culturally and who builds emotional relationships with all of these cultures, while not having full ownership of any of them. By way of example, the third section of the chapter offers a reading of Buck's *The Hidden Flower* (1952) that demonstrates her strategic empathizing and deliberate use of sentimental emplotment to get readers involved in narratives about interracial love and intercultural understanding during the high tide of McCarthyism and Cold War anxieties. While I acknowledge the effectiveness of Buck's approach, I also discuss its potential dangers, as well as the resulting limitations of a sentimental emplotment of cosmopolitanism.

MIXED FEELINGS: THE SENTIMENTAL EMPLOTMENT OF COSMOPOLITANISM

Like cosmopolitanism, sentimentalism has a long and varied history, in the course of which it has been evaluated in very different ways. As a philosophical "moral sense theory," its origins have been traced back to the Chinese philosopher Mencius, who, more than two thousand years ago, suggested that all human beings possess an innate moral sense. In Europe, the history begins with the Third Earl of Shaftesbury's investigations into human virtue in the late seventeenth century. David Hume's *An Enquiry Concerning the Principles of Morals* (1751) and Adam Smith's *The Theory of Moral Sentiments* (1759) are considered important milestones for contemporary moral philosophers, such as Michael Slote, who understand empathy as "the cement of the moral universe" (13). As a literary style, sentimentalism also looks back to a long history, especially in Chinese and other Asian literary traditions, which will become important later on in this chapter when I discuss the influence of the Chinese novel on Buck's literary style.[3] Laurence Sterne's *A Sentimental Journey through France and Italy* (1768) was one of the first important texts in the Anglophone tradition, and throughout the eighteenth century the sentimental novel was valued as a respectable literary genre. Its central premise, as Glenn Hendler reminds us, was "the idea that, through the mediation of textualized sympathy, feelings and experiences can be communicated from one embodied subject to another" (9). The human capacity for empathy thus plays a central role in both philosophical sentimentalism and sentimental literature, and in both contexts is directly related to morality and our capacity to make moral judgments.

The value attributed to sentimental novels during the eighteenth century was crucially related to the belief that by communicating the feelings and experiences of fictional characters, they could refine and shape the moral emotions of readers. However, the nineteenth century grew critical of the possible corrupting influence of the genre's "cheap" emotionalizing strategies and excessive sensuality, and by the turn of the twentieth century, the sentimental novel had all but lost its cultural cachet. As Michael Bell puts it, between the mid-eighteenth and the early twentieth centuries, sentimentalism went from "being one of the most honorific terms in Enlightenment vocabulary" to "a term of near abuse referring to mawkish self-indulgent and actively pernicious modes of feeling" (2). Modernists such as Robert Frost and William Faulkner, who believed in the importance of "making things new," had nothing but contempt for the sentimental novel's conventional narrative strategies and the predictable emotions that these strategies produced in readers. By the end of the twentieth century, little had changed in this regard. "Literary texts, such as the sentimental novel," writes Jane Tompkins in her 1985 *Sensational Designs*, "that make continual and obvious appeals to the reader's emotions and use technical devices that are distinguished by their utter conventionality, epitomize the opposite of everything that good literature is supposed to be" (125). For the most part, this still holds true today, but it does not change the fact that sentimentalism is an important feature of a great number of the most successful popular culture texts, in particular popular literature and Hollywood film. From Stephenie Meyer's romantic *Twilight* series (2005–2008) to James Cameron's melodramatic science-fiction epic *Avatar* (2009), something clearly continues to attract readers and viewers to sentimental narratives that are built on the prototypical structure of the romance plot, and many scholars agree that this "something" is directly related to these narratives' emotionalizing techniques.

For a better understanding of these techniques, it is helpful to look at the work of cognitive film scholars and psychologists who have considered sentimentalism in the context of the melodrama. Ed Tan and Nico Frijda offer a helpful working definition of "sentimental emotions" that I will use as a starting point. Rather than a single emotion in the narrow sense, the two scholars explain, "sentimental emotions may be blends of several emotions" (48), and thus more complex in nature than more basic emotions, such as fear or anger. Generally, a sentimental emotion is "characterized by an urge to cry or a state of being moved with a strength in excess to the importance we attach to its reason" (49). If we are moved to tears and *know* what it is that moves us so, and if we feel that its importance indeed matches the intensity of our emotion, then we are not being sentimental according to this definition. A second characteristic of sentimental emotions, according to Tan and Frijda, is that they "mostly occur as a response to the fate of others. You watch someone else's fortune or misfortune, and suddenly you find yourself crying, without understanding exactly why the precipitating event would touch you so" (49). Finally, the two scholars define sentimentalism by its lack of action tendencies. Sentimental emotions, they argue, "have a certain measure of gratuitousness. They are not of such a nature as to motivate taking or abstaining from action. Hence, often though not always, the judgment of insincerity or superficiality of the emotions under concern" (49).

According to this definition, sentimental emotions are thus characterized by three attributes: they are excessive in relation to their causes, they are other-directed rather than self-directed, and they involve no action tendencies. In addition, they tend "to be associated with the response to cultural products rather than to real-life situations" (Tan and Frijda, 48), supposedly because literature and film allow us to experience empathic emotions in a different way. This is related to the argument that Suzanne Keen has made about the "disarming" quality of fiction: by taking away "some of the protective layers of cautious reasoning that may inhibit empathy in the real world" ("Narrative," 69), it allows readers to feel more strongly for imagined characters than they would for similar real-life people. After all, they know—or believe—that what they read or watch will have no effect on their own lives, nor can they interfere in any way in the unfolding of the events that they witness.

Other theorists, too, have made the claim that sentimental emotions by

nature are reader or spectator emotions, and that we must therefore associate them with the reception of cultural texts. Hermann Kappelhoff has
argued that they are special not only because they involve a certain lack
of understanding concerning the eliciting conditions of the emotional response, but also that the purpose of our empathic engagement is deeply
egoistical. When we cry in response to a sentimental movie, he explains,
it is not so much because we feel *genuine* compassion for a fictional character, but rather because we sentimentally enjoy our own empathic feelings of sadness (see 40). At first glance, this attested "egoism" of the sentimental emotion seems to contradict Tan and Frijda's observation that it
tends to occur in response to the fate of (fictional) *others.* But things are
more complicated than that. As Tan and Frijda point out, it is important
to realize that the viewer's emotion is not "a reduplication of the one represented in the fiction" (53), and the same is true for the relationship between readers and literary texts. Sentimental emotion displayed by characters does not necessarily provoke a parallel emotion in the reader. It is
actually much more likely that sentimental emotions in readers occur in
response to a *nonsentimental* emotion in the character, such as the deep
grief over the loss of a child or the sadness and despair over having been
separated from one's lover. The character's emotion may, therefore, have
very good reasons, but according to Kappelhoff, this is not true for the
viewer (or reader) who is responding in a sentimental mode. His claim
is that when we watch (or read about) the fate of fictional others in this
mode, we are in fact exploiting our built-in capacity for empathy for the
problematic enjoyment of our own parallel emotional response.

This is a somewhat puzzling claim, at least if we assume, as I do here,
that the experience of strong emotions is one of the main reasons why
people engage with fiction in general. A certain kind of "egoism" seems
to be a given in such engagement, regardless of whether the fictional text
is sentimental or not. But Kappelhoff's point is in fact a little more radical than that: he asserts that in the sentimental mode, we cry simply because crying sometimes *feels good*, and without any genuine regard for
the fate of the character. This is what makes such emotional responses insincere and "inauthentic" in the eyes of many, and I will later return to
the question of whether this is really true and, if so, what it means for the
sentimental emplotment of cosmopolitanism. First, however, I would like
to explore what is also implied in Kappelhoff's claim, namely, the intriguing fact that sentimental narratives somehow make it possible for us to *enjoy* negative emotions, such as fear or grief. In doing so, I will turn to the
work of another cognitive film theorist, Carl Plantinga, who has written

insightfully about the curious mix of positive and negative emotions in the reception of sentimentalist narratives, such as the melodrama.

In *Moving Viewers* (2009), Plantinga dedicates a chapter to the "paradox of negative emotion" (173). Taking James Cameron's melodramatic disaster blockbuster *Titanic* (1997) as an example, he offers a theoretical argument about how what he calls "sympathetic narratives" manage to elicit negative emotions in a way that is ultimately enjoyable for the reader or viewer. "Sympathetic narratives," he explains, "encourage 'closeness' to central characters *and* put those characters into unpleasant and sometimes catastrophic situations. The spectator or reader is typically invited to respond to favored characters with sympathy, and when such characters experience unhappy events or even catastrophe, this elicits negative emotions" (*Moving*, 170–171). Building his argument on David Hume's deliberations on the "paradox of tragedy,"[4] Plantinga argues that in successful sympathetic narratives—regardless of whether we find them in literary texts or in films—various techniques are used that make such eliciting of negative emotions bearable and in the end enjoyable: first, in the narrative's most traumatic moments "painful affect is both attenuated in its effect *and* mixed with pleasurable affect"; second, in the course of the story, "negative emotions are gradually replaced by positive emotions" (187). Third, such positive emotions gain additional strength through what Plantinga calls "the spillover effect": the moment when "the physiological residue of the painful emotions" helps increase the strength of positive emotions evoked later on in the narrative (184). Although sentimental literature lacks the visual component of melodramatic film, Plantinga makes it quite clear that sentimental emplotment works in very similar ways in both creative practices.

From the perspective of what Patrick Colm Hogan has called the "perceptual model" of emotion (*Affective*, 54), such parallels between filmic and literary modes of sentimental emplotment are unsurprising. As I have explained in the Introduction, in this model it is irrelevant for our emotional response whether something is directly perceived (as in real life or film) or imagined (as in literature). What counts is the *vivacity* of the image we perceive, and if a writer is able to evoke detailed, concrete, and powerful images in readers, we must expect a forceful emotional response. Rather than claiming, as Kappelhoff does, that we *enjoy* feeling our own negative emotional response when witnessing the suffering of a protagonist, Plantinga argues that in the case of the sentimental narrative, writers and filmmakers actually "manage [such] negative emotions" (*Moving*, 179) by eliciting "other emotions that in fact are pleasurable"

(181). These pleasurable or positive emotions, according to Plantinga, include experiences of awe and excitement about the depicted events or the moral elation at a character's noble intentions (as, for example, in the case of self-sacrifice). To this, we should add the "curiosity and interest" about a protagonist's future fate and the hope for a turn for the better (182). In fact, as Plantinga reminds us, when we experience negative emotions in a sentimental narrative, we have the "strong expectation" that there will be "subsequent emotional compensations" (182), such as a happy ending.

In order to understand the intricacies of sentimental emplotment, we must also consider the role of what Plantinga calls "meta-emotions" (*Moving*, 182) in our enjoyment of—or, more precisely, *tolerance for*— negative emotions, and the often gendered nature of this tolerance. Citing the work of communication researcher Mary Beth Oliver, Plantinga explains that "For many women, sympathetic sadness, when experienced, is self-enhancing because it is just the sort of emotion a woman *should feel* in relation to such events" (182).[5] Clearly, such gendered responses are a result of societal and cultural conditioning, which over time leads to a greater tolerance for certain kinds of emotions that are negative or aversive. Hogan reminds us that there is "a social and ideological function in the gender division that links male tolerance for aversive emotions to combative or heroic situations (e.g., in war stories) and female tolerance for aversive emotions to bonding relations (e.g., stories of parental self-sacrifice)" (*What Literature*, 29). This typically female tolerance at least partially explains why sentimental films and novels, with their strong emphasis on both positive and aversive emotions in response to bonding relations, tend to draw mostly female audiences, especially in Europe and North America.

In addition to mixing negative and positive emotions in individual scenes or passages, sentimental narratives also tend to *gradually replace* negative emotions with positive ones as they progress. Plantinga demonstrates how at the end of *Titanic* "The sadness, fear, and pity characteristic of the earlier scenes are replaced, for many audiences, by positive emotions [such as] elevation, admiration, hope, and exhilaration" (*Moving*, 186). He further speculates that the positive emotions of this final moment of the film are in fact *enhanced* by the previous experience of negative emotions, and that this "spillover effect" is another reason why viewers tend to be exhausted but happy at the end of the film. Sentimental novels, such as Harriet Beecher Stowe's *Uncle Tom's Cabin* or Buck's *The Hidden Flower*, to which I will turn in the third section of this chapter, tend to include similarly elevating endings that make the reading experience ultimately pleasurable despite—or even because of—the fact that they include many painful moments. And while Plantinga rejects the notion of a "purgative" catharsis as it has been defended by the psychologist Thomas Scheff,[6] he argues that sympathetic narratives can offer a "working through" or "dealing with" negative emotions "that takes into account the negative circumstances of the narrative and frames them in such a way that their overall impact is both cognitively and emotionally satisfying, comforting, and pleasurable" (179).

This final satisfaction, comfort, and pleasure, in combination with the sentimental narrative's tendency to use gross simplification, stereotyping, and exaggeration, are why many of its critics have insisted on its depoliticizing and ultimately problematic nature. Perhaps the most famous critique in this regard was leveled at the sentimental novel by the African American writer James Baldwin, who vehemently denounced the sentimentality of Stowe's *Uncle Tom's Cabin*. In Baldwin's eyes, such sentimentality is nothing but "the ostentatious parading of excessive and spurious emotion, [which] is the mark of dishonesty, the inability to feel; the wet eyes of the sentimentalist betray his aversion to experience, his fear of life, his arid heart; and it is always, therefore, the signal of secret and violent inhumanity, the mask of cruelty" (*Notes*, 14). Baldwin's indictment much more fervently emphasizes what Tan and Frijda have called the "gratuitousness" of sentimental emotion. He insists that a reader's excessive emotional response to a piece of fiction actually masks or even furthers an *inability* to feel about real-life people and situations in more authentic ways, and that it does not tend to induce action. As Shari Dromi and Eva Illouz point out, "via an interesting detour, Baldwin claims that the excessive solicitation of moral emotions in Stowe's novel leads to a denial of the very experience which gives rise to those moral emotions" (361), a phenomenon that equates with escapism.

Given that many sentimental novels—including all of those that were written by Pearl Buck—rely on what Hogan has called the "romantic narrative prototype" (*Understanding*, 324), and that I have claimed in chapter 1 that, because of its inherent antidivisive tendencies, this prototype is particularly well suited for the emplotment of cosmopolitanism, the question arises of whether we will have to exclude *sentimental* love stories from such a claim. If it is indeed true that such stories, because of their generic narrative properties, lead to an egoistic enjoyment of only seemingly compassionate emotions, and if it is further true that such stories actually *prevent* readers from caring about real-life others, then they clearly are by definition not suited for a "cosmopolitan education" through imaginative texts as it has been advocated by philosophers such as Martha Nussbaum and psychologists such as Martin Hoffman. Although sentimental stories would still crucially rely on readers' empathic capacities and might encourage them to empathize and sympathize with the members of an out-group during the reading process, the pleasures of such reading would indeed be "selfish rather than social" (22), as Harold Bloom has insisted they are.

The problem with this conclusion is that Stowe's *Uncle Tom's Cabin*, as is well known, was one of the most successful literary texts of the nineteenth century not only in commercial terms, but also in political terms. Tompkins has famously argued that Stowe's novel "offers a critique of American society far more devastating than any delivered by better-known critics such as Hawthorne and Melville," calling it "the most important book of the century," whose "impact is generally thought to have been incalculable" (124). Sentimental narratives, then, must have the capacity to move readers in ways that do not just evaporate into self-contented happiness once they close the book, and the sentimental emotions produced by such narratives can clearly provoke rather serious actions. As Tompkins points out, Stowe's novel "helped convince a nation to go to war and to free its slaves" (141). She has suggested that we should look at the book as "an act of persuasion aimed at defining social reality" (140), as a piece of rhetoric that tried to change history by "convincing the people of the world that its description of the world is the true one" (141). Understood this way, *Uncle Tom's Cabin* is indeed "not only a work of fiction but what we may call a *critique*" (Dromi and Illouz, 352), and it is Stowe's use of *strategic empathy* that makes it one. Her novel is in fact a fine example of what Keen has called "broadcast strategic empathy," since it "calls upon every reader to feel with members of a group, by emphasizing common vulnerabilities and hopes through universalizing representations" ("Narrative," 71–72). Certainly, we should not uncritically embrace sentimental narrative strategies; as many critics have rightly pointed out, some of the stereotypes Stowe uses are racist, her plotlines are meandering and often implausible, and the story as a whole is controlled by her Christian framework.[7] This does not take away, however, from the cultural work her novel has done, and since many of Pearl Buck's novels did very similar work in the Cold War atmosphere of the 1940s and 1950s, we must ask ourselves what this cultural work really is and how it is related to the sentimental emplotment of cosmopolitanism.

The literary scholar Philip Fisher, I believe, has offered at least a partial answer to these questions. He locates the cultural power of popular culture forms, such as the sentimental novel, exactly in what has so often been considered their greatest deficit: their tendency toward conventionality and repetition. In Fisher's view, this tendency—and readers' obsession with it—is a key quality of popular literature because it creates a "process by which the unimaginable becomes, finally, the obvious" (8). Importantly, the repetitiveness enhances readers' emotional engagements with such texts. Fisher reminds us that artful literature is often believed to invent new patterns of feeling, while popular culture texts are thought to keep rehashing emotions that are all too familiar, thus cementing the status quo. But he suggests that "when we look back candidly we can see that often the popular art forms . . . were massing small patterns of feeling into entirely new directions" (19). *Uncle Tom's Cabin*, for example, uses familiar narrative patterns and emotionalizing strategies, but the *objects* of readers' empathic emotions were new and quite radical at the time. In the same manner, Pearl Buck's novels offered the new and radical—in this case stories about interracial love and intercultural understanding—in the guise of the familiar and comfortable form of the sentimental love story. Like Stowe's *Uncle Tom's Cabin*, Buck's novels were "act[s] of persuasion aimed at defining social reality" (Tompkins, 140), and she quite deliberately chose the narrative prototype of the romantic tragicomedy for an emplotment of cosmopolitanism that would speak to the (female) masses. "Making familiar or making ordinary is the radical 'work' done by popular forms" (19), argues Fisher, and Buck's best-selling romance novels, such as *The Hidden Flower*, certainly did such radical work in the anxious political climate of the early Cold War period. The interesting fact, however, is that both her sentimental cosmopolitan imagination and her preference for the romance plot can be traced back to her complex emotional relationships to what she called her "several worlds."

TALES OF A THIRD CULTURE KID: BUCK'S MULTIPLE ATTACHMENTS

"I grew up in a double world" (10), writes Pearl Buck in her 1954 autobiography *My Several Worlds*. "Geographically, my worlds are on opposite sides of the globe and for me, too, only the years of my life tie them together" (3). Here and elsewhere, Buck stresses the perceived distance and even incommensurability between the two cultural spaces in which she grew up, and the fact that both were *her* worlds. Taken by her missionary parents to China when she was only three months old, Buck grew up in the small town of Chinkiang in the province of Kiang-su, spending her early childhood *in between* a home that was firmly marked by Christian and American values and a surrounding world that was 100 percent Chinese. Between these two distinct worlds, Buck explains in her autobiography, "the small white clean Presbyterian American world of my parents and the big loving merry not-too-clean Chinese world . . . there was no communication. . . . When I was in the Chinese world I was Chinese, I spoke Chinese and behaved as a Chinese and ate as the Chinese did, and I shared their thoughts and feelings. When I was in the American world, I shut the door between" (10). Buck's experience in China was therefore very different from that of her missionary parents. Although they allowed Chinese influences to at least partially invade their house, the Sydenstrickers clung to their cultural roots and thus made it necessary for their children to move in and out of this little Christian-American enclave, shutting the door to surrounding China whenever they went inside. Buck soon learned to move back and forth between these two worlds effortlessly, participating in both of them almost without restrictions. As a result of these transcultural experiences, and because of the many international dislocations she would experience during her formative years, she became what David Pollock and Ruth Van Reken have termed a Third Culture Kid (TCK).[8]

In the eyes of Pollock and Van Reken, there are two central factors that, in combination and *only* in combination, produce TCKs, and that make their experiences significantly different from those of children who grow up in their birthplaces, as well as from those of first-generation immigrants. First, they are raised in a genuinely cross-cultural world, implying that they grow up in more than one cultural realm. Second, their world is a highly mobile one, implying that "Either the TCKs themselves, or those around them, are constantly coming or going" (17). In addition, Pollock and Van Reken stress the central importance of the age factor. Cultural dislocation, they explain, has very different effects on adults, who have formed their identity in a relatively stable home culture, than on children, who are confronted with the challenge of forming their identity in the midst of constantly shifting and often conflicting cultural patterns and norms. The creation of a hybrid third culture identity only happens when permanently mobile transculturation occurs during the developmental years of an individual (see 56). The identity formation process is thus a very specific one, and it is further intensified by the fact that the parents of most TCKs are affiliated with some sort of transnational entity—such as diplomatic corps, transnational corporations, nongovernmental organizations, armies, or missionary boards—that inflects the family's belief and value system. As a result of these various and often conflicting influences, TCKs tend to build private "third cultures" from available cultural components.

Buck's internalized diversity—resulting not only from a wide variety of cultural inputs, but also from the understanding that there were at least two radically separate perspectives on almost any given thing—is what Pollock and Van Reken would consider her third culture.[9] And since both the Chinese perspective and the American perspective seemed normal and natural to the young girl, she accepted both of them, bearing the contradictions and shifting her behavior according to whatever was needed in the current cultural environment. Despite her dual cultural competence, however, Buck was, like most TCKs, acutely aware of her own otherness and foreignness in her host culture, of being, in her case, "pitied for my blue eyes and yellow hair" (My Several, 24). Throughout her life, she insisted on the lasting effect that this early experience of marginalization had had on her, despite the happy times that she seems to have experienced during her childhood years in China. And while Karen Leong does have a point when she criticizes Buck's later tendency to blindly equate her own experience of marginalization in China with that of African Americans in the United States, because white American missionaries were a privileged and well-protected minority (see 31), Conn is right, too, when he emphasizes that privilege does not necessarily remove the psychological aspects of marginalization. "Legal entitlement," he writes, and the protection that came with it for the Sydenstricker family, "could not conceal the universal evidence of Chinese contempt, nor did it prevent periodic outbursts of murderous violence. All of China's white intruders knew that their presence was resented and their safety was fragile" (24). Conn thus points to the emotional impact of the experiences Buck had during the early years of her life, and he insists that these experiences, and the episodic and emotional memories that resulted from them, had a major impact on her worldview as an adult and on her literary imagination.[10]

One of the central emotional experiences in Buck's early life was the Boxer Rebellion in 1900, during which the anti-imperialist, peasant-based Boxer Movement attacked foreigners—many of them missionaries—associated with the foreign domination of China. The uprising, during which approximately 230 foreigners and thousands of Chinese Christians were killed, forced the Sydenstricker family to leave their mission and flee to Shanghai, and from there to the United States. For Buck, who was eight years old at the time, the experience of being shunned and the fear of being killed because of her nationality, religion, and race were deeply shock-

ing, and they did much for her evolving understanding of human same-
ness and equality (see *My Several*, 33–36). Despite her, in several ways,
privileged (if also very poor) upbringing as a daughter of American missionaries, she experienced the problems and potential dangers of marginalized existence at an early age, which did not get much better when she
found herself in the country that was supposed to be her "real" home:
the United States. First, she did not know the country and its culture very
well, a point she stressed over and over again in her later writings, and
that critics such as Leong appear to not quite believe when they assert that
Buck *was*, after all, an American. However, relative ignorance and the
resulting insecurity with regard to the cultural rules of the "home" culture are typical for TCKs.[11] Beyond Buck's insecurity about American cultural codes, there was the fact that she was, again, marginalized. Buck's
American peers considered her, with her strange, outdated clothes made
of Chinese grass linen, "a freak who could speak Chinese" (Buck quoted
in Henry Lee, 18). As a child, Conn explains, she "felt continuously dis-
oriented and displaced. She knew that China was not her home," but the
United States did not much feel like home either. "Her feeling of separation," according to Conn, "was the central fact of her childhood, and did
much to shape her adult relationship to the world. . . . She was never quite
sure where she belonged, or whether she belonged anywhere" (24). As a
result, she developed confused and often insecure attachments, living with
a constant feeling of loss.[12]

Like most TCKs, Buck had to deal with the unresolved grief she experienced whenever she moved from one place and culture to another:
leaving behind her childhood home during the Boxer Rebellion, leaving
behind her newly met grandparents in West Virginia when her family decided to return to China, leaving behind her home in China again to attend college in the United States, and leaving behind her college friends
and the job she got after graduation when her mother fell so ill that Buck
was forced to return to China to take care of her. This pattern of recurring dislocation, loss, and resulting grief was to continue into Buck's life
as an adult. Her marriage in 1917 to John Lossing Buck, himself a missionary to China, brought about another move, this time to Nanhsuchou
in the rural Anhwei province, the region she later described in *The Good
Earth* (1931). Three years later, the couple moved to Nanking, where Buck
gave birth to her only (and profoundly retarded) biological child, and also
adopted the first of her seven nonbiological children. After a one-year ten-
ure in Ithaca, New York, where Buck received a master's degree in English at Cornell University, the Buck family went back to Nanking, until,

after the so-called "Nanking Incident," they had to leave the city in 1927 to temporarily seek refuge in Unzen, Japan.[13] One year later, the family returned to Nanking, where they continued to live as missionaries until Buck's permanent departure from China in 1934.

It was not only the difficult political situation in China that prompted Buck to return to the United States in the early 1930s. There were plenty of more personal, but just as pressing, reasons. After a lifetime of exposure to the self-evident "truth" that American Christianity granted women freedoms of which the oppressed women of patriarchal China could only dream, Buck became increasingly aware of her own oppression as the wife of even such a relatively progressive missionary as was her husband.[14] In addition to this newly emerging vision of her own role as a woman, Buck was less and less convinced of the cultural, social, and spiritual benefits that Western missions claimed to be bringing to China. As a result of both developments, she became increasingly estranged from her husband, and gradually came to despise the fact that American missionaries in China "were free to preach a religion entirely alien to the Chinese, nay, to insist upon this religion as the only true one and to declare that those who refused to believe would and must descend into hell" (*My Several*, 49). She had come to understand the missionary intrusions in China as "a form of 'spiritual imperialism'" (Conn, 28), and she began to deeply resent such one-sided intercultural "conversations." The early 1930s would see not only the publication of her first novels and nonfiction books, but also her first public speech on racial equality in the United States—in front of a group of African American women in Harlem—and, in 1932, a speech at a conference about missions to China.

In this speech, Buck offered a rather scathing criticism of the cultural arrogance and insensitivity of the American missionary,[15] championing *empathy* and personal interaction as appropriate means to deal with a foreign culture such as the Chinese. These are, as Karen Leong points out, "stereotypically feminine forms of communication" and human relations (32),[16] but as we have seen, they are also important components of the cosmopolitan imagination. Accordingly, Buck concluded her speech with the demand that American missionaries should stop trying to make the Chinese more American, and that they should focus instead on developing a better intercultural understanding and a more respectful interaction with Chinese individuals. As one might expect, the Presbyterian Missions Board was not enthusiastic. Buck, however, resisted the Board's demands for a revision or repudiation of her statements, and requested instead to be relieved of her commission. Making the break a complete one, she also asked her missionary husband for a divorce and moved to New York City, marrying soon after her publisher and longtime supporter, Richard Walsh.

At age forty-two, Buck certainly was a grown-up woman when she left China, but that does not mean that her experiences as a Third Culture Kid had simply slipped into the past. Quite to the contrary, they served as the foundation of her fiction and nonfiction writing during the 1930s, 1940s, and 1950s. Moving back and forth between China, the United States, and Japan in the late 1920s and early 1930s, she wrote the manuscripts for *The Good Earth* (1931) and three other novels that, together with the two biographies of her parents, won her the Nobel Prize for Literature in 1938.[17] In addition, she translated the Chinese fourteenth-century classic *All Men Are Brothers* by Shui Hu Chuan into English (1937).[18] Her professed intention at the time was to actively influence the American/Western view of China, so that it would more adequately reflect what she understood as the "real" China and the "real" Chinese people. However, despite this urge to communicate a more *realistic* image of China to the West, Buck's style was near-unanimously categorized as "sentimental" by her American contemporaries, as well as by many later critics.[19] As such, it seemed to many a holdover from the eighteenth and nineteenth centuries, not only unrealistic, but, from the vantage point of high modernism, also effeminate, trite, and hopelessly old-fashioned. However, this does not do justice to the complex influences on Buck's literary style. One of them might indeed be related to a certain time delay. On the American side, Buck's cultural mold was, after all, not only shaped by the missionary fervor of her parents, but it was also, as Dody Thompson puts it, "irrevocably set a generation behind what would have been her 'normal' one" (89). Growing up in rural China, Buck "missed out" on the cultural and aesthetic dissatisfaction and iconoclasm that suffused the American cultural air of the 1920s. Her often didactic style, a particularly offensive trait in the eyes of her Western critics, can also be at least partially traced to her upbringing in a missionary family.

Another crucial factor in Buck's literary style, however, was her exposure to Chinese storytelling traditions, and specifically the Chinese novel, which was a genre she knew well enough to make it the topic of her Nobel lecture. In this speech, she emphasized that "it is the Chinese and not the American novel which has shaped my own efforts in writing" (*The Chinese*, 3). And, as Kang Liao explains in his monograph on Buck (1997), the Chinese literary traditions she inherited "favor fast-moving action, simplicity of style and vocabulary. . . . The point of view is always the omniscient third, which [Buck] constantly used in her fiction" (37). Buck's style, Liao declares, "is Victorian and . . . affected by the Chinese story-telling tradition" (37). The Chinese novel, according to this definition, indeed shares some features with the sentimental novel, with its emphasis on accessible language and familiar narrative patterns.

The same is true for the genre's reliance on an emotional ethos that celebrates human connection. Hogan argues that while there are undoubtedly some differences in the precise working out of romantic relations in Chinese and European cultures, these differences cannot be "profound and uniform," since if the two cultures "differed fundamentally in the development of emotions, then we would not have paradigmatic works with the romantic structure (such as *Romance of the Western Chamber* and *Romeo and Juliet*) in each tradition" (*What Literature*, 34). In her Nobel lecture, Buck explains that the famous eighteenth-century Chinese novel *The Dream of the Red Chamber* "is simple in its theme but complex in implication, in character study and in its portrayal of human emotions" (*The Chinese*, 42), and that she understands her own championing of emotions as another legacy of her cross-cultural upbringing. "Life in China and with the Chinese," she writes in *My Several Worlds*, "ha[s] taught me much about human beings. . . . To know how a person feels was to my Chinese friends more important than anything else about him, for until one knows how another feels no friendship can be established" (370). Emotions are thus seen, by Buck, as key to proper human interaction and friendship. As she further explains in her autobiography, she later "applied" her Chinese "education" about the importance of feelings to her American readers. She did so by first finding out how they felt about the Chinese (or other foreign nationals), and then trying to change these feelings—and by extension their thoughts—by engaging them in the fate of fictional foreign "friends" in her sentimental love stories (see 370).

There is a third point of connection between Chinese and European traditions. Joanne Dobson reminds us that the sentimental novel's emphasis on empathic engagement and transparency is "generated by a valorization of connection" and by "an impulse toward communication with as wide an audience as possible" (268). Reaching as wide an audience as possible was certainly one of Pearl Buck's primary concerns, but this, too, was taken from Chinese traditions. In her Nobel Prize lecture, she explains to her audience that "The novel in China was never an art" (*The Chinese*, 4), and that she "grew up believing that the novel has nothing to do with pure literature" (11). Instead, the Chinese novel has always been part of popular culture, and Buck insists that "like the Chinese novelist,

I have been taught to write for [the] people. If they are reading their magazines by the million, then I want my stories there rather than in magazines read only by a few. . . . [A] novelist . . . must be satisfied if the common people hear him gladly" (52–53).[20] Buck thus derived her populist, "sentimental" aesthetic from both Anglo-American and Chinese traditions, and she very deliberately *used* it because she thought it was effective for her purposes. She wanted to make Americans familiar with the everyday thoughts and feelings of people from another culture, and she deeply believed that an empathetic portrayal of these people would indeed evoke sympathy in readers, helping them to imaginatively transcend racial and cultural, as well as national, borders.[21] In order to do so, she tended to use a double approach. On the one hand, she appealed to her readers' rational cognition by filling them with factual information about a more or less unknown culture (she also did this in her many articles and nonfiction books). At the same time, however, she also appealed to her readers' emotions by building engaging imaginative worlds filled with foreign characters whom American readers could empathize with and thus relate to and care for.

There are literally dozens of novels that would lend themselves as examples for Buck's sentimental emplotment of cosmopolitanism, among them *The Promise* (1943), *China Sky* (1941), *Pavilion of Women* (1946), *The Hidden Flower* (1952), *Come, My Beloved* (1953), and *Letter from Peking* (1957). All of these novels feature love relationships between characters of different race, citizenship, or religion (one of them generally being American), asking their reader to *feel* with the suffering lovers who struggle against blocking social authorities. And in case the reader has not understood quite yet, each of them also offers rather direct moral appeals targeted at the more rational capacities of its audience; however, such appeals are always supported by and suffused with emotion. I have selected *The Hidden Flower* as an example, partly because it is a little unusual in that it focuses on Japanese-American (love) relationships, thus engaging with an American trauma that—in 1952—still was relatively fresh and recent, the resulting anxieties and prejudices of which were in dire need of attention.

THE HIDDEN FLOWER: COSMOPOLITAN LOVE STORY OR SENTIMENTAL FAILURE?

Sentimental narratives often focus on young and beautiful women who get into trouble. "The central theme of the sentimental novel," Tan and

Frijda remind us with recourse to the work of R. F. Brissenden, "is the virtuous character who finds himself or herself in distress due to circumstances not his or her fault" (50). Buck's *The Hidden Flower* is no exception. Conceived and published in the early 1950s, this "challenging novel of interracial love"—so the subtitle states—tells the story of the American occupation officer Allen Kennedy and the Japanese girl Josui Sakai. The first half of the novel is set in Japan, the second in the United States, and all but the last fifty pages of the narrative conform closely to the romantic prototype structure described by Hogan. As he explains, "the union of lovers—the prototype eliciting conditions for personal happiness" defines "the outcome goal" of the romance plot, "with romantic love as the sustaining emotion" (*The Mind*, 102). And in fairly predictable fashion, Buck introduces us to a beautiful young girl and a handsome, charming young man whose budding love is opposed by their parents because they belong to two different nations, cultures, and ethnicities. Nevertheless, they fall for each other with a passion that surprises even them. In fact, the argument could easily be made that their feelings for each other are sentimental in the sense that they seem a little excessive in their sudden force, but then this is a typical feature of romantic love in general, and Buck *does* offer some reasons for why, against all odds, the unlikely couple falls in love.

In Allen's case it is an irresistible mixture of attachment and sexual desire, according to Hogan, the most intense happiness goal (in a personal context) known to humans (see *Affective*, 182). We learn that after Allen's first brief encounter with Josui, "desire burned in his blood. . . . He loathed the coarse and casual ways of common men in wartime, and yet he felt the same lusts in himself. . . . He wanted to think of the girl as a pretty picture, but he thought of her only as a female, a creature made for taking" (33). In a rather obvious way, Allen's powerful emotions are—against his will—producing a certain kind of imagination, and that imagination in turn triggers even more powerful emotions. Allen is depicted as a virile young male filled with passion and thus a potential threat to female virtue, but because he is—at this point in the narrative at least—a romantic hero and not a "common" man, he struggles to contain his desire and channel it into a direction that is more morally acceptable: "Some delicacy instilled in him, he supposed, by his mother, that small and dainty creature of immense will nevertheless, had made love and desire inseparable for him. . . . He was compelled to love before desire could be fulfilled" (33–34).

Given that Allen is a young man and an American occupation officer in

postwar Japan, the high moral ground he takes here is quite remarkable—
one might also say that his character is *idealized* in a sentimental fashion
for the simple reason that this will make him more attractive to female
readers (if they can tolerate mothers being called small and dainty crea-
tures). "A successful work," posits Hogan, "is a work that enhances the
reader's emotional response" (*What Literature*, 25), and it is a frequent
misconception that realistic or accurate representation produces such enhanced responses. Rather, "it may be the case that increased representational accuracy will, in certain respects, diminish empathic response,"
which is why some literary texts, such as, for example, the sentimental
novel, may "deviate from depictive accuracy through *idealization*" (25).
Such idealization can occur either in reference to "arousal" components
of emotional experience or in reference to the "modulation" components
of emotional experience. In the first case, the idealization is manifested
in characteristics of the beloved that make him or her particularly attractive to the reader as well (such as physical beauty or a noble character). In
the second case of idealization, the reader's simulation of a character's attachment to his or her lover may not be disrupted by negative emotions,
as may be caused by (perhaps more realistic) depictions of infidelity or uncertainty of attachment (see Hogan, *What Literature*, 26). Both of these
modes of idealization are typical for the sentimental version of romantic
emplotment, but as we will see, Buck relies only on the former in her characterization of Allen—a choice that has direct effects on plot development
and readers' empathic engagement.

Josui, on her part, has her own reasons for falling in love with Allen.
One of them is her awakening sexuality. She too feels a mixture of desire
and attachment, but there is something else, and that is her own confused
identity. We learn that Josui was born in the United States, and that she
spent the first fifteen years of her life there until, after the Japanese attack
on Pearl Harbor, her family was confronted with the choice to go into an
internment camp or return to Kyoto.[22] The wartime events have left her
father, a well-respected doctor, embittered, not only because he feels be-
trayed by his former host country, but also because his only son died fighting for the U.S. Army in the European theater of war. As a result, he is
"punishing America . . . for sending him away and the punishment was to
love Japan only and all the old Japanese ways and beliefs" (13). Because
he lived in California for so long, this is difficult for him, but he is determined to give it his best attempt. For Josui, the situation is even worse.
"I do not know what I am exactly, whether more Japanese or American"
(58), she tells Allen, and it is clear that she cannot, as her father struggles

to do, bury the memories and habits she acquired as a young girl in Los Angeles. Although she is not a Third Culture Kid, she is thoroughly acculturated to American society, and even after five years in Japan, it is nearly impossible for her to become the quiet Japanese woman her father now wants her to be.

Buck's heroine is interesting indeed, and she too is idealized. Josui is portrayed as a mixture of stereotypical "exotic" Japanese traits, such as beautiful "Oriental eyes" (34) and "skin as white as almond kernels" (28), and more familiar "American" attributes that make it easy for the (female) American reader to feel empathy and sympathy for her. Buck thus uses a somewhat different strategy than does Kay Boyle: whereas Boyle encourages her American readers to empathize with an American heroine who feels strong attachment to and/or sympathy for members of an out-group, Buck asks them to empathize *directly* with a member of an out-group. But she makes this easy by having her heroine walking and often thinking "like American women" (7), a rhetorical trick that likens her to members of the readers' in-group. Given Josui's peculiar background and her amiable character, it is easy for such readers to feel sympathy for the young girl and to imagine why meeting Allen, who makes her "remember much that I thought I had forgotten" (30), stirs a yearning in her.

In the romantic prototype narrative, the lovers are bound to encounter an obstacle to their union, commonly in the form of some superior social authority. During the first half of the narrative, it is Josui's father who creates the blockage. His deeply ingrained anti-Americanism makes interaction between him and Allen difficult, verging on impossible, since a union between his daughter and the American would be a humiliation in both social and personal terms. Josui's mother is compassionate but does not have anything to say in the patriarchal Sakai household, and she too realizes the enormous disgrace for the family if Josui were to marry a member of the American occupation army. There is also a rival, a young Japanese man of excellent social standing and the preferred choice of Josui's father. After the first spatial separation of the lovers following Allen's return to his base in Tokyo, Josui even agrees to marry the rival, and it is only Allen's last-minute reappearance that prevents the wedding. These developments of course involve some (rather mild) negative emotions on the part of the reader, since she must fear that things will go awfully wrong and that poor Josui will be relegated to a life similar to that of her docile mother. Realizing that she has barely read a quarter of the novel, however, the reader will likely predominantly experience more positive emotions, including some empathic romantic excitement as she simulates Josui's feelings for Allen and growing curiosity about how their story will develop. The novel becomes what Buck intends it to be: a page turner.

The second part of the narrative is likely to elicit much more profound negative emotions in readers, either because they cannot bear the "cheesy" melodrama or because they can bear it and thus respond with compassion, anger, sadness, and sorrow to the unfolding events. The latter is obviously what Buck was hoping for, and her sentimental narrative strategies seem to have worked well enough with contemporary readers. After Allen's return to the Sakai household, Josui's father grudgingly accepts his fate, arranging an instant Buddhist wedding for the couple. They spend their first night as husband and wife before Allen departs alone to bring the news to his wealthy parents in Virginia. The plan is that Josui— who is an American citizen by birth—will follow, and that they will continue their lives in the United States, since they expect less opposition to their union there. But when Allen meets the "small and dainty creature" that is his mother, he soon has to learn that she will not even allow his Japanese wife into her home, considering the mixed-race relationship as a disgrace to the family. When Allen's father asks her to be a little more tolerant and generous, because, after all, the two are married, she plays her trump card. "They are not married," she declares, because "The law of this state forbids marriage between the white and colored races" (162). When her husband protests that "that law was made against the niggra!" (162), she remains unimpressed. Indeed, it turns out that she is right: Allen's marriage to Josui is illegal under the laws of Virginia, irrespective of the fact that she is, as Mr. Kennedy notices with astonishment and relief, "so obviously not colored" (162).

If one was not aware of her political engagement at the time for the social and legal equality of African Americans, one would have to wonder about Buck's use of racial stereotyping here. Clearly, her aim is to demonstrate to readers both the racist attitudes of the Kennedy family and the absurdity and terrible consequences of American miscegenation laws, but since there are no black protagonists in the story, there is a danger of it being read as supporting racist differentiation between "colored" African Americans and "white" Japanese. Buck's employment of and partial challenges to stereotypical gender roles, however, are quite interesting. While in Japan it is Josui's patriarchal father (as well as Japanese society) who blocks the attainment of the couple's happiness goal, in the United States it is Allen's racist and obstinate mother (as well as American society) who constitutes the biggest obstacle to mutuality and happiness. Allen's father, on the contrary, is shown to be much more tolerant and accepting; he even displays purportedly feminine—and sentimental—reactions, with his "ready and trembling" pity "rush[ing] towards" the Japanese girl (162). Even with his compassion, however, Allen's father is shown to be caught in the logic of both patriarchy and white supremacy, as he keeps treating both his wife and Josui as "childish creature[s]" (164) and cannot help but belittle the wife of his son as "a little bit of a thing" (162). Despite the larger problems I have pointed out above, Buck very clearly controls and fine-tunes this more benevolently discriminating attitude of Mr. Kennedy in such moments, thereby showing the different shades and degrees of American racism and gender oppression.

From here on, Buck's sentimental love story takes some unexpected turns, not least because it no longer strictly conforms to the prototypical romance plot. Allen first reacts with anger to his mother's objections and Virginia laws, taking Josui to New York, where they can legally be man and wife. The social pressure against them, however, is hard for him to endure on a continuing basis, and as a result he grows more and more distant from his wife. The last fifty pages of the novel confront readers with an increasingly unsympathetic lover who is no longer idealized in reference to the "modulation" components of emotional experience. Not only does Allen abandon his wife emotionally, he also shows pronounced interest in his childhood friend Cynthia, and eventually asks her to marry him since his marriage to Josui is not legally binding. It is Cynthia's feelings of moral disgust alone that prevent this union, and the reader is invited to share this disgust, to feel indignation on behalf of Josui, who is unaware of Allen's betrayal.

Josui also makes some remarkable choices. When she learns that she is pregnant, she decides not to burden her husband with a biracial child. Instead, she leaves him and, in her despair, puts the baby up for adoption. For the reader, this is bound to be an unexpected turn of events, and Buck only barely escapes damaging her heroine beyond repair. Providing an unexpected kind of happy ending to her tale, she has an older Jewish woman—a Holocaust survivor who has "never kissed a man" (219)—adopt Josui's little boy, thus saving him from a miserable life in one of the poorly equipped orphanages designated for "colored" children.

These are some heavy-handed plot turns, and few of them are transparent or plausible. But it seems that Buck did not care much about such details. The deus ex machina who saves Josui's baby is not only a doctor, but a cosmopolitan as well, who, like Buck, has a great heart for the abandoned children of the world. Looking at her adopted son, she thinks "suddenly of little dead babies, starved, killed, bayoneted, tossed into heaps, babies who died because of what their parents were: Jews, Catholics, rebels, the hated, the feared, the despised. . . . Along all who were lost, this child she had saved" (234). It is not hard to imagine that such deeply sentimental formulations went straight to the heart of the millions of American mothers who read them. And while the tale's heroine is not quite as virtuous as she was at the beginning, Buck invites readers to feel compassion for the girl who is victimized by the racism and intolerance of her two very different home countries. With no money and no way to make a living in the United States, she—presumably—has no choice other than to abandon her biracial child and return to her patriarchal father, who would not welcome the little boy in his house.

At the time Buck wrote *The Hidden Flower*, marriages between whites and nonwhites were still outlawed in twenty American states. She makes use of strategic broadcast empathizing to put forward her sharp critique of the racist ideology expressed in these laws, combining it with a passionate plea for the adoption of abandoned biracial children, one of her many social projects then.[23] In order to get her political message across, Buck does not hesitate to reduce her major characters to what Conn calls "allegorical signposts." The victims in the story, in Conn's words, "are virtuous, the bigots are relentlessly wicked, and the plot marches inevitably to a sad but morally uplifting conclusion" (329). Buck thus offers her readers a move from negative affects to more positive ones, ending with the elicitation of pleasurable moral emotions, such as admiration and elevation (for the adoptive mother), a typical feature of sentimental emplotment. Readers' anger at Allen is turned into triumph when he is rejected by Cynthia. Their pity for Josui's son is no longer necessary, since he has found the best of all possible mothers, and their sorrow and compassion for Josui herself are attenuated by the fact that she returns to Japan in the company of the good-natured rival, who will be kind to her.

The only character, therefore, who sustains readers' anger at the end of the novel is Allen's heartless mother, along with American society as a whole, which is relentless in its racist prejudice and has "no place" for a perfectly wonderful biracial child such as Josui's son. This is presumably what Buck intended, and she knew well enough that this message would hit home with the kind of audience she was hoping to reach: middle-class American women.[24] Elizabeth Janeway, writing a review of *The Hidden Flower* for the *New York Times Book Review*, emphasizes that these middle-class women, called "idiots" by the journalist and essayist H. L. Mencken, were actually quite important for political change in the United States.[25] "If our mores are changing in the direction of tolerance," she writes, "if our knowledge of the world is broadening, it is she [the middle-class woman] who is accepting the change. It is vital to communicate with this woman" (both quoted in Stirling, 230). And communicate Buck did. As mentioned above, *The Hidden Flower* became a best seller, soon to be republished in condensed form by *Reader's Digest*, the best-selling consumer magazine in the United States.

The Hidden Flower was thus part of a larger political project that Buck had been pursuing since the early 1940s. In a 1942 letter to Edward Carter, who at the time was director of the American Institute of Pacific Relations (IPR), she declared that she was perfectly happy "to get down to the level of the comic strip" (quoted in Shaffer, "Pearl," 12) in order to reach her audience. Complex and highly sophisticated discussions of American-Asian relations, such as those provided by Carter's institute, Buck explained, were not suited to reach the broad masses of the United States. During the mid-1940s, her East and West Association indeed used a comic strip series entitled "Johnny Everyman" to provide average Americans with some cosmopolitan perspective.[26] It appeared in two mass-market quarterly comic magazines—*World's Finest Comics* and *Comic Cavalcade*—which, as historian Robert Shaffer informs us, "had combined sales of over one million copies" ("Pearl," 19).[27] Institutions such as the American Institute of Pacific Relations, in Buck's eyes, were genuinely important for the research work they did. But in order to communicate their findings to the American "everyman," one had to pack them into a form he or she was willing and able to accept. And if that had to be in the form of the comic strip or the popular novel, then she had no problem with it.[28]

Others, however, have seen problems in such an approach. Literary scholars have rightly pointed to the danger inherent in sentimental narratives of becoming (often unwilling) accomplices of imperialist and discriminatory agendas. After all, the well-intended boiling down of complex issues into a simple story risks certain kinds of distortion. If a sentimental writer is committed, for example, to showing her American readers that Japanese are humans *just like* Americans and can thus be related to as such, this might lead to the creation of a Japanese character that appears to be a lot more American than Japanese. This may result in a text that perhaps succeeds in encouraging Americans to relate to Japanese, but only at the cost of rendering the Japanese themselves as American. This line of argument has repeatedly been used by scholars of race and imperialism, who, as Hendler points out, tend to see "the politics of sympathy [as] fatally flawed by its drive to turn all differences into equivalences. . . . [I]f I have to *be* like you and *feel* like you in order for you to feel *for* me, sympathy reaches its limits at the moment you are reminded that I am not quite like you" (8). Buck of course partially evaded this problem in *The Hidden Flower* by making her Japanese heroine a transcultural subject and making her parents longtime expatriates, but the potential categorical boundedness of readers' empathic engagement with her characters still applies. After all, one might easily argue that American readers only responded empathetically to Josui because she—in certain respects—is thoroughly Americanized, and that this in no way prepares them to empathize with a literary character who is "authentically" Japanese, let alone actually existing Japanese people. This leads us directly into the minefield that is the notion of authenticity, which is worth spending some discussion on because it has played such a central role in the argumentation of many of Buck's critics.

Karen Leong, for example, has taken Buck to task for her complicated relationship with American Orientalism. American Orientalism, Leong explains, draws on European traditions of Orientalism—the "imperialist imaginings of Asia's cultures through the lens of European values, norms and culture"—in order "to affirm the political, social, and cultural superiority of the United States" (2). Asian people, in this Orientalist paradigm, tend to be imagined as exotic, feminine, and timeless, but also as "alien and distant" (1). One of Buck's self-assigned tasks was to change this problematic imagination into something more realistic and respectful, not least through her sentimental fiction. However, there obviously is some paradox involved here, and Leong thus charges Buck with unwillingly helping create a *new* kind of Orientalism, which she calls the *China mystique*: an image of China that was "romanticized, progressive, and highly gendered" (1). Furthermore, while she does recognize Buck's intellectual development from missionary wife to cultural ambassador and her "acute ability to assume multiple perspectives" (55), Leong sharply criticizes the fact that Buck created a "persona" of "someone who was more Chinese than American" (23). For Leong, such "cultural passing" created a "dilemma of authenticity" and, accordingly, is evidence of "Buck's inability to see her limitations as a foreign-born white woman" (52).[29]

It is quite interesting that Leong stresses so much, here and elsewhere, that Buck was *born* in America—although the first three months of her life could hardly have made much of a cultural impression on the infant. Leong insists on Buck's "true" Americanness, and this criticism is in some ways similar to the one that Buck heard for decades from the other side of the Pacific: that, as a white Western woman, she could not possibly communicate an *authentic* image of China, no matter how long she had lived there.[30] Without wanting to dismiss Leong's important critique of Buck, I believe it is necessary to question the adequacy of the idea of "authenticity" as it is used and implied in her text. There is no denying that Buck wrote quite a few mediocre books set in Asia, but I do not think it is helpful to consider her as someone who consciously and fraudulently claimed a Chinese identity to further her career as a writer and spokesperson. Rather, I believe, we should see her as the hybrid person that she was, culturally. Buck indeed was neither fully Chinese nor fully American. Hers was a *third*, much more private, culture, and the result was that she was unable to think about or ever feel anything in a completely American or completely Chinese way.

This suggests adjustment of Leong's critique, but does not challenge her claim that, despite (or because of) Buck's well-intended cosmopolitan engagement, she at times unwittingly helped support the American imperialist project. Reading Buck's nonfiction texts of the 1940s and 1950s in particular, one is amazed at how easily she seems to square her cosmopolitan demands with American patriotism and a deep belief in American exceptionalism, both of which Leong ascribes to her residual Orientalism. However, while it is possible that Buck retained an attachment to American exceptionalism from her childhood, we should not forget that she vehemently rejected the missionary Orientalism of her father. I believe that for a better explanation, it is helpful to, once again, remind ourselves that Buck was an (adult) Third Culture Kid. After all, as Pollock and Van Reken observe, it is not at all atypical for transculturated individuals to seek refuge from their feelings of rootlessness and restlessness in the deliberate embrace of *one* given place or culture. Being tired of moving, as well as of the constant feeling of outsiderness, they at some point, as Pollock and Van Reken put it, "swear they will find a place to call their own, put up the white picket fence, and never, ever, move again" (128). For the Pearl Buck of the 1940s, the place and culture where she decided to put down her white picket fence seem to have been the United States, where she bought an old farmhouse—Green Hills Farm—in Pennsylvania. Her rapprochement with the American nation—in part a result of the fact that for political reasons she could no longer return to China— led to a new cosmopolitan outlook that was inflected by the work of leftist American intellectuals, such as Horace Kallen and Randolph Bourne, who constructed the United States as an inherently transnational and cosmopolitan nation that had the potential to become a moral world leader.[31]

This is not to say that Buck was not critical of American domestic and foreign policy. In fact, nothing in the world made her angrier than the fact that the United States was not living up to what she considered its exceptional potential, engaging instead internally in racial segregation and externally in pronounced racial prejudice, especially toward the Chinese and other Asian people.[32] Rather, she tried to become what Kwame Anthony Appiah calls a "rooted cosmopolitan" or "cosmopolitan patriot" ("Cosmopolitan," 91), with all of the advantages and limitations that such a position entails. In the end, however, she seems to have remained, to some degree, a lonely outsider who wrote obsessively because it comforted her emotionally. As Hilary Spurling writes in her biography of Buck: "Storytelling had been an escape for Pearl ever since, as a small child, she could forget her troubles by reading and rereading the collected works of Charles Dickens. She said that every one of her own novels included a character who was a version of herself, and that her imaginary world of dreams, projections, and fictional presences came to seem to her as substantial as the real world" (233). This illustrates well the reciprocal relationship between a writer's emotional engagements and her creative imagination. While there is no doubt that Buck used her sentimental novels strategically to support political projects that were close to her heart, in the end they also served the very personal emotional needs that she had developed as a Third Culture Kid.

CONCLUSION

The sentimental emplotment of cosmopolitanism is clearly not without its problems. One danger inherent in our emotional responses to sentimental texts is that they have no true basis, in the sense that what they are responding to does not actually exist. Of course, this is the case for *all* of our responses to imaginary fiction. However, in sentimentalism, the object of our emotion is, quite literally, a fantasy—idealized, exaggerated, or vilified—that we nevertheless respond to as if it were real when it is depicted vividly. Sentimental emotions may thus become an egoistical pursuit, removed as they are from the world for our own personal pleasure. The other danger of sentimental emotions lies of course in the possibility that we may mistake the fantasy for reality, imagining noble savages or simply savages when thinking of the real-life members of an out-group. Seen this way, sentimentalism is indeed a dangerous pursuit for cosmopolitans. Given that both sentimentalism and cosmopolitanism have been charged with colonizing tendencies, it seems one has to proceed with extra caution when using sentimentalism to support genuinely (and not just apparently) cosmopolitan agendas. Both sentimentalism and cosmopolitanism are, after all, only valuable when they allow for both equality *and* difference, instead of confusing compassionate solidarity with a "saming" and colonizing of out-group others. Otherwise, they subscribe to the kind of universalism that conflates the local with the universal and therefore is in fact not a universalism at all. However, does this mean, as Carl Plantinga has asked so pointedly, that "idealization [is] always wrong? Is strict adherence to some standard of realism always preferable?" (*Moving*, 194). His answer is no, because while there are doubtless problematic and decidedly *un*cosmopolitan forms of sentimentalism, "presenting idealized representations may encourage and invigorate the spectator [or reader] toward positive action even while the fiction misinterprets the actual world," because such depictions may "serve as worthy goals for emulation" (194, 195). This is a tempting answer, and if we accept the proposition that imaginative texts *in general* can somehow have an impact on their audiences' thoughts and real-world actions, then there is no good reason to believe that highly emotionalizing forms, such as the sentimental novel or the melodrama, cannot because they rely on established narrative conventions.

In the end, the value of a sentimental emplotment of cosmopolitanism may indeed, as Philip Fisher has suggested, lie in the cultural work that is done by "massing small patterns of feeling into entirely new directions" (19), thus participating in a larger "process by which the unimaginable becomes, finally, the obvious" (8). While it may be the case that presenting a sympathetic member of an out-group who shares significant traits with members of the in-group *prevents* readers from engaging seriously with actual members of that out-group, as Baldwin and others have suggested, it may also be the case that the gradual "getting used to" sympathetic if romanticized portrayals helps *open the door* for more realistic portrayals and real-life interaction. Historical evidence points in the direction of the latter, not only because of *Uncle Tom's Cabin*'s spectacular success, but also because of Pearl Buck's own track record. As Shaffer attests, it has by now been acknowledged by many historians that "American sympathy for China in World War II stemmed in part from the runaway success of *The Good Earth*, which provided a very human portrait of the Chinese peasantry" ("Pearl," 2).[33] And even Leong acknowledges that Buck's novels helped change the terms by which Americans imagined Asian people into ones that were still Orientalist, but much more sympathetic. Interestingly, Buck's literary legacy is currently experiencing something of a resurgence among Asian scholars, who are finding it much more interesting than its reputation had previously suggested.[34]

In addition, it is crucial to keep in mind that Buck never intended to have her sentimental novels stand in isolation. Instead, she chose every popular medium possible to transport her messages about human equality and intercultural understanding. As a result of what Mari Yoshihara has called her "consistently populist" approach (169), Buck's perceived authority on American-Asian relations was at times higher than that of the designated "experts."[35] Her influence on the American public with regard to domestic concerns—especially in the context of race relations—was similarly strong. Not only did she protest publicly against the unconstitutional internment of Japanese-Americans in the United States during World War II and do what she could to bring about the repeal of the Chinese Exclusion Act,[36] she also supported the African American struggle for greater equality and civil rights, contributing repeatedly to the NAACP publication *The Crisis* and giving speeches on racial equality in front of black and white audiences. In a 1942 article called "The War for Race Equality," W. E. B. Du Bois recognized and appreciated Buck's public support at a time when segregation was still the most natural thing in the American imagination. Eslanda Goode Robeson—the outspoken wife of the black singer and performer Paul Robeson—agreed to coauthor with Buck *American Argument* (1949), in which the two women conversed about everything from race relations to Communism. Langston Hughes, with a certain double-edged amiability, called Buck the "current Harriet Beecher Stowe of the race" (259). While Hughes's comment captures well the ambiguity we feel when engaging critically with the sentimental emplotment of cosmopolitanism, it also reminds us of the enormous societal impact such emplotment has had historically, from Harriet Beecher Stowe to Buck and beyond.

Buck, however, believed that her engagement was very different from Stowe's in that it was the result of her own painful experience of marginalization in China. In "On Discovering America" (1937), she recounts how she found herself very much distressed by "the amazing hatred among all these Americans for each other" (315) when she arrived in the United States after leaving China for good in 1934. "A sensitive mind," she explains, "at first can not but be frightened and oppressed by the fearful prejudices of race and creed which possess the feelings of the average American" (315). With this emphasis not only on the shaping force of negative emotions, such as hatred and fear in American race relations, but also on the role of *sensitivity* in the perception of such emotions and their social consequences, Buck names the crucial coordinates that would define the literary imaginations of Richard Wright and William Gardner Smith. As Buck explained on another occasion, "People who have suffered, people who have had to live with an inescapable trouble . . . develop either a corroding bitterness, or a deep wide philosophical outlook on life" ("Breaking," 450), and the lives and works of these two African American writers measure the dimensions of this existential choice. While Wright's work is centrally concerned with the way in which fear, anger, and hatred shape the imagination of the black American individual, Smith's fiction and nonfiction explore the precariousness of a heightened empathic propensity in such an emotionally charged atmosphere, and the way in which it is related to the moral emotion of empathic guilt. As I will show in the next chapter, the life and work of Smith, a little-known and vastly underestimated American writer, demonstrate that the notion of sensitivity, and a preference for the romantic emplotment of cosmopolitanism, are restricted neither by gender nor race.

COSMOPOLITAN SENSITIVITIES: BYSTANDER GUILT AND INTERRACIAL SOLIDARITY IN THE WORK OF WILLIAM GARDNER SMITH

IN 1952, WILLIAM GARDNER SMITH welcomed the chief editor of an American magazine into his shabby quarters at the Hôtel Tournon, which at the time was a popular haunt of black American expatriates in Paris. In his autobiographical *Return to Black America* (1970), Smith recalls this moment and the editor's "utterly stupefied look as he stood in the doorway of my little attic room, fresh from his luxurious American apartment, staring at the ugly peeling wallpaper, the lumpy iron bed, the bare lopsided table, the rickety chairs, the worn linoleum, and the washstand attached precariously to the wall" (4). "My God!" the bewildered editor exclaims. "Do you mean to tell me it's for *this* that you turned down the job I offered you?" Smith recollects himself answering with amusement and conviction: "Yes, precisely for this" (4). At the time of this incident, the twenty-five-year-old Smith had turned down a lot more than just a job offer in the United States. His young wife Mary, who had come with him to Paris in 1951 but been unable to deal with their bohemian lifestyle and impoverished living conditions there, had returned to Philadelphia without him. His mother and sister wrote letter after letter, asking when he would finally be coming home. But although Smith cared for his family and felt guilty for leaving behind those whom he loved, he was not planning to return to the United States anytime soon. After all, he had left his native country because he had "had the feeling of stifling" (quoted in Flanner, 165).

Once believed to be on the verge of a great literary career, Smith faded into obscurity after his death, and his work has received very little attention over the years from scholars of African American literature. His biographer, LeRoy Hodges, noted in 1985 that Smith was—unjustly—considered a "minor writer" (i), and, despite Hodges's efforts, little has changed since then.[1] However, Smith's work—particularly his fourth and final novel, *The Stone Face* (1963)—deserves more scholarly attention, as literary scholar Michel Fabre, sociologist Paul Gilroy, and historian Tyler Stovall all have pointed out.[2] Not only is the novel one of the few African American texts dealing with the complicated relationship of the black U.S. community in Paris to the so-called Algerian question, but it is also an impressive exploration of the difficulties and complexities of intercultural understanding, and of the crucial role played by empathic imagining in the development of such an understanding. Like Smith himself, the novel's African American protagonist Simeon starts out as a man habituated to American patterns of racism, haunted by terrifying memories of violence and abuse, and, in his relief to have gotten away, rather oblivious to French racialization of and discrimination against Algerians. In the course of the story, however, he develops a reflexive and critical cosmopolitan perspective, changing his understanding of both France and his own identity and responsibility as a black American expatriate. The catalysts of this changed ethical stance are both positive emotions, such as his growing *emotional attachment* to people belonging to various outgroups, and profoundly negative emotions, such as feelings of *guilt* and *shame*. The condition that enables this development, however, is his *sensitivity*, a trait Simeon considers so dangerous that he calls it a "curse" (23).

In this chapter, I will look at *The Stone Face* as another example of the romantic emplotment of cosmopolitanism, but my focus will be on two different aspects of the cosmopolitan imagination. Critical and reflexive modes of cosmopolitanism, I will argue, are dependent not only on positive empathy-based responses, such as sympathy and compassion, as I have demonstrated in previous chapters, but also on more negative empathic emotions, such as anger, guilt, and, to some degree, shame. Empathic guilt and shame are particularly important here, because they are directed at the self and thus crucial for the process of reflection, which is central to concepts of critical, reflexive, and "thick" cosmopolitanism. Smith's novel, I argue, imagines complex processes of empathic engagement and critical self-reflection in ways that are particularly lucid and engaging. While celebrating cosmopolitan modes of thinking and feeling, Smith does not shy away from exploring the potential risks and dangers involved in caring for distant others. And not by coincidence, he relies on what Patrick Colm Hogan has defined as the "romantic narrative prototype" (*Understanding*, 324) for his emplotment of critical cosmopolitanism. Like Kay Boyle and Pearl S. Buck, Smith felt drawn to this prototype for the narration of human engagements that stretch beyond the parochial, evidenced by the fact that all four novels he published during his lifetime were centrally concerned with emotional attachment and romantic love. What differentiates Smith's fictional work from that of Boyle or Buck, however, is that negative and painful emotions, such as fear, anger, guilt, and shame, play an important role in his protagonists' experience of themselves and the world, and that any affective engagement with other humans has to transcend inhibitions that result from aversive past experiences and the resultant habits and memories. Therefore, there is an emotional burden that pervades *The Stone Face*, a burden that is grounded in the African American experience. The achievement of Smith's sensitive protagonist is that he learns to overcome his fears and inhibitions, and to connect his own painful experiences to those of others. One achievement of the novel is that it allows the reader to simulate its protagonist's thoughts and feelings, thus learning not only about the process by which one learns to relate to the members of an out-group, but also about what Stovall has called "The single bloodiest event in the history of postwar France" ("Preface," 305): the massacre against the Algerian minority on October 17, 1961.

In the first section of this chapter, I look more closely at the role of sensitivity in the emergence of moral emotions, such as guilt and shame, and their relationship to critical, reflexive, or "thick" modes of cosmopolitanism. In this context, I pay particular attention to factors that may *inhibit* empathy and thus prevent the development of empathic feelings, such as compassion or guilt, as well as to the consequences that such inhibition may have for intercultural understanding. The second section briefly considers the romantic emplotment of cosmopolitanism in Smith's early novels, demonstrating that in all cases, the protagonist's sensitivity is shown to be crucial for his cosmopolitan worldview, but at the same time, also a hazard to his own well-being. The third section then turns to *The Stone Face*, paying particular attention to the novel's representation of its protagonist's inner struggle with painful emotional memories and a wide range of empathic emotions. Among other things, this representation demonstrates that empathic guilt can arise in response to direct perceptions as well as to memories and imaginations, and that it is a vital component in the emergence of the critical cosmopolitan imagination.

SENSITIVITY, GUILT, AND THE CHALLENGES OF CRITICAL COSMOPOLITANISM

Sensitivity, according to *Oxford Dictionaries Online*, is "the quality or condition of being sensitive," which means, among other things, being "quick to detect or respond to slight changes, signals, or influences," being "easily damaged, injured, or distressed by slight changes," and "having or displaying a quick and delicate appreciation of others' feelings." As we will see in the third section of this chapter, *The Stone Face* plays with all three of these meanings, portraying them as fatefully interrelated and interdependent. For now, however, I will concentrate on the third meaning, which roughly translates into what psychologist June Tangney has called an "enhanced empathic responsiveness" (603). Empathy, as I have explained in chapter 1, is crucial not only for moral emotions, such as sympathy and compassion, but also for our imaginative engagement with literary texts, where it may be manipulated or at least guided by "*authorial strategic empathizing*" (Keen, "Narrative," 83), leading us to have stronger feelings for some fictional characters than for others. When an author uses strategic empathizing for the emplotment of cosmopolitanism, as is the case for all of the writers I consider here, we should expect that we are either invited to empathize directly with a member of an out-group, as American readers are in Buck's *The Hidden Flower,* or to empathize with a member of the in-group who feels empathy or sympathy for members of an out-group, as in Boyle's *Primer for Combat* as well as Smith's *The Stone Face.* While the strategies are somewhat different, the goal in both cases is to encourage readers to extend their empathic imagining beyond narrow parochial boundaries. We have also seen, in chapter 2, that empathic engagement can lead to negative or painful emotions, such as sorrow, pity, and grief. As Carl Plantinga has shown, sentimental narratives tend to aggrandize such emotions, while at the same time controlling and attenuating them through more positive emotions, ultimately offering more rewarding and morally uplifting reading or viewing experiences (see *Moving,* 169). Empathic guilt and shame, however, are different from sorrow, pity, and grief, in that they are in part *directed at the self.*

The important process that links empathic capacity to feelings of guilt is what psychologist Martin Hoffman has called "empathic distress" (30): negative and painful emotions that result from observing or imagining someone else who is in actual distress and from sharing that person's feelings. In *Empathy and Moral Development* (2000), Hoffman argues that empathic distress is a "prosocial motive" in the sense that it precedes and contributes to people's helping behavior, but he also investigates the factors that partially or fully impede such behavior. Empathic distress, he explains, strongly compels people to help others whom they perceive to be in distress, but if the perceived costs of such helping are high, then people may "be leery of feeling empathy in the first place for fear of what it may lead them to do" (34). For this reason, they may "try to forestall feeling for victims in order to escape the motivational consequences of that feeling" (34). Egoistic motives thus compete with empathic distress and may lead to an attempt to cognitively suppress the empathic response.

Sociocultural factors also play a crucial role. As Hogan has pointed out, in-group/out-group divisions are among the most important forms of empathy inhibition (see *What Literature*, 177). What Hogan calls "categorical identity"—a kind of labeling that signals the "inclusion of ourselves in particular sets of people" (*Understanding*, 8)—defines where people locate themselves in terms of in-group/out-group divisions, and they generally tend to be much more inclined to feel with the members of their in-group than with members of an out-group. As I will show in my discussion of *The Stone Face*, categorical identity and egoistic motives can interact in very powerful ways in the inhibition of an empathic response.

If we accept Hoffman's claim that empathic distress is a strong prosocial motive, then the fact that empathy can be inhibited—that humans, in fact, may even be hardwired to feel empathy more easily for the members of their in-groups—has some important consequences for cosmopolitan ethics. After all, as sociologist Gerard Delanty has argued with reference to the work of Hans-Georg Gadamer, the challenge of the "Other" is in fact needed for the development of cosmopolitan imaginations (see 11).[3] This challenge, however, is not only rational, as is so often assumed. Gadamer's (and Delanty's) "good-willed" conversations require both the *willingness* and the *capacity* to put oneself into the shoes of another person, and this requires empathic responsiveness. The inhibition of empathy for egoistic or socially conditioned reasons will necessarily stand in the way of such good-willed conversations.

Therefore, we would have to assume that a certain degree of sensitivity is an essential characteristic of the cosmopolitan individual, and I would posit that this is indeed the case. Although, as we will see when I discuss Smith's early novels, the increased vulnerability that comes with sensitivity may under certain conditions become a hazard to the sensitive individual's own well-being, it is nevertheless a precondition for cosmopolitan attitudes and behaviors, not least because it can trigger reflection and prosocial behavior through the elicitation of negative emotions that are directed at the self. And while we must assume that some individuals naturally have higher empathic capacities than others, it may often be a question of consciously *working against* the empathy inhibitions that one notices in oneself in certain circumstances. This is something I will come back to in my analysis of *The Stone Face* in the third section of the chapter.

An *uninhibited* empathic response can lead to a number of emotions beyond one's feeling of another's pain or distress. The two that most interest me here are *empathic anger* and *empathic guilt*. In empathic anger, according to Hoffman's definition, "one's attention [is] diverted from the victim to the culprit. One may feel angry at the culprit because one sympathizes with the victim or because one empathizes with the victim and feels oneself vicariously attacked, or both" (96). The distinction Hoffman makes between sympathy for and empathy with the victim is important. In both cases, the empathizing person may get angry at the perceived culprit; however, in the first case, it is because one feels sorry for the victim, whereas in the second case, it is because one is empathizing to a degree that one perceives the injury as if it were done to oneself. Of course, the two responses may commingle, but it is important to see the difference and keep in mind that painful emotional memories of a similar situation in one's own past may facilitate the second response. Hoffman admits that it is often difficult to distinguish empathic anger from direct anger, because the behavioral outcomes are very similar (see 99). Empathic anger, however, will always involve a sympathetic concern for the person with whom one is empathizing.

Empathic guilt in cases where the empathizing person has not herself harmed the victim is a response that is related to empathic anger, but in this case, the empathizing person is not so much focused on blaming a culprit (although that might happen as well), but rather on blaming him- or herself for not helping the victim. Hoffman calls this phenomenon "bystander guilt over inaction" (102).[4] It is important to keep in mind that bystander guilt is not the result of *causing* the person's distress. This latter form of guilt is what Hoffman calls "transgression guilt," and I will return to it in chapter 4 when looking at the literary work of Richard Wright. Bystander guilt, on the other hand, is of central importance in Smith's *The Stone Face*, and it was also an emotion Smith himself struggled with throughout his short life. I believe it is a particularly important emotion in the development of critical and reflexive cosmopolitanism, because it includes a feeling of responsibility—and a tendency to act—even in cases in which one has not *personally* or *directly* harmed the victim(s).

Hoffman offers two examples that are interesting both because they involve a transcendence of in-group/out-group boundaries and because they are equivalents of the kind of bystander guilt that is at work in *The Stone Face*. He cites a 1968 study by Kenneth Keniston in which white civil-rights activists explain their involvement in the movement as being a result of the feelings of guilt they *would have* experienced had they done nothing to prevent the further discrimination against and victimization of African Americans. Hoffman's second example is taken from Samuel and Pearl Oliner's *The Altruistic Personality* (1988), in which a German citizen who saved several Jews from the Nazis reports that "Unless we helped, they would be killed. I could not stand that thought. I never would have forgiven myself" (168). Note how in both cases the people felt responsible, although they were not personally harming the victims. In addition, the people in both cases were acting so as to avoid the *emotional distress* involved in feeling guilty. Helping the victim—while at least in the second case extremely risky for the helper—led to *empathic relief*, because the victim was no longer in distress. It also led to a different kind of relief, however; the relief of not having to feel guilty in the future. This is what Hoffman calls *"anticipatory* guilt" (105), and it involves a high degree of cognitive processing because it springs from the imagination. When the German who saved Jews from the Nazis says that he could never have forgiven himself, he comments on how, when confronted with the distress of others, he imagined himself in the future, knowing that he would not be able to live with the feelings of guilt he *assumed* he would have if he did not help. Therefore, his altruistic act was partially based on his compassion for the people he saved and partially on avoiding the pain he associated with future feelings of guilt.

Part of our motivations for caring and indeed helping others in distress is thus egoistic, but this should not devalue the response in any way. On the contrary, I argue that we must take empathic guilt—especially bystander guilt over inaction—into consideration when thinking, as both Andrew Linklater and Andrew Dobson have done, about our cosmopolitan obligations to the members of out-groups. In "Thick Cosmopolitanism" (2006), Dobson argues that an "appeal to the mechanism of empathy" (171) will not be enough to motivate people to act in the interest of strangers, because this will at best lead to what Linklater has called "thin" forms of cosmopolitanism.[5] To produce a cosmopolitan "nearness," Dobson argues, one needs "less empathy" and "more causal responsibility" (172), because the recognition of our own involvement in the suffering of others is much more compelling than our vague feelings of compassion for the same people. While this is a valid point, I think Dobson makes a mistake when he dismisses empathy and identification altogether. After all, most citizens in affluent societies actually *do* know that the distress experienced by distant others in less privileged regions of the world is in part the result of their own comfortable lifestyle. However, this does not, as Dobson insists it should, lead most of them to acknowledge their obligations and to stand in solidarity with those distressed, even if it means that they themselves will be losing some of their privileges, as would be the cosmopolitan thing to do.

Bruce Robbins addresses this problem when he remarks in *Feeling Global* (1999), "To get the haves mobilized behind a significant transfer of resources to the have-nots, you need . . . something like religious fervor" (153). In thinking of religious fervor, it seems quite helpful to keep in mind the idea that strong beliefs and passions form a part of people's cognition. Graham Long reminds us that "emotions can undermine—or reinforce—an agent's willingness to do the right thing. In motivational terms, emotions move us to action" (328). This is why, in his view, it is vital to "reshape" people's emotional attachments in ways that make them "more responsive to cosmopolitan demands" (327). Of course, there is always the question of who is in charge of such reshaping and by what means the reshaping is or can be done. Long, Nussbaum, and Hoffman all believe that this is the task of formal education, and that literary texts and other media forms can also aid in this process. Hoffman is the only one of the three, however, who gives detailed consideration to the ways in which the "mechanism of empathy"—to use Dobson's term again—can mobilize not only positive emotions, such as sympathy or compassion, but also negative emotions, such as guilt, which may in fact be a crucial motivational force for the acknowledgment of *obligations* that Dobson considers so important for thick and binding modes of cosmopolitanism. After all, Hoffman insists that empathic distress strongly compels people to act on behalf of others whom they perceive to be in distress, and that empathic guilt reflects an acceptance of *responsibility* and a willingness to take corrective action (see 31–33).

The crucial point, then, for the emergence of thick cosmopolitan ties might indeed be to sensitize people in the sense of enhancing their empathic responsiveness, working against, that is, the various modes by which they inhibit empathy for egoistic or socioculturally determined reasons. It might indeed be the case that feelings of guilt are at least as crucial a motivational force for cosmopolitan solidarity as the more positive emotions that may result from an empathic engagement with others. The emotion of shame is also interesting in this context, because psychologists have connected it with a *lack* of empathy, rather than with enhanced empathic responsiveness. I will give much more attention to this fascinating relationship when I consider the literary work of Richard Wright in chapter 4, but it is nevertheless worth looking briefly at the distinction between guilt and shame here, because shame also plays a role in Smith's novels.

Shame is generally understood as a feeling of *self-disgust* (I will discuss disgust in chapter 5) directed at the self as a whole, rather than just a bad feeling about a specific action performed by the self, as is the case for guilt. According to Tangney's clinical research, the presence of shame in subjects tends to correlate with the absence of empathy. "When faced with a distressed other," Tangney explains, "shame-prone individuals may be particularly likely to respond with a personal distress reaction, in lieu of a true empathic response" (600). This may be the case because the extraordinarily painful and overwhelming experience of shame inevitably "draws the focus away from the distressed other, back to the self" (600). Whereas shame is an "ugly feeling," guilt "is a bad feeling but it is not ugly. Guilt may be uncomfortable enough to motivate reparative action but not aversive enough to squelch empathic tendencies" (600). As we will see, the protagonist of *The Stone Face* struggles with both shame and guilt, and the two emotions in fact have effects on his cognition and cosmopolitan action tendencies that are very much in keeping with Tangney's research results.[6]

Before I turn to *The Stone Face*, however, I want to first briefly look at Smith's earlier literary work and at some of the life choices and emotional engagements that led him to write these texts. In this context, it is important to stress that Smith developed his cosmopolitan imagination from the standpoint of a black man who had grown up in a segregated country, and who in fact needed the emotional challenge of foreign people and places to move imaginatively beyond what he had learned and internalized at home. In his 2005 *Postcolonial Melancholia*, Paul Gilroy expresses his regret about the fact that "Today, any open stance toward otherness appears old-fashioned, new-agey, and quaintly ethnocentric" (4). Like a number of other scholars, among them Walter Mignolo, Ross Posnock, and Fujuki Kurasawa, Gilroy insists on the value of a reconceptualization of (critical) cosmopolitanism that includes diverse and nonwhite or non-Western perspectives.[7] As Gilroy himself has pointed out (see *Against*, 308), Smith's literary work offers us an opportunity to consider and value such marginalized perspectives—what Mignolo calls "border-thinking" (744)—and it is valuable in the context I discuss here, not only because it shows that a critical cosmopolitanism conceived from an African American perspective must inevitably be different from that developed by Boyle or even Buck, but also because it demonstrates that, despite these inevitable differences in attitude and perspective, the cosmopolitan imagination of these three American authors also *shares* important elements. Among those elements is not only the insistence on the equal value of all human beings, but also an emphasis on their protagonists' emotional engagement with others, the use of authorial strategic empathizing for explicit political purposes, and the preference for a romantic emplotment of cosmopolitanism.

OPEN TO OTHERS: SMITH'S NOTION OF SENSITIVITY

William Gardner Smith's life as a transnational subject began in December 1945, when he received his letter of induction into the U.S. Army. He was drafted in early 1946 and sailed to Europe soon thereafter, where he was assigned to the 661st Truck Company in Berlin as a clerk-typist. He was only nineteen years old, but he was already a writer. Coming from the shabby black ghetto of Philadelphia's South Side and having been an excellent student, he had been offered scholarships to Lincoln and Howard Universities, but declined, having set his mind on becoming a journalist. In 1944, the year of his high school graduation, he had started working full-time for the *Pittsburgh Courier*, one of the most influential black newspapers of his time, and when he was dispatched to Berlin, it was clear that he would also write a few pieces about his experience there. What Smith was unprepared for was the nature of that experience. As a member of the occupation forces, he enjoyed freedoms unthinkable for a black man in American society, and it was about this that he wrote in the articles he sent home to the *Pittsburgh Courier*. When he returned to the United States in 1947, he was already working on a novel that would somehow capture what had happened to him, the overwhelming feeling of a freedom he had never known. When the novel was published as *Last of the Conquerors* by Farrar, Straus and Company one year later in 1948, it was an immediate critical and commercial success. And because it featured Smith's first incarnation of the sensitive hero and was his first attempt at the romantic emplotment of cosmopolitanism, it is worth rendering it in a bit more detail here.

Last of the Conquerors is an unabashedly romantic, but also finely tuned and courageous, novel, which does not shy away from depicting the situation in the segregated U.S. Army as Smith himself experienced it. While the interracial love story between the black GI Hayes Dawkins and the German girl Ilse is at the heart of the narrative, it also succeeds in portraying a sentiment that was very common among African American soldiers in postwar Europe: the bitterness that springs out of the realization that black people are actually not second-class citizens everywhere, but only at "home" in the United States. In the novel, the overall tenor among the black soldiers is perhaps best summed up in the words of one of the major characters, Sergeant Murdoch, who explains after a few drinks to his compatriots why he likes Germany:

> It's the first place I was ever treated like a goddamn man. . . . You know what the hell I learned? That a nigger ain't no different from nobody else. I had to come over here to learn that. I hadda come over here and let the Nazis teach me that. They don't teach that stuff back in the land of the free. (67–68)

The bitterness in Murdoch's words reveals his feelings of anger and disgust when he points to the almost absurd irony that of all people, it is the "Nazis"—that is, the postwar German population—who teach him the meaning of racial equality. Murdoch is deeply moved by the experience of being treated simply as a human being, and not as a "black man" or "nigger." It is an experience that has completely changed his outlook and self-understanding, and so he fears nothing more than going home, back to the Jim Crow South. The same is true for most of his black comrades. This is why they desert, disappear, or flee into the Soviet Zone, where, so they have heard, blacks are treated much better than in the United States.

Because Smith was a journalist, and *Last of the Conquerors* is in part an autobiographical book, many of the experiences described in the novel closely mirror those of actual black GIs in postwar Germany. The German reception of black U.S. soldiers was—after 1945, that is—indeed often a warm and even cheerful one. If American GIs in general were the Germans' favorite group of occupation soldiers—much preferred to the French and British, and especially to the Russians—then black GIs were considered by far the most compassionate and least condescending among the occupiers.[8] The German population returned the favor with friendliness and respect. Such thriving intercultural contact did not go unnoticed. As historian Maria Höhn points out, "the encounters of black GIs with Germans were so positive that the African American press in the United States repeatedly described the experience of the GIs in Germany to indict American racism at home" (*GIs and Fräuleins*, 91). Over time, these articles (some of which were written by Smith himself) had a lasting effect on U.S. race relations.[9] Few today would dispute that the experiences of black GIs in Europe—and the portrayals of those experiences in the American press—played a significant role in both the desegregation of the U.S. Army and the strengthening of the civil rights movement in the 1950s.[10]

Smith's novel contributed its share to this process at the time, not least because it offered its explosive political message in the shape of a pleasant and emotionally engaging love story, narrated from the first-person perspective of a black American who for the first time in his life is able to speak freely with a white-skinned woman to whom he is attracted. A good example of Smith's predilection for sensitive heroes, Hayes is a perceptive and thoughtful man, longing for friendship, love, and modes of human connection that are uninhibited by racist ideology. When he lies next to Ilse on the Wannsee beach, he is surprised how "Here, away from the thought of differences for a while, it was odd how quickly I forgot it. It had lost importance" (*Last*, 44). Hayes's genuine love for Ilse, and the fact that their love crosses color lines, allow him to develop a new understanding of the nature of interracial relationships and, by extension, of human relationships in general. He is—as Smith was himself at the time—a budding cosmopolitan thinker who grasps the truth of human equality, not least through his emotional attachment to a member of an out-group.

Smith separates his two lovers, after a few happy months in Berlin, when Hayes is transferred to an all-black unit in southern Germany, evocatively nicknamed "nigger hell" among the soldiers. The narrative thus continues to adhere closely to the prototype of the romantic tragicomedy, which by default involves the separation of the lovers by a "blocking social authority" (Hogan, *What Literature*, 34). However, the interesting detail here is that the blocking authority in question is not the parents of the lovers, nor, indeed, German society. Instead, it is solely and exclusively the *white* members of the U.S. Army. From here onward, Smith presents readers with a disturbing, yet historically accurate, picture of the life of a black soldier in the segregated occupation army,[11] showing Hayes's love for Ilse and his friendship with other black soldiers to be not only his greatest assets, but also his biggest liabilities in such atrocious surroundings. Sensitivity, and a yearning for attachment, are bound to become dangerous in an atmosphere that is charged with racial hatred. The most heated racial animosities between black and white GIs—in historical reality, as well as in Smith's novel—centered on interracial dating.[12] In the novel, Ilse—who has followed Hayes to southern Germany—is kept in custody for two full days for a venereal disease check, during which she is emotionally assaulted and informed "that the colored man was dirty and very poor and had much sickness" (*Last*, 196). Ilse, however, remains unimpressed by American racial ideology, and neither she nor Hayes is willing to end their relationship because of external pressure.

At the end of the novel, it is his continued attachment to Ilse that gets

Hayes into trouble. Although he has been warned from the beginning that missing bed check is regularly used as a pretense to punish black GIs for fraternization with German women, he ignores the warning and ends up being ostentatiously punished for just that offense. The real issue at hand, however, is his knowledge of a (historical) fraud in the U.S. Army, the goal of which was to have one-third of the black GIs dishonorably discharged.[13] It is his emotional attachment to Ilse and to other black GIs that, in the end, provokes Hayes's forced choice between court-martial and the return to the Philadelphia ghetto that is his home. Hayes's final decision to return to the United States rather than heroically face a court-martial, as Hodges has pointed out, could be understood as "a flaw in [his] character" (16). It is, however, one that is in keeping with the flaws of Smith's other sensitive heroes. Like them, Hayes is a cosmopolitan intellectual rather than a fighter, but he is also a man in touch with his emotions, and his first-person narration is both emotionally engaging and thought-provoking.

This is perhaps why Carl Van Vechten wrote in a 1948 letter to Smith's publisher John Farrar that "William Gardner Smith is a remarkable new writer, with remarkable skill, charm, and power. It has been a long time since I have read a more arresting and moving book than Last of the Conquerors."[14] While many contemporary reviews were similarly positive,[15] more recent critics tend to have views similar to that of Gilroy, who observes that Smith's work is interesting "not because his novels manifest the greatest literary qualities but because, with an exemplary bravery, they dare to approach complex and important questions" (Against, 308). Last of the Conquerors, however, presents readers not only with a sad piece of American history, but, as Gilroy also points out, with decidedly cosmopolitan ethics.[16] Spatial and cultural displacement—and the resulting confrontation with the members of an out-group—are necessary prerequisites for cognizance in Smith's novel, and empathic emotions are shown to play a central role in such confrontations.

What may be seen as more problematic, however, is the novel's eclipsing of German antiblack racism.[17] While it is certainly true that of all occupation soldiers, black GIs were the favorites of the German population, this enthusiasm went only so far. The line was clearly drawn at possession of the German woman, perhaps partially in response to the loss of social and sexual privilege that was one of the most shocking aspects of defeat and occupation for German men.[18] We might attribute this oversight to Smith's youth, and his enthusiasm for a social space in which he, for the first time, could move without restrictions. Another possible reading, however, is that he made the deliberate choice to *idealize* German society in order to provoke stronger affective and cognitive responses among his American readers. As Brian Richardson has pointed out, minority and postcolonial writers often "have had to address different, incompatible audiences" (12), and this need has influenced their narrative and stylistic choices. Although we must assume that the majority of Smith's readers were black, the reviews suggest that there were white readers as well, and for both audiences the idealization of the situation in Germany would have had some obvious advantages.

Black readers—and especially black men—must have felt encouraged by imagining a European world devoid of antiblack racism, which was a myth that was already well established at the time for France and other European countries. A second likely response is *empathic anger* at the rampant racism of the blocking social authority in the novel and, by extension, *direct anger* at the blocking social authority at home.[19] And while some white readers must have felt a sense of shock when imagining what, in their understanding, was an amoral and illegal love relationship, they hardly could ignore the bitter irony involved in purging a racist country with a segregated army. Even if we acknowledge the likely political motives behind Smith's choices, however, the problem remains that the novel eclipses racist attitudes in a national out-group for the sake of castigating racist practices in the in-group. Much more than Buck's *The Hidden Flower, Last of the Conquerors* is indeed a *challenging* novel of interracial love, but it shares with the former the problem that can be involved in strategic idealization: that it offers a distorted image of reality.[20] As we will see in the final section of this chapter, Smith's *The Stone Face* is a much more careful and nuanced novel in this regard.

Last of the Conquerors made Smith a star in Philadelphia's African American community, and, at the age of twenty-one, he was celebrated as an up-and-coming black writer in the tradition of Richard Wright. He married Mary Sewell, whom he had met in his final year of high school, and they both studied at Temple University until Smith decided to break off his studies to become a full-time writer. He already had an advance contract in his pocket for a second novel, but there soon emerged differences of opinion between him and the editors at Farrar, Straus and Young. Their correspondence at the time makes quite clear that Smith was not willing to be labeled, after the success of *Last of the Conquerors*, as a "black protest writer." This is why he was planning to write about white people and universal themes instead.[21] John Farrar and his partners tried to talk Smith out of writing a "white life novel,"[22] but given his notorious stubbornness, it is not surprising that Smith's second novel, *Anger at Innocence* (1950), is exactly that and concerned with "the almost universal dream of complete happiness," as well as "the effects of conscience, of guilt."[23]

Clearly, Smith attempted to write a story about universal human values and problems, and he could easily have, as Richard Wright did on the jacket of *The Outsider* (1953), attested that his characters could have been "of any race." He kept retelling this story, which fascinated him, for the rest of his life: The problem of sensitivity, the effects of racial hatred, the turn to brute strength, the dream of peace and happiness, the tormenting effects of guilt—these are the themes that dominate all of Smith's books. In *Anger at Innocence*'s story of the thin-skinned night watchman Theodore and the abusive relationships he finds himself in, Smith probes the limits of sensitivity, concluding that in an unlimited and uncontrolled fashion, this human quality is not only dangerous, but potentially fatal. All major characters in the novel are white and are among the working poor, and have thus not seen much more of the American dream than the average African American. The racial theme in the story is addressed through the figure of Juarez, a dark-skinned Mexican immigrant who struggles with his racialized status in U.S. society and fights desperately to be accepted as a white American male.

Unfortunately, *Anger at Innocence* is an underdeveloped book that his editors thought would have much profited from further revision (which Smith was unwilling to do).[24] Still, the novel is important in the context of Smith's developing cosmopolitanism, not only because he attempts to write about topics that are all-inclusive and universal, but also because he points to one of the major problems of cosmopolitan ethics: how can one be sensitive, compassionate, and cosmopolitan in noncompassionate, noncosmopolitan surroundings? Writing hard on the heels of his return from Germany, Smith uses U.S. society as a prime example of such an environment, showing how it produces row upon row of angry, desperate, insensitive, and even insensate subjects. Theo is a man who does not understand that, in such an environment, his unabashed sensitivity and the resulting compassion and care for others are nothing but a danger to himself. That Smith allows this to destroy his main character suggests a desire to demonstrate the validity of his own assertion that sensitivity is—in the wrong environment—a curse for not only the black man, but any human. He seems to suggest that, as long as the world is the way it is, particularly but not exclusively in the United States, sensitive human beings must engage in some self-shielding and self-saving if they want to survive. Smith attempts to work out the possible strategies available for such shielding and saving in his next novel, *South Street* (1954).

In sharp contrast to *Anger at Innocence*, *South Street* features a nearly all-black cast, but it is again set in Smith's native Philadelphia. The novel centers on three African American brothers who have developed very different philosophies in dealing with American society. Michael is, as Hodges notes, something like an "early version of the late Malcolm X" (44), while the hypersensitive Philip is diffident and pacifist. Claude, the third brother and protagonist of the story, is somewhere in between. He is the critical intellectual of the family who prefers reflection to thoughtless violence. As so often occurs in Smith's books, the story builds a tension between interracial love and racial violence, and the love relationship—in this case between Claude and the white violin player Kristin—in the end is deeply damaged by the racial hatred that surrounds it.

Claude, however, does not want to be limited by other people's discriminating attitudes. He wants to understand "the universal human experience," while at the same time exploring the "range" of human existence to its fullest extent, "emotionally, spiritually, and intellectually" (*South*, 244). This is a cosmopolitan yearning, and the fact that, in Claude's eyes, the human range consists of emotions, spirituality, and intellect alike suggests that he sees the universal human experience as lived through these different but interconnected meaning-making faculties that are shared by *all* human beings. Such a life experience, however, is close to impossible in a society built on racism. Unlike Theo in *Anger at Innocence*, and unlike his brother Philip, whose hypersensitivity gets him murdered in the end, Claude understands that he cannot make American society fit his needs, and that expatriation is therefore the only possible way out (literally) of his dilemma. Only in a less hostile, less racist, and more cosmopolitan environment will he and Kristin be able to live the kind of life that they want.

This conclusion is in many ways congruent with the lessons Smith seems to have drawn in *Last of the Conquerors* and *Anger at Innocence*: a sensitive, cosmopolitan life is not possible in the United States, and those Americans—particularly those African Americans—who want to live it must leave their home country and go to other, more open-minded societies. In *South Street*, Claude's decision to leave the United States comes too late. At the end, his and his wife's bags are packed for their departure to Montreal, but they will not go and their love will not survive.[25] And so it is perhaps not a coincidence that *South Street*, with its disheartening ending, was written when Smith was already living abroad. Having left the United States in the summer of 1951, he was now working as a journalist for the English-language service of Agence France-Presse (AFP) in Paris and had become, as Michel Fabre puts it in *From Harlem to Paris* (1991), "what he had chosen to be: a cosmopolitan, worldly mind, inclined to enjoy the more leisurely pace of European life . . . and capable of adapting to diverse cultural milieus" (238). Fabre's emphasis on the fact that Smith was fluent in French and "shared the French lifestyle to the point of marrying a Parisian and raising a family there" (238) underlines Smith's quickness in adapting to new cultural surroundings. Although he had initially planned to go to Paris for only one year, he felt at home in France and had at this point already put behind him the idea that he would ever return to the United States.[26] In a 1953 letter to his mother, he wonders whether "there are any people left in the States," since it seems to him that everybody he knows is leaving.[27] The idea that one could fight one's way forcefully to a mutual engagement and respect with the abusive "Other" now seemed absurd to him.[28] In Paris, he writes, he can live the free and open-minded life he wants to live, enjoying the company of "people with common interests from all over the world" and relishing the liberal and multihued atmosphere of the beautiful city.[29] This attitude began to shift nine years later, in 1963, when he was working on *The Stone Face*. With this novel, Smith goes far beyond the blinkered celebration of a racism-free Europe that we find in *Last of the Conquerors* as he combines his indictment of American racism with a critical, cosmopolitan gaze at the political situation in France.

THE LITTLE LULU BELLES: BYSTANDER GUILT AND CRITICAL COSMOPOLITANISM IN *THE STONE FACE*

The Stone Face is, to my knowledge, the only African American novelistic engagement of its time with the so-called "Algerian question" in France.[30] Written at roughly the same time as Richard Wright was working on his "Island of Hallucination," Smith dared to put at the center of his novel what Wright tried to avoid under all circumstances: an open critique of French policies and attitudes toward Algeria and Algerians on French soil. As such, *The Stone Face* is important, not least, as Tyler Stovall has emphasized repeatedly, for historical reasons. In "Preface to *The Stone Face*" (2004), Stovall emphasizes that of all the texts about the 1961 massacre of Algerians in Paris, "surely none is more unique" than Smith's novel, which "almost certainly represents the only literary account of the . . . massacre written at the time of the actual events by someone who witnessed them"

(305).[31] Literary critic Kristin Ross similarly asserts that Smith is one of the few fiction writers (white or black) who "kept a trace of the event alive during the thirty years when it had entered a 'black hole' of memory" (44). The massacre occurred when the French police attacked an unarmed and peaceful demonstration of some forty thousand Algerians and sympathizers who had been organized by the Algerian Front de Libération Nationale (FLN) in reaction to the decree of an indefinite nightly curfew for Algerians in Paris. It is unclear to this day how many people, exactly, died at the hands of the police during the massacre. After decades of silence, the French government finally acknowledged forty deaths in 1998; historians, such as Stovall, estimate the number of victims at "over two hundred" ("The Fire," 195). The realistic description of the massacre in *The Stone Face*, which can almost certainly be attributed to the fact that Smith was also a journalist and a great fan of Ernest Hemingway's simple and direct style, thus makes it an important document for historians and other scholars concerned with a long-repressed part of French colonial history.[32]

However, the historical relevance of Smith's novel does not end here. In addition to denouncing French racism against Algerians, *The Stone Face* also views critically the ways in which the African American expatriate community in Paris dealt with this issue. Smith's story of the black American expatriate Simeon, who, in his comfortable Parisian exile, is confronted with the question of which side he wants to choose—that of the oppressor or of the oppressed—lays bare the various and often egoistic reasons that led black American intellectuals to inhibit their empathic engagement with the Algerian minority in France and stay silent about the abuses of another nonwhite ethnic group that they were witnessing on a daily basis. The Algerian War, Stovall explains, "challenged cherished African American beliefs about French color-blindness" ("The Fire," 183) as the open violence of French authorities against Algerians both in Algeria and on French soil called "into question this cozy unity between African American expatriates and their French hosts" (189). Many black Americans in France were angered by the behavior of the French government, but they also knew that open criticism would cost them their residence permits in France. Simeon Brown, Smith's alter ego in *The Stone Face*, is confronted with these realities, and he must make his own choices in the face of them.

Simeon is perhaps the best example of Smith's general tendency to create sensitive, thoughtful, and intellectual heroes who are distinguished by the ambiguous privilege of being particularly insightful and at the same time particularly tormented by their insights. Like so many fellow black expatriates, Simeon has escaped to Paris to find peace and safety. "Violence," he thinks in relief upon his arrival in Paris, "would not be necessary, murder would not be necessary" (*Stone*, 3). Simeon has left his hometown Philadelphia in order to prevent himself from one day running amok, killing the man who had stabbed him in the eye, or killing some other man who might try the same. Artistically, the young painter is at an impasse. He can only paint a single motif: the face of the man who blinded his eye, an "inhumanly cold face with dull, sadistic eyes, a thin mouth, tightly clamped jaw and deathly pale skin" (27). The man who presented him with this "stone face," Simeon is convinced, "felt no human emotion, no compassion, no generosity, no wonder, no love! The face was that of hatred: hatred and denial—of everything, of life itself" (27). There is, of course, a contradiction in this statement: a man who feels "no human emotion" is unlikely to feel hatred, which is, after all, a forceful emotional response. But my conjecture is that what Smith is really after here is not a lack of feeling, but rather a lack of *empathy*. The stone face is the face of *insensitivity*, of complete indifference toward others.

The fact that, despite its lack of empathy, the stone face expresses an emotion—the insensate and uncaring expression of hatred—determines Simeon's feelings for it. That is true not only because he is sensitive, but also because he keeps remembering, imagining, and in fact *painting* the stone face. All of this allows him (or condemns him) to perceive its image vividly, and as I have explained in chapter 1, facial emotion expressions tend to trigger immediate emotional responses in empathic perceivers. These responses can be either parallel (resulting in the same emotion) or complementary (resulting in an opposite emotion). In Simeon's case, it is mostly the latter, since most of the time the hatred of the stone face fills him with a deep-seated fear. Nevertheless, he is also obsessed with it; indeed, one could argue that in a bizarre way, the face has become an attachment figure, and as Hogan reminds us, "Attachment enhances the likelihood of emotional contagion" (*Affective*, 33). The stone face represents for Simeon what he himself is not: not only is it insensate and pitiless, it also stands for unlimited power and domination. His own sensitivity, Simeon declares early on in the novel, "was a curse" in the black Philadelphia ghetto in which he spent his childhood, as it is now as an adult, because the world as a whole is "violent and brutal" (*Stone*, 25). At the same time, however, this same sensitivity, and the empathic distress that comes with it, prove vital for his cosmopolitan development.

Apart from the haunting images of his past, Simeon seems to indeed have found in Paris the kind of racism-free paradise that Hayes Dawkins in *Last of the Conquerors* imagined—at least we are tempted to believe so at the beginning of the novel. Simeon enjoys the liberties of his new life in Paris and the friendships he makes within the black American expatriate community, a fictional version of the historical African American community in Paris, which, as Stovall notes, "was cosmopolitan not just in its internal makeup but also in its broader perspective" and its close connection to African intellectuals ("Harlem-sur-Seine"). The biggest obstacle to a happy life in this cosmopolitan city, it seems initially, is Simeon's habituation to American patterns of racism and his related emotional memories. In an early scene, Simeon sits on the terrace of the Café Tournon and enjoys his new quarters when he notices a beautiful French woman a few tables away from him. Simeon at first feels too shy and self-conscious to approach "an unfamiliar woman, white to boot" (*Stone*, 5), but finally brings himself to ask if he can buy her a drink. The woman declines without even looking at him, and Simeon is "mortified." Certain that everyone is staring at him, he feels "alone and naked on a stage, a blazing spotlight on him" (6). Simeon's reaction is too violent for embarrassment; what torments him is *shame*. With shame, we typically feel that we are watched (and judged) by others, and we feel distress because of what we believe they see in us. What at first seems like an excessive response becomes more understandable when Simeon reveals its true cause: "Slowly, against his will, the old insidious thought came to him, the conditioned reflex. *Racism*. It was omnipresent. It was here in Paris, too" (5). Not only does Simeon feel self-disgust for having been naïve enough to believe that the French capital is free of racism, but he now also detests the French girl "with her mocking smile" (6). People's attitudes in Paris, it seems, are just as discriminatory as those of the society "at home" in the United States.

Just a few seconds after this quick indictment of both the girl and his new surroundings, however, Simeon has to learn that things are not as he had thought:

> [T]he young woman's face lighted as she looked toward the street. . . .
> A tall African, black as anthracite, walked smiling up to her. They embraced and kissed. The people on the terrace continued to talk . . . ignoring this scene as they had ignored the scene with Simeon. (6–7)

In a clever rhetorical move, Smith introduces the topic of "omnipresent" racism only to dismantle it in the next moment as the paranoid imagination of a man who is haunted by his American past. No one had in fact been staring at Simeon, and the French girl did not decline his offer be-cause he is black—her boyfriend is blacker than he is. She simply was not interested because she is spoken for, irrespective of skin color or race. Re-gardless of Simeon's generally sensitive nature, the waves of shame and anger that wash over him during this brief episode make it impossible for him to put himself into the girl's shoes, to even consider that there may be reasons for her behavior other than racism. These emotions are, as he puts it, a "conditioned reflex," acquired by decades-long exposure to rac-ist practices.

Using Simeon as a focalizer in this scene, Smith aligns readers with his protagonist, allowing them to first share his strong negative emotions, and then his surprise and perplexity when things are different than they seemed. Through an avoidance of "intrusive editorial comments," notes Bernard Bell, Smith encourages "identification with the moral and polit-ical awakening of his central character by generally restricting the focus to his double-consciousness" (185). The scene also captures what Sue Kim calls "the possible dynamics of literary representation of anger, includ-ing such issues as the dangers of erroneous judgments as the bases for emotions" (99). In addition, it makes readers aware of "the *histories* and *structures* that produce emotions, beyond a single person's subjectivity, not only in characters but also in readers" (Kim, 99). Here and elsewhere, the reader is invited to see both the United States and France through Simeon's eyes, and since Simeon's vision is impaired—both physically and metaphorically—such a perspective cannot but be limited and skewed. Consequently, it must be modified and adapted as the focus of perception changes. Simeon's perception only gradually adapts to his new surround-ings, and so it takes time until he can see—and respond emotionally to—the forms of discrimination that actually exist in Paris. Racism, it turns out, is indeed far from absent in France. It is just different, targeted at a different group of people.

The novel in fact provides the first hints of French racism toward the Algerian minority early on in the story. At first, such eruptions of rac-ist rhetoric or physical violence seem only incidental. Simeon glances at a newspaper that says "MOSLEMS RIOT IN ALGIERS. FIFTY DEAD" (*Stone*, 7), but does not give much thought to the headline. Not much later, he witnesses a French policeman brutally clubbing a man whose lan-guage he cannot understand, and "this violent scene of *matraquage*," as Kristin Ross observes, "jars loose a flashback," causing him to relive "his own beating at the hands of police in Philadelphia" (46). There is, for Simeon, an eerie proximity between his vivid memories of his past experiences in the faraway United States and what he observes, as an innocent bystander, on the streets of Paris.

This uncomfortable proximity is not least the result of Simeon's sensitivity, which makes it difficult for Simeon to dissociate and distance himself from the destiny of the Algerians, like other members of the African American expatriate community do. As a result, he feels increasingly uncomfortable about his own position as a well-respected American expatriate. When asked one day by an Algerian how it feels "to be a white man" (*Stone*, 55), the label at first seems absurd to him, but he also recognizes that it is true: here, in the Paris of the early 1960s, he is indeed enjoying, in spite of his skin color, the privileges of a white man, and it is the Algerian minority that takes the place of, as one of them puts it, "the niggers" (57). He now understands that Algerians in France are faced with a dominant "Other" that is just as hostile as the nonblack part of American society was and is for Simeon.

Once Simeon makes his first personal contact with Algerians, he soon befriends one of them, Ahmed, and accepts an invitation to visit his home in the Goutte d'Or, the immigrant-populated "Drop of Gold" in the north of Paris. The sight of the shabby and overcrowded quarters that he finds there again triggers memories of the South Philadelphia ghetto for him. And the similarities continue. Not only does he learn that Algerians for the most part cannot find housing in any other, and less run-down, parts of town, but he also experiences a police raid in which he has to show his papers to an armed French policeman. After recognizing that Simeon is "not an Arab" (94), the policeman wants to know what he is doing in this part of town. "Visiting a friend" is Simeon's answer, upon which the police officer suggests that he should "stick among the foreigners. You've got nice cafés over there on the Left Bank. Stay out of trouble" (95). This advice to stay out of French affairs was, of course, familiar to all American expatriates, but at this point in the novel Simeon is already too much involved with the Algerians to heed it.

This involvement is mostly a result of his increasingly close friendship with Ahmed, who tells him early on that he believes that he and Simeon are "similar in some way" (82). Despite their differences in nationality and ethnicity, Ahmed explains, they are connected through a shared sensitivity, and they are both "repelled by hatred and violence," even as they see themselves occasionally compelled to use force and brutality "when there is no other way" (82–83). The friendship that develops between the two men out of this shared sensitivity—and certainly also out of similar experiences—has a number of far-reaching consequences for Simeon. Not only does it profoundly change his view of France and its attitude toward the Algerian minority, he also grows increasingly distant from other black Americans. "Identifying with the Algerians," Ross points out, means for Simeon "first *dis*identifying with his own social group, the black Americans in France. . . . It is that displacement which allows him to see what the other black expatriates, in their clannishness, do not" (46–47). Disidentification and reorientation are thus important elements in Simeon's cosmopolitan development from a mostly immersive to a critical and reflexive style of cosmopolitanism, which "demonstrates a broad willingness to step outside stable, privileged and established power categories of selfhood" (Kendall, Woodward, and Skrbis, 122). How difficult and painful this process can be, and how much it depends on a willingness to deal with the consequences of empathic distress, are demonstrated in one of the most intriguing moments of *The Stone Face.*

After spending the evening with Ahmed and three other Algerians, Simeon spontaneously decides to take his friends to one of his favorite hangouts in Paris, a highly exclusive nightclub. The usually friendly waiter stares at them coldly, and Simeon suddenly feels like he is "back in Philadelphia" (107). The French guests in the club, too, react with icy silence. Because of his association with the Algerians, Simeon realizes, he has become "a nigger again . . . to the outside eyes" (108). Most distressing for him, however, are his own thoughts and emotions:

> For one horrible instant, he found himself *withdrawing* from the Algerians—the pariahs, the untouchables! He, for the frightening second, had rejected *identification* with them! Not me! Not me! Can't you see, I'm *different*! the lowest part in him had cried. He looked down with shame. (108)

Here, Smith powerfully demonstrates the role of social pressure in the creation of racism and social stigma. It is other people's alienating stares—stares that this time are disconcertingly real—that make Simeon feel humiliated and ashamed, which is why, for a moment, he responds "with a personal distress reaction, in lieu of a true empathic response" (Tangney, 600). Insisting on his categorical identification as a black American, he mentally abandons the men who just a minute ago were his best friends. Having lived for months as a foreign yet accepted member of French society, Simeon suddenly realizes not only how quickly these privileges can be lost again, but also how much he *desires* them. His sudden urge to reject identification with the Algerians is an egoistic urge to inhibit empathy and the resulting empathic distress. It is the first step in the direction of becoming an insensitive and uncosmopolitan stone face himself.

However, Simeon's second emotion episode is just as interesting: cognitively monitoring his own urge to empathically withdraw from his friends, he experiences a different kind of shame. We must assume that when Simeon looks "down with shame" (108), he is ashamed of his overwhelming desire to be accepted as a worthy human being, mixed with some bystander guilt about letting down his Algerian friends. The outcome of this mixture of bystander guilt and shame is interesting. After the initial moment of shock has passed, Simeon realizes that he has "crossed the bridge" and now feels "at one with the Algerians" and "strangely *free*—the wheel had turned full circle" (109). In this important moment of (re)identification, Simeon overcomes his egoistic urge to distance himself from the Algerians, consciously choosing solidarity with his friends over the privilege of being a "white man." This, he believes to be the morally right and—in the term I have chosen here—cosmopolitan thing to do.

Critical and reflexive cosmopolitanism, as Kendall, Woodward, and Skrbis note, tends to emerge, as in Simeon's case, "from bonds of solidaristic sentiments and the imagination" (152), which are necessary to think and feel oneself into the position of another person. That does not mean, however, that it is an easy thing to do. As a result of his solidarity with his Algerian friends, Simeon has to give back his key to the private nightclub, to which he now, as a "nigger lover," can no longer belong. Like Smith himself, who was good friends with Algerians and publicly assumed a pro-Algerian position even though it was potentially unsafe for his own status in France, Simeon now takes personal risks and accepts personal disadvantages and injuries to stand in solidarity with someone who used to be the "Other." Although this is quite remarkable, one could still argue that Simeon's act of solidarity must not necessarily be truly cosmopolitan in kind, but simply the expression of a newly chosen kinship and identification with a particular ethnic group, or even a simple projection of his own experiences onto the "Other." And indeed, Simeon's act of solidarity with the Algerians is only a first step in a much larger personal development.

Another important factor in that development is his love relationship with the Polish girl Maria. It should be mentioned at this point that *The Stone Face* is as much an attachment story as it is a love story; indeed, it could be argued that the attachment story—Simeon's friendship with Ahmed—is the true center of the novel.[33] Nevertheless, Simeon's love for Maria plays a crucial role in the emergence of his cosmopolitan imagination. A Jewish concentration camp survivor who hopes to make a career as an actress in Paris, Maria presents herself as a lighthearted young woman, determined to leave the horror of the camp behind. But Simeon soon comes to understand that behind the beautiful façade, she is haunted by the same face that keeps troubling him. She, too, suffers from impaired vision as a result of the physical violence she has endured, and when she talks about the German camp commander who kept her, and for a time her parents, alive, but also regularly raped the then nine-year-old girl, we realize that she, too, is haunted by a stone face. Remembering the dreadful moments when the commander's "face would change," she explains that it was "like the face in your portrait; his eyes would be hard, the blood would go away and his skin would be white like ashes, cold like stone" (*Stone*, 76). The stone face here emerges as the abstract image of racial oppression, transcending the concrete historical situations and conditions of such oppression.

However, this connection between Simeon's and Maria's fate, and the implied linking of Jewish and black histories of abuse, are only the beginning. Smith also uses the figure of Maria to make clear that not even the Algerians—who clearly stand for *the oppressed* in the novel—are without discriminating attitudes toward others. When Maria shows Simeon a new bracelet and feels she might have been overcharged by the shopkeeper, one of the Algerians blurts out that "probably some dirty Jew sold it" to her (121), and Simeon is "stunned" at this racist remark from one of his friends: "Abruptly a whole mental and psychological structure he had built up . . . seemed to collapse" (122). Maria, for her part, reacts with icy anger: "I am dirty Jew," she tells Hossein, who feels guilty at the realization of his faux pas (122). After all, he cares for Maria, and realizes only when he empathizes with her reaction that he has hurt her feelings with his thoughtlessly voiced prejudice. This important moment in *The Stone Face*, in which the oppressed prove just as susceptible to racial prejudice as the oppressor, not only shows Smith's capacity as a writer, but also gives evidence of his own critical cosmopolitanism. He uses his novel to voice a passionate critique of racism, and he manages to do so without romanticizing or idealizing the victims of that racism.

The vehicle of this critique remains his alter ego Simeon, who, after the incident in the nightclub, gets more and more involved with the Algerian liberation struggle as a political project. He has heated discussions with fellow expatriates about the question of whether they should get involved in the Algerian fight for independence or whether the intensifying civil rights movement in the United States obligates them to go back "home" to join the struggle there. Simeon feels increasingly guilty about enjoying a convenient life in Paris while others are fighting for their freedom. These feelings verge on the unbearable when he learns that Ahmed has joined the FLN and that in the American town of Little Rock, there are now children facing racist mobs. Simeon imagines himself "walking with the image of [a] little girl he had named Lulu Belle" to the schoolhouse in Little Rock (137). He cannot get rid of that mental image, and the more he ponders it, "the more disgusted he felt with himself. He was over here, comfortable in Paris, leaving the *fighting* to the little Lulu Belles" (143–144).

The vivid mental image of the little black girl braving an onslaught of discrimination triggers bystander guilt over inaction in Simeon, as well as self-disgust, and it is important to see that his reflexive cosmopolitanism critically depends on both of these emotions. Other black Americans, however, react differently. Simeon's friend Babe Carter insists that black people have "enough trouble in the world without going about defending white people" (105), thus explaining his lack of solidarity with the Algerians, whom he, rather conveniently, constructs as white. At the same time, he feels unable to go back and support the civil rights movement, because he believes that he has been away from the United States too long to adjust again to its racist politics (see 145). Disengaging from both the distressed Algerians around him and the more distant black people at home, Babe has found a mental stance that allows him to continue his convenient life in Paris. Because Simeon is unwilling or unable to inhibit his empathy for both of these groups, he feels the need to take on personal responsibility, be it by returning to the United States or by supporting the independence struggles in Algeria or sub-Saharan Africa.

It is in Paris, however, that Simeon finally feels compelled to take action. Personally witnessing the massacre of Algerians in October 1961, he cannot control himself when he sees a French policeman beating an Algerian woman and her baby on the streets of Paris.[34] Coming to the rescue of woman and child, he suddenly recognizes in the policeman's face "that face he knew so well, the face . . . he had tried to escape" (203). It is the *stone face* that Simeon sees in front of him, another incarnation of the face of insensitivity, cruelty, and hatred. As usual, the emotional expression in the face triggers an empathic response in him, but this time it is not complementary, but parallel. Tormented by the pain in the socket of his missing eye, Simeon swings "his fist into that hated face" (203). The man who abhors violence feels forced into violent action himself, in defense of the helpless woman and child as much as in desperate and helpless revenge for his own injuries. The moment is interesting, because it demonstrates that *empathic anger* can indeed be the result of both empathy with and sympathy for the victim. While Simeon clearly is concerned for the woman and her baby, he just as clearly hits the policeman because he perceives the injury as if it were—once again—done to him. His violent response is fueled by his emotional memories and his uneasy attachment to the ever-present image of the stone face.

After attacking the policeman, Simeon is arrested and shipped to a prison camp outside of Paris; there, surrounded by thousands of Algerians, he comes to the realization that is the central thesis of the novel and the message the reader is supposed to grasp:

> [T]he face of the French cop . . . the face of the Nazi torturer at Buchenwald and Dachau, the face of the hysterical mob at Little Rock . . . and, yes, the black faces of Lumumba's murderers—they were all the same face. Wherever this face was found, it was his enemy; and whoever feared, or suffered from, or fought against this face was his brother. (205–206)

Simeon, who has understood that being on or taking the side of the oppressed is the only way to avoid becoming an insensate stone face himself, also realizes here that being the subject of oppression links him to every other oppressed being in the world. And that realization puts him at the same time in opposition to the oppressor. As Bernard Bell notes, the main theme of *The Stone Face* is that "wherever oppression exists, it dehumanizes the oppressor as well as the victim; and anybody who lives in its shadow is guilty of social and moral blindness and irresponsibility" (184). It is bystander guilt over inaction that leads Simeon to critically reflect on his own responsibilities in the face of discrimination, injustice, and suffering. Although his physical vision is still impaired, his intellectual insights have, as a result of his empathic engagement with others, progressed greatly by the end of the novel. Cosmopolitans, he now understands, cannot afford to just *enjoy* cultural difference; they have a moral obligation to fight racial and social injustice everywhere they go, and their opponents can assume any nationality, race, or skin color.

Gilroy's reading of *The Stone Face* is especially sympathetic to the above-quoted passage, which he interprets as an expression of Smith's insight "that the face of racial hatred could be fought when and wherever it appeared" (*Against*, 323). All the more regrettable, in Gilroy's view, is Smith's choice of an ending for his story. Deviating from the typical romance plot, Smith has Maria leave Simeon at the end of the novel because she hopes to make a career for herself in the United States. Even more devastating for him is the news that Ahmed has died fighting for the liberation of Algeria. Wondering where he can go now, Simeon believes he knows "the inevitable answer—even though repugnance swept through him whenever he thought of it" (210). Despite his feelings of disgust for his home country, he believes he must go back because "America's Algerians were back there, fighting . . . the stone face" (210). This decision, in Gilroy's view, marks a sudden change from a complex to a simplistic narrative, since it "is neither illuminated nor justified and becomes an explicit if unconvincing repudiation of the cosmopolitan alternative involved in taking responsibility for the struggle against injustice in its immediate manifestations" (*Against*, 323). Gilroy's final verdict, I believe, does not do the novel justice, since Simeon's feelings of bystander guilt in relation to the civil rights movement have been a constant thread throughout the novel. The same feelings also haunted Smith himself. In a letter to his sister Phyllis in 1964, he notes: "I sometimes feel guilty of living way over here—especially when I read of 'freedom marchers' and the like. Maybe we'll come back eventually."[35] In light of this, Gilroy might well have sensed a tension in *The Stone Face* that stems from Smith's attempt to work out a real-life conflict within his novel.

Such a tension, however, must not necessarily mean that Smith "was either unprepared or unable to follow the logic of his own [cosmopolitan] insight to its obvious conclusion" (Gilroy, *Against*, 323). In my view, Smith actually does "follow the logic of his own insight," only there is more than one conclusion to draw from this logic. One such conclusion might have been to have Simeon stay in Paris and fight the French government. Another might have been to have him go to Algeria—as he plans at one point in the novel—or join the anticolonial struggle elsewhere. As it turns out, this is exactly what Smith originally had in mind. From his correspondence with his publisher, we learn that Smith had written a different ending for the novel, one in which Simeon left for Africa instead of the United States. It was his editor at Farrar, Straus and Company who took up a remark in a letter of Smith's and suggested that the book might sell better in the States if the hero went back to support the civil rights movement.[36] Smith agreed and made the change. Whether he did so for ideological or for commercial reasons, we will never know.

However, even with the published ending of the novel as it is—in which Simeon books a ship passage to return to the Unites States and tears up his painting of the stone face because "the reality had penetrated" (213)—I see no final collapsing of Smith's or Simeon's cosmopolitanism. After all, the civil rights struggle in the United States is, in Gilroy's own understanding, as much a part of the black Atlantic as the decolonization movement in sub-Saharan Africa. If anything, Simeon's solidarity with both the Algerian struggle *and* the civil rights movement constitutes an *extension* of the idea of the black Atlantic that also allows for the participation of the Arabic (post)colonial context, which makes it an even stronger affirmation of a transracial cosmopolitanism that transcends and transgresses national or race thinking. This is why Moustafa Bayoumi calls *The Stone Face* "a brilliant novel," asserting that "this little-known novel is a triumph in transcultural empathy, a way of feeling one's connection in the world through a shared experience with another 'Other'" (21). Bayoumi's statement nicely underscores the importance of sensitivity for the plot and theme of the novel, as well as the central role it plays in critical and reflexive modes of cosmopolitanism more generally.[37]

Unlike his protagonist, Smith did not go back to the United States, but instead made the choice that Gilroy seems to find preferable: a year after the novel's publication, Smith left Paris and moved with his wife Solange Royez and their daughter Michelle to Kwame Nkrumah's Ghana. There, he helped Shirley Graham Du Bois build Ghana Television, as well as the Ghana School for Journalism and the first African news service. As he writes in his unpublished "Through Dark Eyes," he went to Ghana because he "wanted to participate in what was going on in the world," instead of "rotting in Paris" (18–19). Unlike his protagonist, he chose one of the newly independent countries in Africa for this local participation. After the coup d'état in 1966, Smith and his family returned to Paris. In 1967 he briefly visited the United States in order to report on the "race riots" for Agence France-Presse. It was his first visit in sixteen years, and he recorded his experience of the civil rights struggle, together with his thoughts on Ghana and Paris, in his last book, the nonfiction *Return to Black America*. When the book went to press in 1970, Smith was living with his third wife, the India-born Ira Reuben, in Paris. A year later, they welcomed their daughter Rachel, Smith's third and last child. As a special correspondent for AFP, he continued to cover important events in the decolonization process, such as the nonaligned nations' conference in Belgrade, the Arab summit in Morocco, and the 1971 economic meeting in Peru, until his quickly worsening health no longer allowed for such strenuous trips.

Smith died of lung cancer in 1974 in a suburb of Paris, at the age of forty-seven, without having ever returned to the United States again. In "Through Dark Eyes," he sums up how his experiences abroad contributed to the development of his cosmopolitan imagination. "It is fascinating," he writes, "to shift vantage points, change worlds, turn the prism slowly before the eye" (10). Such shifting of vantage points, he makes clear, inevitably transforms one's identity and self-understanding, but there are some things that remain constant as well:

> I was, once, an American, albeit a black one. . . . The outward trappings of my "Americanism" faded as the years went by, but one thing did not change: the blackness of my skin. I was, in the United States, a black man in a racist white society; in Europe, particularly France, a black man in a less racist society; and in Africa, for the first time in my life, a black man in a black society. (10–11)

This progression, Smith explains, "was psychologically stupifying [*sic*]" (11), and its psychological impact helped him reflect critically on both the differences and the important continuities between his own experiences and those of other humans around the world.

CONCLUSION

Sensitivity, then, I have shown in this chapter, is not only the capacity to be aware of what is going on in one's human and nonhuman surroundings, but also includes the *willingness* to engage empathetically with them—*even if* such engagement is painful or potentially dangerous for one's own well-being. This, in turn, means that it involves actively working against the "natural" inhibition of empathy through egoism or categorical in-group/out-group divisions. I have also discussed the potential value of empathic guilt—specifically bystander guilt over inaction—and milder forms of shame for the development of critical and reflexive cosmopolitan ethics. *The Stone Face* imagines how such a process might work, and since it invites readers to simulate Simeon's thoughts and feelings, it may trigger such processes in readers as well. That is at least suggested by the anecdotal evidence that I gain from teaching the novel to my students, and it is indeed quite remarkable how much they tend to like the novel, and how strongly they react both to its vivid portrayals of racial violence and to the protagonist's increasing engagement with the Algerian liberation struggle. While they tend to differ strongly in their opinions about the ending—some feel that Simeon makes the right choice, while others believe he should have stayed in France or Algeria to help the people there—none of them ever suggests that he should simply have stayed out of all of it. Instead, they start reflecting and discussing the advantages and disadvantages of sensitivity and the related moral choices that they can see, and I believe that this is really all we can ask for from a cosmo-politan literary text.

There is little doubt that Smith thought of himself as a sensitive man, and that he believed sensitivity to be a particularly precarious quality in a black man like himself. In his novels, sensitivity is consistently depicted as something for which a black American male—and perhaps anyone— must inevitably pay a high price. At the same time, it seems Smith could not help but affirm the importance of this delicate quality, which attunes people's thinking and feeling to what is going on around them and makes them *care* about it. It is out of this tension that much of Smith's cosmo-politanism—fictional and actual—arises. It was quite unusual, even dar-ing, for a black male writer at the time to openly advocate a quality such as sensitivity. While the quality itself had traditionally been coded as fem-inine, Smith's pairing it with love and attachment relationships at the cen-ter of what often amounted to protest novels, or at least deeply political novels, was a risk. If he thus insists on the sensitivity of his characters, as well as on his own, he consciously moves away from the conventions of black masculinity of his time. To acknowledge sensitivity and emotion-ality as important parts of our meaning-making faculties was not and is not generally seen as an adequate (or masculine) approach to problems of racial and social injustice, but when we compare Smith's heroes with the angry and often violent protagonists that populate the novels of Richard Wright, we are struck by their openness, compassion, and overall paci-fism.[38] Most of them despise violence (including the violence they feel in-side themselves) and become violent only if there is no other way to defend themselves or someone they love.

At heart, these characters all firmly believe in the universality of the human experience, and Smith himself shared that belief. His dim hope, in spite of his general skepticism, was that this universality might pro-vide some common ground for cosmopolitan understanding and solidar-ity. In "The Negro Writer: Pitfalls and Compensation," published in 1950 in *Phylon* when Smith was only twenty-three years old, he wrote that "the Negro writer of strength and courage stands firmly as a champion of the basic human issues—dignity, relative security, freedom and the end of savagery between one human being and another" (303). In this, the young Smith hoped in a truly cosmopolitan spirit, the black writer "is supported by the mass of human beings the world over" (303). Richard Wright, to whom I will now turn, certainly agreed with Smith about the nature of these "basic human issues," but, as we will see in the next chapter, the rhetorical strategies he used to convince his readers of their value could hardly have been more different.

COSMOPOLITAN CONTRADICTIONS: FEAR, ANGER, AND THE TRANSGRESSIVE HEROES OF RICHARD WRIGHT

"I'M A ROOTLESS MAN," RICHARD WRIGHT declares boldly in *White Man Listen!* (1957), "but I'm neither psychologically distraught nor in any wise particularly perturbed because of it" (xxxviii). With this audacious statement, Wright claims for himself, and decidedly embraces, the status of the rootless cosmopolitan, the man who does not "hanker after, and seem[s] not to need, as many emotional attachments, sustaining roots, or idealistic allegiances as most people" (xxviii). This radical emotional independence, Wright "confesses" to his reader, is by no means a coincidence, nor is it a "personal achievement" of his (xxix). Instead, he has "been shaped to this mental stance by the kind of experiences that [he has] fallen heir to" (xxix). His historical situatedness, as a black man in racist America and as a foreigner experiencing the French and African political climates of the 1950s, Wright argues, has produced an outlook in him that rejects tradition and community in favor of rootless cosmopolitanism. Wright's angry professions of rootlessness were in part the result of his conflicted feelings toward the United States, the "home" country that he passionately loved and deeply despised at the same time. When he said he was free of *all* attachments, he was mostly insisting on being free of America, the country that had rejected him as a full citizen and a whole human being, the country that, as a result of a very painful emotional process, had *driven* him to a cosmopolitan position. However, not only did the practical enactment of this "rootless" position turn out to be much more difficult than Wright had hoped, his actions and writings as a whole were also quite inconsistent with his repeated proclamations of radical independence. If he kept insisting on his complete detachment, then at the same time, he lived and passionately advocated a cosmopolitan solidarity across national and racial boundaries.

I will argue in this chapter that Wright's cosmopolitan contradictions can only be truly understood if we pay attention not only to their intellectual, but also their emotional, dimensions. Kwame Anthony Appiah is right when he says that "There's a sense in which cosmopolitanism is the name not of the solution but of the challenge" (*Cosmopolitanism*, xv), and in his fiction and nonfiction, Wright lays bare just how great that challenge can be. I will look at three of his novels—*Native Son* (1940), *The Outsider* (1953), and the to-this-day-unpublished "Island of Hallucination"—to explore how negative emotions, such as fear, anger, and shame, can hinder or at least complicate the emergence of cosmopolitan imaginations because they involve the inability to engage openly and empathically with others.[1] As we have seen in chapter 3, William Gardner Smith believed that empathic responsiveness is something that a black man in America cannot really afford, because he grows up in sociocultural conditions that make sensitivity a liability rather than an advantage. Smith's protagonists are sensitive men who deeply care about others and, as a result, learn to stretch their moral imagination across in-group/out-group boundaries. However, only those who leave the United States can thrive and develop cosmopolitan practices—those who remain at home are condemned to disappointment, failure, and death. Wright's novels arrive at similar conclusions, but their protagonists are much less compassionate than Smith's, and they are also more angry and violent. Wright's rhetorical strategy in the three novels I will consider is to condemn his readers to empathize with a protagonist they find morally ambiguous, disgusting, or even threatening, in the hope that this will shock them into realizing the immorality of their own conduct and society. In the end, he has his protagonists fail and/or die, but not without giving them some insight into the problematic nature of their condition. I will demonstrate that this insight amounts to an affirmation of the human need for attachment, empathy, and compassion, and although none of the novels is a prototypical love story, we find that in two of them, there is an emplotment of cosmopolitanism that foregrounds romantic love and attachment.

The first section of the chapter explores the negative and often debilitating emotions that tend to dominate Wright's novels: fear, anger, and shame. I argue that in order to understand the relationship between these negative emotions and Wright's emplotment of cosmopolitanism, we need to pay attention not only to their eliciting conditions and actional outcomes, but also to their temporal dimensions and potential interwovenness. To illustrate these points, I use examples given by Wright himself in his well-known essay "How 'Bigger' Was Born" (1940), a piece of self-reflection that also demonstrates the centrality of Wright's own negative experiences and resulting emotions in the creation of his influential first novel, *Native Son*. The second section of the chapter looks more closely at the development of Wright's cosmopolitan imagination after his permanent departure from the United States in 1947. I pay particular attention to the allegation, uttered by James Baldwin and others, that Wright's life abroad and his association with French existentialist intellectuals interfered with his authenticity as a black American writer. I turn to Wright's second novel, *The Outsider*, which was influenced by French existentialism, as an interesting example of Wright's romantic emplotment of cosmopolitanism. Like *Native Son*, *The Outsider* features a protagonist who almost drowns in negative emotions, but they include not only dread and anger, but also transgression guilt and remorse. The latter emotions, which are a direct result of the novel's love story, are what allow him to move away from radical and murderous solipsism toward an understanding of the importance of human community. A similar development can be observed in Wright's "Island of Hallucination," which I will consider in the third and final section. Like Smith's Simeon Brown, the novel's protagonist has left the United States and lives as an expatriate in France, but because he is much less willing than Simeon to engage openly with his new surroundings in Paris, he is at first unable to change his habituated outlook. My focus in the discussion of all three novels is on the ways in which they align readers with morally transgressive protagonists in order to promote cosmopolitan ethics.

FEAR, ANGER, AND THE DARK IMAGINATION OF BIGGER THOMAS

In chapters 2 and 3, I have been concerned with negative empathic emotions, such as sorrow, pity, grief, empathic anger, (bystander) guilt, and mild forms of shame, and with their potential value for the development of cosmopolitan imaginations. While these sentiments are not absent from Wright's literary work, his novels tend to foreground a different group of negative emotions: fear/anxiety, (direct) anger, (transgression) guilt, and (self-)disgust. At first sight, none of these emotions seems particularly conducive to open-minded and respectful interactions with others; nevertheless, they often dominate such interactions, especially when strictly policed boundaries between in-groups and out-groups are involved. As a black American who grew up in Mississippi and Tennessee, Wright was well aware of this reality, and he had learned his lessons about what Ryan Schneider has called the "emotional dimensions of race" (3): the fact that race is "an affective-cognitive phenomenon" that is "best apprehended in terms of the feelings that specters of miscegenation or racial extinction . . . can provoke" (11). In Wright's novels, *fear*, and its more sustained relative, *anxiety*, tend to precede and sometimes cause other negative and potentially dangerous emotions. Therefore, I will consider this first.

Fear is generally conceptualized as a "basic" emotion, which, as philosopher Robert Solomon explains, "consists of a complex more-or-less fixed response, a syndrome involving certain parts of the brain, the endocrine system, and characteristic 'hard-wired' behavioral expressions, especially facial expressions. This all gets 'triggered' by some provocative event" (*True*, 14). As with all basic emotions, fear is a product of evolution, even though it tends to be modulated by personal and sociocultural factors. The fear system, explains neuroscientist Joseph LeDoux in *The Emotional Brain* (1996), is "a system that detects danger and produces responses that maximize the probability of surviving a dangerous situation in the most beneficial way" (128). The motivations involved in fear are thus clearly self-interested, and in order to secure a rapid and potentially life-saving response, part of the fear system operates independently of consciousness. LeDoux's model differentiates between two pathways by which we process our perceptions: the "low road," which moves directly from the sensory thalamus to the amygdala, and the "high road," which moves from the sensory thalamus to the sensory cortex and only then to the amygdala. The "quick and dirty processing system" (163) of the low road allows for an immediate response, whereas the "high road" allows for a somewhat slower but more precise processing of perception. In the case of fear, the two systems will lead to what LeDoux calls "defensive behavior" (128): one or several actional outcomes that secure survival in the face of danger.

These possible actional outcomes tend to be hierarchized. In fear, explains Patrick Colm Hogan, we tend to "first try flight, but if that does not work, [we will] try to fight (or in certain cases, freeze)" (*Affective*, 37). Typically, our first response to an object we perceive as threatening will be that we try to flee and thus avoid it, regardless of whether it is a physical threat or whether we fear that someone will say something hurtful. A subsequent response option, which normally occurs only if flight is not possible, is to try to fight the threatening agent. The third response option is freezing, but, as Hogan points out, "it is preferential only in cases where one is not already the target of gaze, motion, and/or address from the threatening agent" (38). Finally, there is the option of appeasement, which we might try if we are certain that the threatening agent has noticed us and believe that we can neither flee nor successfully fight back. In this case, we may attempt to somehow placate the aggressor with the hope that she or he can be convinced not to hurt us. The same emotion—fear—can thus lead to a number of very different actional outcomes, and these outcomes can also involve other emotions. As Hogan points out, the fight response "relies on a feeling of anger being connected with the anxiety" (*Affective*, 38), and while this can make a lot of sense in moments of danger where a brief moment of aggression may successfully scare the threatening agent away, the combination of anger and fear/anxiety becomes more problematic if it is sustained over a long period of time.

Anxiety is an emotion that is closely related to fear, but has a different temporal dimension. For people suffering from anxiety, explains Solomon, "fear is not just an occasional emotion" but "what Heidegger would call 'a way of being.' In such cases, fear seems to lack any particular object. Or rather, it seems to take *everything* as its object" (*True*, 40). Anxiety, which is also called dread in existentialist parlance, behaves like a mood in the sense that it becomes the background of one's everyday life.[2] In Greg Smith's helpful definition, a mood is "a preparatory state in which one is seeking an opportunity to express a particular emotion or emotion set. Moods are expectancies that we are about to have a particular emotion, that we will encounter cues that will elicit particular emotions" (38). Moods thus focus our attention in certain ways, and in Smith's words they "orient us toward our situation, encouraging us to evaluate the environment in mood-congruent fashion" (38). This involves the imagination and thus complex cognitive processes, which is why it is not quite correct to say that moods have no object. As Solomon puts it, "emotions, such as anxiety (angst) and dread . . . in fact have very peculiar objects," whether that be an existentialist "nothingness" or one's own death (*True*, 41). Anxiety can also result from a permanent expectation of a threatening object to appear because one *remembers* it having appeared in the past and/or because one is certain that it is going to appear in the future, but one just does not know when it will occur. In this form, anxiety is bound to give way to spurts of fear, but it can easily also lead to another related emotion: terror. This, as Solomon points out, is a form of fear that "is marked by its obsessional quality" (*True*, 46). Together, this cluster of fear-like emotions is a constant presence in Wright's fiction, and because his black (anti-)heroes are often trapped in ways that do not allow them to flee, it tends to be closely intertwined with anger.

Anger, like fear, is a basic emotion that often arises spontaneously, leading to defensive or aggressive behavior. However, it can also develop into a more drawn-out, mood-like emotion. As Solomon points out, someone may continue to be angry although we can no longer discern a distinctive physiological response, and in some extreme cases, anger may even become "a continuous structure . . . in one's thinking and behavior, what one pays attention to, what one remembers, what one imagines, even what one dreams" (*True*, 17). As in the case of fear, protracted forms of anger are bound to shape what we will or can imagine, and these imaginings will in turn trigger more anger responses. However, there is another temporal dimension that we need to consider, since, as Hogan reminds us, anger "may actually be intensified in retrospect" (*Understanding*, 111). The reasons for this phenomenon, he explains, are related to the emotion's actional and expressive outcomes: "The retrospective reexperiencing of anger invariably leads to the imagination of some response to the provoking event (e.g., punching the initial offender). However, the fact that we cannot act on that imagination is itself a cause of frustration and thus a trigger for anger" (110–111). Dwelling on anger-provoking incidents therefore necessarily multiplies the triggers of anger because of the inevitable "discrepancy between our imagined response and our real action" (111). Because this process repeatedly activates the same emotion circuit, it tends to be self-perpetuating, with anger eventually becoming the "continuous structure in one's thinking and behavior" that Solomon finds so problematic.

Such ruminative anger may commingle and interact with long-standing feelings of anxiety if, as is often the case in Wright's novels, the affected individual believes that he has been morally wronged. As Hogan points out, anger is also a moral emotion, and as such "centrally a response to perceived harm" (*What Literature*, 238). A simultaneous activation of the fear system, which involves the anticipation of *future* harm, will necessarily lead to the enhancement of anger-based actional outcomes in the present that have the aim of eliminating the threatening object or agent. The degree and type of violence we will see in such moments, explains Hogan, are "in part a function of the extent to which the fear and anger systems are activated" (239). Wright's novels read almost like case studies on the ways in which internalized social norms combined with a desperate rebellion against the perceived injustice and immorality of these norms can lead to the near-permanent activation of anger and fear systems. Over time, such protracted activation transforms the way in which his protagonists see the world, and once the combination of fear and anger has begun to dominate their memories and imaginations, there is little that will stop their atrocious behavior short of death.

For a good example of the complex interaction among moral anger, fear, and aggression, it is helpful to turn to Wright's "How 'Bigger' Was Born," in which he recalls how his lifelong observations of a certain type of black man led him to create Bigger Thomas, the protagonist of *Native Son*. In the Jim Crow South, Wright explains, the typical African American was dominated by a sense of fear, and only occasionally would one hear a statement like "I feel like I want to burst" (xiii). This is clearly an expression of anger, but as Wright makes clear, it tended to be a short-lived emotion episode. He offers several examples of such quick spurts of anger, in response to a highly unjust and discriminatory social system, that also quickly subsided again, allowing the subject to return to his "normal" feeling state of frustration and anxiety. However, with a certain type of black man, whom Wright calls the "Bigger Thomas" type, things are different. Like the "Bigger Thomases" in other parts of the world, these American men feel unusually "tense, afraid, nervous, hysterical, and restless" (xix). Acutely aware of the fact that they are "dispossessed and disinherited" (xx), they become human time bombs. "[G]ranting the emotional state," writes Wright, "the tensity, the fear, the hate . . . the sense of exclusion, the ache for violent action, the emotional and cultural hunger, Bigger Thomas . . . will not become an ardent, or even a lukewarm, supporter of the *status quo*" (xx). Instead, he will sooner or later revolt in some terrible outburst of violence against his oppressors.

It is this inevitable process and its detrimental consequences for American society that Wright wanted to put on paper when he wrote *Native Son*, and his own conflicted emotions helped produce and shape his creative imagination. Thinking about his own motivations for writing, he explains, the writer "comes to regard his imagination as a kind of self-generating cement which glued his facts together, and his emotions as a kind of dark and obscure designer of those facts" (vii). The problem with the author's emotions, he believes, is that they are subjective and that the author "can communicate them only when he clothes them in objective guise" (viii). However, "the moment he does dress up an emotion, his mind is confronted with the riddle of that 'dressed up' emotion, and he is left peering with eager dismay back into the dim reaches of his own incommunicable life" (viii). Despite these challenges and limitations, Wright believed that the story of Bigger Thomas was one that America needed to hear in 1940.[3] He was afraid that white readers would say, "See, didn't we tell you all along that niggers are like that?" (xxi), but he also felt that if he were not to depict Bigger as he believed he was—"resentful toward whites, sullen, angry, ignorant, emotionally unstable"—he would "be reacting as Bigger himself reacted" (xxi–xxii). This is why he—against all odds—decided that he had to write the story, "not only for others to read, but to free *myself* of this sense of shame and fear" (xxii). Wright hoped that expressing these painful and potentially damaging emotions in *Native Son* would have a purgative effect on himself.

While it is an attractive thought, the viability of a "purging" of negative emotions through artistic creation seems more than doubtful. The perceptual account of emotion, at least, suggests that the vivid imagination of the eliciting conditions for fear or shame will perpetuate these emotions rather than obliterate them. Arguably, what helped Wright to at least temporarily alleviate his feelings of fear and shame during the gestation of *Native Son* was instead the *anger* he experienced when he realized in 1938 that, with his short story collection *Uncle Tom's Children*, he "had written a book which even bankers' daughters could read and weep over and feel good about" (xxvii). This is a typical case of what Suzanne Keen calls "empathic inaccuracy" ("Narrative," 81), and one that in fact involves both *failure* and *falsity*, since Wright's short stories evoked empathy in readers in ways that were against his own representational goals.[4] As Paul Gilroy explains in *The Black Atlantic* (1993), Wright "was especially horrified at the possibility that his mass white readership might discover deep pleasures in the images of blacks as victims of racism" (153). He feared that white Americans "might be completely comfortable with the representations of black pain and suffering which inevitably flowed from attempts to deal seriously with the systematic operation of racism in American society" (153–154). For this reason, he decided that if he ever wrote another book, he would make absolutely sure that there was nothing sentimental about it, leaving readers no chance to feel the intriguing mix of sadness, pity, and pleasure that, as I have shown in chapter 2, is so typical for the sentimental novel. As Wright famously declares in "How 'Bigger' Was Born," he wanted *Native Son* to "be so hard and deep that they would have to face it without the consolation of tears" (xxvii).

The result is a narrative that almost brutally forces its reader to share the frightening experience of a young black man who has little orientation in life. Because of the hostile environment in which he has grown up, Bigger is engulfed in emotions of anxiety, fear, anger, hate, and shame, which ultimately cause him to become a multiple murderer. As the cognitive film scholar Murray Smith has pointed out, "Moral perversity . . . is an enduring subject of fictional representation, both filmic and literary" (219). What is important, however, is the way in which such moral perversity is depicted and how the reader/viewer is positioned with respect to a morally transgressive protagonist. In this context, it is important to understand the difference between *allegiance* and *alignment*. Alignment, Smith explains, is a result of "our access to the actions, thought, and feelings of a character" (220). If we see the events from a certain character's perspective, we are aligned with that character in the sense that the character is the focalizer of the story. Allegiance, by contrast, refers to the way in which a narrative "elicits responses of sympathy" toward that character. Such responses are "triggered—if not wholly determined—by the *moral structure*" of the narrative (220). Typically, alignment with a character is combined with allegiance to that character, but in *Native Son* Wright aligned his contemporary (white) readers with a main character whom they found to be extremely disconcerting and even threatening.

Keen suggests that "empathic distress at feeling with a character whose actions are at odds with a reader's moral code may be a result of successfully exercised authorial empathy" ("Narrative," 71), and I argue that this is exactly what we find in *Native Son*. As I have shown in previous chapters, although authors may use strategic empathizing to help readers feel empathy and sympathy with a member of an out-group by portraying that person as particularly likeable, virtuous, or attractive, they may also try the opposite strategy in order to change a reader's dispositions or attitudes. In *Native Son*, Wright offers a haunting psychological portrait of a double murderer while suggesting at the same time that the overwhelmingly negative emotions that drive him to these crimes are produced by a racist and unjust society. As John Reilly has pointed out, the novel's "realism . . . is concerned not so much to report objective conditions as to show the way it *feels* to be imprisoned by the social facts of Negro life in America" ("Afterword," 394; emphasis added). The fact that Bigger has no means to address or change the social conditions that frighten and enrage him is shown to be directly responsible for his immoral attitude and his violent actions.

Bigger's first, and in a way accidental, murder is preceded by a disturbing emotional mix of "helplessness, admiration, and hate" (81) when he is alone with his white employer's drunken daughter. Breaking the taboo of miscegenation, he touches the girl's body, first to help her and then in response to her sexual advances, only to be "seized" by "a hysterical terror" when he realizes that the "white blur" of her blind mother is in the room (84). While this is a spontaneous startle response,[5] it is Bigger's imagining of what might happen to him when discovered in the bedroom of a white girl that whips his conditioned fear into self-centered "frenzy" (84). To him, the only important thing is that the girl does not make a sound;

he does not even realize that he is smothering her to death in the process. And once he sees that this is what happened, he can only think about what it will mean for *him*: "She was dead and he had killed her. He was a murderer, a Negro murderer, a black murderer. He had killed a white woman" (86). Bigger's personal distress reaction is so overwhelming in this moment that it leaves no room for an empathic response; his subsequent brutal murder of his own girlfriend betrays the completeness of his emotional detachment and empathy inhibition. *Fear*, therefore, is not only the name of *Native Son*'s Book One, but indeed the all-consuming emotion that drives the novel's disenfranchised protagonist into a downward spiral of anger, hate, violence, and murder.

Readers' emotional relationship to this protagonist is bound to be a rather complex one. On the one hand, they will likely feel *sociomoral disgust*, and since, as I explain in more detail in chapter 5, this emotion involves the urge to distance oneself from the object of disgust, they will want to withdraw from Bigger's consciousness, thus severing their empathic ties with a protagonist whose moral universe they reject. On the other hand, they may be fascinated by his ruthless immorality, and may also be curious to learn whether he will be punished for his transgressions. At times they may even feel *compassion* for Bigger and empathic anger at the racist society that drives him to murder. As Mark Bracher has shown, the novel over and over again presents Bigger's aggression as the product "of his fear, which is itself a consequence of his threatening situation" (Bracher, 248), thus helping readers understand that his actions cannot be condemned without also condemning the social situation that has produced both the actor and his deeds. It is in this recognition that Martha Nussbaum locates the "possibility of a deeper sympathy" (*Poetic*, 94). Because we are aligned with Bigger, "we cannot follow the novel without trying to see the world through [his] eyes," and this, in turn, leads us to "take on, at least to some extent, his emotions of rage and shame" (94). Readers are thus likely to develop an uneasy allegiance to this black murderer, one that is likely inflected by their own life situations. For contemporary *white* readers, the fact that Wright was quite deliberately playing with the stereotype of the black rapist and murderer must have had some very immediate emotional dimensions. When Bigger is sentenced to death for his crimes but still believes that what he "killed for must've been good" (*Native*, 392), there was indeed no "consolation of tears" for such readers, since they knew that American social conditions ensured that sooner or later another Bigger Thomas would be standing next to *their* daughters.

Wright's reliance on the "dark and obscure" shaping power of his emotions in the creation of his first novel was therefore extremely successful with contemporary black and white audiences. Despite its often attested weaknesses—many of them related to Wright's portrayal of Communism in the third part of the book—*Native Son* became an immediate best seller and one of the most influential books of its time.[6] As Arna Bontemps remembers in a 1953 piece for the *Saturday Review*, "Thousands of readers were shocked speechless . . . and most of them had not completely recovered five years later when [Wright's autobiography] 'Black Boy' was published" (15). It is perhaps because of this "shocking" success that we also find similar narrative strategies in Wright's second novel, *The Outsider*, and in his final novel, "Island of Hallucination," which were both shaped by the emotions that grew out of Wright's increasingly cosmopolitan engagements during the late 1940s and the 1950s.

EXISTENTIAL DREAD AND TRANSGRESSION GUILT: THE CONFLICTED EMOTIONS OF *THE OUTSIDER*

Wright was among the first of the exodus of African American writers who left the United States in the mid-to-late 1940s to settle in Paris. Despite the runaway success of *Native Son* and his status as *the* black American writer of his time, he was less and less inclined to put up with the daily dose of racist abuse, which often was centered on his interracial marriage to Ellen Poplar, daughter of Jewish Polish immigrants. In 1946, Wright accepted an invitation by the French government to stay for a year in Paris and soon after moved his family permanently to France, where he was welcomed as a famous African American writer.[7] Soon, he was joined by other black Americans, many of them ex-soldiers taking advantage of the GI Bill,[8] and he quickly became one of the leading figures of this "new lost generation,"[9] which included James Baldwin, Chester Himes, Ollie Harrington, and, from 1951 on, William Gardner Smith. As Brent Hayes Edwards has shown in *The Practice of Diaspora* (2003), for all its imperfections, Paris "allowed boundary crossing, conversations, and collaborations that were available nowhere else to the same degree" (4). Wright was very much a part of these conversations and collaborations. Like Smith, he did not want to be confined in the identity of an American protest writer, and therefore he turned his attention in the 1950s increasingly away from the United States and toward international politics, especially the Pan-African and decolonization movements. As Kevin Gaines observes, however, Wright's position in the Pan-African movement was complicated by the fact that he was critical of "Negritude, the politically charged assertion by some Francophone African nationalists of a transhistorical, transnational black cultural unity" ("Revisiting," 75). Wright rejected such black essentialism in favor of political coalitions and, in the same vein, found allies in certain circles of France's intelligentsia, among them prominent existentialist philosophers such as Albert Camus, Jean-Paul Sartre, and Simone de Beauvoir.

These new and "foreign" influences on his writing were regarded by many of Wright's black friends and critics in the United States as problematic, if not dangerous, for his career. Wright's biographer Hazel Rowley writes that "letter after letter" addressed to Wright in the 1940s and 1950s carried the message that it would be best for him to give up his exile and to come back "home" to write about the topics he knew and understood ("The 'Exile'").[10] Moreover, it was not only people back in the United States who were concerned about Wright's intellectual reorientation. His co-expatriates in Paris had qualms as well. James Baldwin, for example, took Wright's sudden and premature death in 1960 at the age of fifty-two as incentive to speculate publicly about "the uses and hazards of expatriation." Some of Wright's former friends in the expatriate community in France, Baldwin argues, felt that he had perhaps been away from "home" for too long and had made a mistake by "cut[ting] himself off from his roots" (Nobody, 166). Many of them, like Baldwin himself, particularly "distrusted his association with the French intellectuals, Sartre, de Beauvoir, and company," because it seemed to them "that there was very little they could give him which he could use" (Nobody, 151). American peers at home as well as abroad thus suspected that Wright's race-transcending contact with the French existentialists had corrupted, if not destroyed, the authenticity of his black vision. Baldwin remembers how an African once told him "with a small, mocking laugh, *I believe he thinks he's white*" (Nobody, 166).

The challenge of the French existentialist philosophy, however, was important for Wright's development as a cosmopolitan thinker. Sartre's political and artistic vision especially resonated in important ways with his own background and experience. Like Sartre, Wright believed in the importance of political commitment, which was expressed in their joint engagement in the Rassemblement Démocratique Révolutionnaire (RDR), a radical left group that rejected both American capitalism and Soviet Communism, and that was committed to finding a third (transnational) political way. According to Michel Fabre, Wright developed three major preoccupations while in France, which led to his involvement in the RDR: "how to inject a personal philosophy into Marxist theory; how to restore morality to political action; and how to save mankind from atomic destruction through the reactivation of humanistic values" (*World*, 159). Sartre's claim that "existentialism is a humanism" profoundly influenced Wright's literary vision of the early 1950s.[11] After departing from the United States, he had continued to expand the scope of his thinking, looking for political allies in his struggle against racism and imperialist oppression.

In order to conduct this struggle, it seems that he found it necessary to be radically free, and free to choose his own way to live as well as his allies. His bold declarations of cosmopolitan detachment, accompanied by his official abandonment of the United States, suggest a desire to transcend the constraints imposed on him by American history. If he described himself in *White Man Listen!* as a "rootless man," then he renounced his belonging even more radically in *Pagan Spain* (1957): "I have no religion in the formal sense of the word. . . . I have no race except that which is forced upon me. I have no country except that to which I'm obliged to belong. I have no traditions. I'm free. I have only the future" (21). Wright's perspective in such statements parallels that of Cross Damon, the black antihero in his second novel *The Outsider*, who makes the conscious decision to leave behind everything that previously determined his life: family, religion, social responsibilities, and, almost absurdly, race. Regarding race as a social construct rather than a preordained essence, Cross not only violently confronts the normative power of a racialized American society, but also believes that he can exist as an *outsider* to human society in general.

While there is much in *The Outsider* that is reminiscent of *Native Son*, Damon Cross is an even more violent and ruthless protagonist than Bigger Thomas, making the empathic challenge for readers even greater. One contemporary reviewer complained about the "almost psychopathic lust for violence" in the novel, and another called it "an assault on our nerves" (both quoted in Reilly, *Richard*, 206, 207). The assault was, of course, calculated, and it was deeply informed by the notion of radical freedom that Wright had come to embrace. "Strongly Existentialist in tone," writes Lewis Vogler in his more sympathetic review of the novel for the *San Francisco Chronicle*, *The Outsider* is "not for the squeamish, still less for those who are disinclined to admit the psychological realities of industrial civilization" (quoted in Reilly, *Richard*, 212). With this acknowledgment of the existentialist dimensions of the novel, Vogler indirectly confirmed what Wright had spelled out on the dust jacket of *The Outsider*: that the protagonist of his story "could be of any race" (quoted in Fabre, *World*,

172). What he was depicting, Wright felt, was the dilemma of modern human existence: the tremendous inner conflict between a yearning for freedom from oppression and an emotional need for attachment. Even more drastically than in *Native Son*, Wright uses his novel to explore the emotional dimensions of this dilemma. If fear and hot anger are what dominated his first novel, then we find existential dread, cold anger, and shame in the second. The most striking feature of *The Outsider*, however, is that its protagonist is a pensive and indeed sensitive man who acts violently because he cannot bear the *empathic distress* he experiences when his ruthless pursuit of individual freedom hurts people to whom he is emotionally attached. Wright's second novel is therefore an investigation into the psychology of oppression and violence, exploring the fateful dynamics among desire, attachment, and transgression.[12]

At the beginning of *The Outsider*, the most defining feature of the twenty-six-year-old Cross is his feelings of entrapment and resentment: He dislikes his low-paying job at the Chicago post office, where his coworkers tease him about what they call "his four A's. *Alcohol. Abortions. Automobiles.* And *alimony*" (4). He feels trapped in the unhealthy relationship that he has with his deeply religious mother, whose "accusing eyes" leave him "fighting down a feeling of defensive guilt" (24), and feelings of "self-loathing" (71) are intensified by the even more harmful relationship he has with his wife Gladys. After committing adultery, he feels for her "compassion mingled with disgust" (72), and, disliking this feeling, he physically abuses her in order to cure "her of her love for him" (71). Finally, Cross resents his mistress Dot, who is both underage and pregnant, and who threatens him with going to court unless he gets a divorce and marries her. Although there is no question that he is at least partially responsible for the distress experienced by the women in his life, Cross feels that this distress is something they deliberately display in order to manipulate him. Like Smith's protagonists, Cross is a sensitive man, but in his case, perceiving the distress of others does not lead to prosocial action, but rather to a personal distress response that sheds an interesting light on Martin Hoffman's notion of transgression guilt.

Hoffman defines interpersonal transgression guilt as "a painful feeling of disesteem for oneself, usually accompanied by a sense of urgency, tension, and regret, that results from empathic feeling for someone in distress, combined with awareness of being the cause of that distress" (114). It is different from bystander guilt in that the person experiencing it is planning to harm or has actually harmed the victim. Like anger and fear, guilt is a moral emotion, and according to Hoffman, it can lead to several actional outcomes: "To keep from feeling guilty, a person can avoid car-rying out harmful acts, or, having committed such an act, he can make reparation to the victim in the hope of undoing the damage and decreas-ing the feeling of guilt" (114). This is why Hoffman conceptualizes it as a prosocial emotion that can inhibit harmful behavior toward others, and instead further helping behavior. However, like anger, guilt can become problematic when it is sustained over a long time and/or when the trans-gressing agent is certain that no actional outcomes are possible that would relieve the empathic distress associated with transgression guilt. This seems to be the problem faced by Cross Damon in Book One of *The Out-sider*. He believes he has no power to behave in ways that will not hurt the people—and especially the black women—around him, and so his strat-egy is "to escape this fountain of emotion that made him feel guilty" (29). When flight is not possible, he tends to attack, as in the case when he vi-ciously beats his wife to "make her hate him" (71). A negative response, such as hate or anger, is much easier for him to handle than expressions of pain and suffering that remind him of his moral transgressions and the fact that he is personally *responsible* for the suffering.

We must also assume that he tries to fight off feelings of shame, which, as Hogan notes, "counsels concealment. Shame is bound up with our acute sense that we are the target of other people's aversion, particularly disgust, physical or moral" (*Affective*, 36). This is particularly obvious in Cross's interactions with his mother, who "evoked in him that shame-ful mood of guilt born of desire and fear of desire" (*Outsider*, 26). Unable to respond in any constructive way to his mother's reproaches, "he would listen with a face masked in indifference and he would know that she was right; but he would also know that there was nothing that neither he nor she could do about it, that there was no cure for his malady, and, above all, that this dilemma was the meaning of his life" (24). A sense of shame, Hogan explains, is likely to make the affected individual "intensely aware of his own emotional expressions" (*Affective*, 37), and so it is not sur-prising that Cross is adamant about controlling his outward expressions, whether he "masks" his face with indifference or distorts it with "an imi-tation of rage" (*Outsider*, 81). His defensive behavior, however, does little to rectify the situation, and so when the opportunity finally arises, Cross "act[s] upon the impulse of flight" (51). After being involved in a freak ac-cident in the Chicago subway, he manages to switch identities with one of the fatalities and walks away to become what he always longed to be: completely free.

This complete freedom in the existentialist sense, however, comes at a high price. Although a "keen sensation of vitality invade[s] every cell of his body" (*Outsider*, 106) after his escape, Cross soon yearns "for just one more glimpse of his mother" and the three sons he has with Gladys (114). But he knows he cannot look back and that he can now "map out his life entirely upon his own assumptions" (115). This includes defending his absolute freedom when it is threatened, and this necessitates Cross's first murder when he is recognized by a former colleague. For the reader, this is a crucial moment, similar to that of Bigger Thomas's first murder in *Native Son*. Unlike Bigger, however, who kills in a state of frenzy, Cross is overcome with a *desire* to kill, his "fingers ach[ing] to blot out this black man who grinned with bewilderment" (134). He murders the man with an empty whiskey bottle and then pushes him out of the window "in one swift, merciless movement" (136–137). If Cross wasn't a particularly sympathetic protagonist to begin with—especially for female readers—then his moral transgressions are now of a kind that evokes responses of shock and sociomoral disgust in readers. If readers are familiar with *Native Son*, then they might expect dark plot developments from a Richard Wright novel, but this in all likelihood will not prepare them for Cross's behavior from this point onward. He brutally kills—in fact *executes*—three more people, one of them a fascist, two of them Communist Party members, and insists that these are "acts of ethical murder" (311) because these men are "insect[s] [that] had to be crushed, blotted out of existence" (303). During his executions he is "disdainful, detached" (302), and even in retrospect can "find nothing remiss in how he had deported himself" (311). It is this apparent lack of guilt that will make most readers shudder, and then attempt to inhibit their empathy with him.

The novel thus invites a certain critical distance, which allows readers to have (negative) feelings *about* the protagonist rather than an uncritically empathic and sympathetic relationship *with* him. That distance will never be complete, however, since Cross continues to be the focalizer of the narrative, and this alignment does not allow readers to distance themselves completely from him (unless they stop reading and leave the book unfinished). This is what makes the reading experience so challenging and "an assault on our nerves." Wright's use of authorial strategic empathizing in *The Outsider* is thus very similar to that in *Native Son* in that it shocks the empathizing reader into a critical distance, asking her to think about and judge the character's immoral actions, while at the same time keeping the reader aligned with the protagonist she finds so problematic. As in *Native Son*, there are a number of factors that ease this strained relationship somewhat. Despite his assertions to the contrary, Cross cannot shake a deep feeling of *shame* about his moral transgressions, disgusted as he is by the fact that he "had acted like a little god . . . had judged them and had found them guilty of insulting his sense of life and had carried out a sentence of death upon them" (308). Cross's helpless revulsion at his own hubris is mirrored by the moral feelings of the hunchbacked district attorney Ely Houston, who investigates the case and serves as moral compass for the reader. The third, and in my view most important, element that allows readers to stay in (troubled) touch with the protagonist, however, is the fact that Wright involves him in a tragic love story.

Although it seems hard to believe, given his problematic attitude toward women, Cross falls in love with the wife of the Communist leader whom he murders. He believes that Eva Blount is different from the women he used to have in his life, not because she is white, but because she is a "sensitive" outsider and "a victim like he" (285), a talented painter who has been used by her husband as a figurehead for the Communist Party. Having secretly read Eva's diary makes it "impossible for him to regard her with detachment" (292), and his love for her helps provide the insight that distinguishes *The Outsider* from *Native Son*. Cross feels compelled to open up to Eva about his crimes, but she fails to understand his desperation or his motives and, in her horror, kills herself. Cross is devastated: "She had taken one swift look into the black depths of his heart, into the churning horror of his deeds and had been so revolted that she had chosen this way out" (538). Eva's tragic (one might even say melodramatic) death—and his responsibility for it—make it impossible for Cross to go on, having "in him to the full the feeling that had sent him on this long, bloody, twisting road: self-loathing" (541). Unable to fight back any longer his feelings of shame and transgression guilt, freedom becomes senseless to Cross, and so it hardly matters when he is, in the final pages of the book, shot dead by members of the Communist Party. As Robert Bone has pointed out, Cross's immoral behavior "leads to abandonment" (45), and this is the most terrible punishment Wright could have given him. By making Cross's struggle for absolute autonomy a failure, Wright seems to argue that such autonomy is both inhuman and impossible. While Kierkegaardian dread characterizes the larger part of the novel, which is often observed,[13] it is a decidedly *humanistic* and cosmopolitan version of existentialism that the novel acknowledges in the end.

If it is Cross's sincere love for Eva and his despair over his responsibility for her death that allow the reader to feel some amount of sympathy for him, his final words rectify him as a moral agent. On the last pages of *The Outsider*, Wright has Cross openly renounce his nihilism, realizing that he needs the recognition of others to constitute a meaningful identity. "I wanted to be free," he tells Houston, but "[t]he search can't be done alone. . . . Alone a man is nothing. . . . I wish I had some way to give the meaning of my life to others. . . . To make a bridge from man to man" (585). A comparison to Sartre's "The Humanism of Existentialism" reveals the parallels between Cross's final epiphany and Sartre's plea for a humanist existentialism: "We want freedom for freedom's sake and in every particular circumstance. And in wanting freedom we discover that it depends entirely on the freedom of others, and that the freedom of others depends on ours" (*Essays*, 57–58). The responsibility of intersubjectivity is what, according to Sartre, constitutes the humanism of existentialism. While each individual is free and therefore fully responsible for his or her actions, he or she is at the same time also dependent on the recognition of others and responsible for the consequences that chosen actions have on others.

This is exactly the realization that Cross has at the end of his life: other humans matter and the development of a meaningful life cannot be accomplished alone. It is a realization that refers not to a specific nation or race, but to mankind in general, and it is brought about by Cross's emotional attachment to Eva. The romantic emplotment of cosmopolitanism we find in *The Outsider* is clearly quite different from what we see, for example, in the sentimental novels of Pearl Buck. As Gilroy points out, "*The Outsider* is marked from end to end by [Wright's] resolution to write a powerful, unassimilable prose which could be read only 'without the consolation of tears'" (*Black*, 164). Nevertheless, the love story is central to the novel's ultimately cosmopolitan message, because it is his interracial love for Eva that allows Cross to acknowledge that his desire for radical outsiderness, independence, and individualism stands in the way of what he needs most in the world: attachment, solidarity, and recognition. It is this message that the reader is supposed to take away from the book.

It seems almost bizarre that Wright would reward Cross Damon's outsider perspective with such a terrible epiphany, only to proclaim four years later, in *Pagan Spain*, his own radical independence from all markers of belonging: religion, nationality, traditions, and race. This inconsistency, however, is symptomatic of Wright's central dilemma; we find it not only in *The Outsider* and *Native Son*, but also in his later nonfiction and fiction. He seems to have been torn between a view that sees sociohistorical context as determinative and the individual without agency, and an existentialist view that gives the individual full agency and freedom as well as the associated responsibility. Above all, though, he yearned for ties based on individual insight, bonds that would be open to individuals of every ethnicity or nationality. Maryemma Graham is therefore right when she notes that "*The Outsider* must be seen against t[he] background of anti-colonialism, anti-fascism, and anti-racism, sentiments all shaped by Cold War politics and Wright's own personal experiences in organized political movements" (xx). I would add, however, that the novel must also be viewed in light of Wright's own emotional needs and his desire for attachment and transracial solidarity.

In his *Black Power* (1954), which records his trip to the Gold Coast (today's Ghana),[14] Wright repeats a speech that he gave during one of Kwame Nkrumah's political rallies, in which he claimed that the specific "heritage" of African Americans "has brought us a sense of unity deeper than race, a sense of humanity that has made us sensitive to the sufferings of all mankind, that has made us increasingly human in a world that is rapidly losing its claim to humanity" (84).[15] Although Wright gives much less thought than Smith to the exact value of sensitivity in the recognition of a common humanity, his professed yearning for solidarity with and compassion for all human beings is nevertheless at odds with his proclaimed detachment from human bonds.[16] As Fabre has noted, Wright remained all his life "very much a humanist" (*World*, 159), but his was what Gilroy has called "an agonistic, planetary humanism capable of comprehending the universality of our elemental vulnerability to the wrongs we visit upon each other" (*Postcolonial*, 4). While sharing many interests and goals with Nkrumah, George Padmore, Léopold Senghor, and other Pan-Africanists, Wright did not ultimately want to stop at a community of the transnational African diaspora. Instead, he hoped for a system of living that would respect "the sacredness that I feel resides in the human personality" (quoted in Fabre, *World*, 189). This is why he bonded with Sartre and other French intellectuals, with whom he also shared a Marxist—and internationalist—vision. While not personally victimized in the way people of color were, these intellectuals shared a political vision with Wright, regardless of their ethnic background.

Wright had, of course, already crossed the color line for political reasons with his membership in the CPUSA, but then broke with the Communist Party in 1942. However, his turn away from Communism did not mean the abandonment of his Marxist outlook, which, in its decided internationalism, certainly prefigured and facilitated his cosmopolitan vision.[17] The Stalinist practice of Communism, however, did not gel with Wright's personal beliefs. He explained the reasons for his break with the Communist Party in his essay "I Tried to Be a Communist" (1944).

His deep disappointment, and even embitterment, are also powerfully expressed in his final novel "Island of Hallucination," to which I will now turn. As in my discussion of *The Outsider*, however, my primary concern will not be with Wright's critique of Communism. Rather, I am interested in the novel's emplotment of cosmopolitanism and the role of empathy and emotion in that emplotment. Nevertheless, as will become clear, it is hardly possible to approach these narratological issues without first considering the conditions of their emergence, and so I will begin by briefly looking at these conditions before I turn to the novel itself.

MEMORIES, DREAMS, AND EMOTIONS: LIVING ON THE "ISLAND OF HALLUCINATION"

The fact that Wright had moved to France, many sea miles away from the United States, did not mean that he, as a former member of the CPUSA, was able to escape the anti-Communist paranoia that engulfed his home country during the 1950s. For one thing, he had not really left that country behind, either emotionally or materially. The question of what "America" meant to Wright emotionally is perhaps best addressed in an unpublished piece that he presumably wrote for a French audience. In that work, which was reproduced in Fabre's *The World of Richard Wright* (1985), he offers not one, but eighty-six, answers to the question "Am I an American?" Every single answer starts with the phrase "I am an American but . . . ," and Fabre suggests that the "but" is the most important point of these answers. However, given his speculation that the text was written in the late 1950s, it is quite remarkable that Wright identified himself as an American at all, much less eighty-six times in a row. The American he presented himself as being, of course, was an American with a twist: "I am an American but tomorrow I could surrender my citizenship and still be an American. . . . I am an American but I can live without America and still be an American. . . . I am an American but I insist on talking about the meaning of being an American" (quoted in Fabre, *World*, 188–189). It would not be going too far, it seems, to say that Wright still felt attached to the United States when he was writing these lines, but much more to an America of ideas than to an actually existing place.

The idea that connected him emotionally to America was one with which he had grown up, but it was also an idea that conflicted so brutally with his experiences of the United States that he had to leave the country in order to keep it alive. Only in a non-American framework could he experience freedom, equality, justice, and all the other values that were so inextricably linked to the concept of America. Therefore, for Wright, to be American was not to pledge allegiance to the American flag or to possess an American passport; to be American meant, and this may come as a surprise, to be cosmopolitan. "I am that sort of American," he writes, "an amalgam of many races and many continents and cultures, [and] I feel that the real end and aim of being an American is to be able to live as a man anywhere" (189).[18] Although clearly he is acutely aware of American realities, he does not, and perhaps cannot, disconnect his cosmopolitan ideals from their perceived Americanness, not even in the late 1950s after a decade of expatriation.[19]

Wright was still very much connected to the United States in a material manner as well. As Rowley points out, he had, and continued to have, "an American passport, an American literary agent, an American publisher, American readers, and American friends and associates" ("The 'Exile'").[20] The fact that he remained an American citizen continued to affect his liberty. Like all American expatriates at the time, he had to have his passport renewed every two years at the American embassy. And it was made quite clear to him and his fellow renegade compatriots that they would not get new passports if they spoke too critically against the United States. The daunting examples of Paul Robeson and W. E. B. Du Bois, both of whom had their passports revoked during the 1950s, made clear that such warnings were not without teeth.[21] Another significant uncertainty for Americans in France, as Rowley reminds us, "was that the French government could deport them at any time if they in any way stirred up trouble in their adopted country. This meant that Wright could say nothing about French foreign policy in Indochina or Algeria" ("The 'Exile'"). As we have seen in chapter 3, this statement is not quite correct, since other writers, such as Smith, *did* say something about French foreign policy in Indochina or Algeria. Smith, in fact, was centrally involved in the so-called "Gibson Affair," which—in highly distorted form—is at the heart of "Island of Hallucination."

Wright seems to have tried to kill at least three birds with one stone in "Island of Hallucination." He wanted to write a scathing critique of organized Communism, paint a grim and spiteful picture of the black American community in Paris (which he had come to despise), and assert once again the deeply damaging influence of American racist ideology on the black individual. In doing so, however, he did not want to get in trouble with the French government. That last he would have had to expect, had he written about what the Gibson Affair was really about—French colonial policy in Algeria and the treatment of Algerian immigrants in

France.[22] Richard Gibson—the African American writer and journalist from whom the "Affair" took its name—argues that it is for this reason that Wright "carefully sets the action [of the novel] three years before the beginning of the Algerian War on 1 November 1954, and rather during the Korean War and the riots by the French Left against the visit to Paris at the end of May 1951 of General Mathew Ridgeway [sic] who had been the American military commander in Korea" (901–902). This historical context, of course, had the double advantage of being critical of American politics while being much less "touchy" for French officials.

One certainly can accuse Wright of cowardice or opportunism with regard to his silence about the oppression of dark-skinned people by the French government. In comparison with Smith's *The Stone Face*, which courageously criticizes both French politics and the African American silence about it, Wright's novel indeed pales as a politically engaged piece of writing. The ethical position he assumes in "Island of Hallucination," however, is nevertheless interesting, because it shows that until the end, Wright stayed committed to the planetary humanism that Gilroy accords him in both *The Black Atlantic* and *Against Race*. It also shows, however, that such theoretical stances may not always translate into practical cosmopolitan solidarity. While avoiding a critique of contemporary French politics, Wright uses his last novel to once again assert that in the United States, as a result of American race relations, the black man fatally degenerates to the point where he becomes an inhuman "monster" or, in this case, a machine. However, there is an important difference between "Island" and the two earlier novels I have discussed. In both *Native Son* and *The Outsider*, the black "monster" is the protagonist, thus forcing readers into an uneasy alliance with such a monster. In "Island," Wright uses a different rhetorical strategy. Here, the black monster is even more "monstrous" as a result of his life in the United States, but he is no longer the protagonist and thus no longer invites readers' empathic alignment. Instead, the monster now is the antagonist of the story, thus allowing readers to inhibit empathy and condemn his actions. The protagonist himself is a much less drastic figure, morally questionable perhaps, but with the potential to overcome his defects if he can leave the painful emotional memories of his life in black America behind.

A planned sequel to Wright's earlier novel *The Long Dream* (1958), "Island of Hallucination" starts on board Flight 409 from New York to Paris via Dublin, an obligatory stopover at the time, since planes could not make the entire distance in one flight.[23] Aboard the plane are forty-odd passengers, most are American, and only one is black. This latter character is the novel's protagonist; however, we do not learn his name until after we have seen him through the eyes of four of the other American travelers on board: a middle-aged assistant manager from Texas, a ten-year-old boy from Arkansas, an appellate court judge from Alabama who is a member of the Ku Klux Klan, and a Roman Catholic missionary from Chicago who is headed for the Gold Coast. All of these white Americans eye the young black man in their midst with varying mixtures of apprehension, spite, hate, and contempt, all of them considering it an imposition that a "goddamn nigger" (2) should be traveling with them in the same cabin, served by the same white flight attendant. However, as the omniscient narrator informs us, all of them are "a long way from home" (2) in this airliner above the Atlantic, and because American law is not in force here, they can do nothing about the African American's presence, and as a result must bear it. At the center of all of this unwanted attention is eighteen-year-old Rex Tucker from Mississippi, a young man known as Fishbelly. He has escaped from the negative energy around him by sinking into a deep slumber, but his dreams keep him caught in the same logic; they have him running frantically among coffins, from one of which a white girl is calling out incessantly to him. Fishbelly, we learn right away, is an ex-convict, having served two years in jail for allegedly raping a white woman—a crime he claims not to have committed, attributing his conviction instead to American racism.

In the all-white environment of the transatlantic airplane, Fishbelly feels more than just a little uncomfortable. While he is used to being constructed as a disenfranchised black subject under the gaze of white Americans, the changed ideological context that they are all in on this flight to Europe deeply unsettles him. He knows that in this new context, he is allowed to share the cabin with white people, but having never experienced anything else but American "separate but equal" ideology, he cannot simply switch his understanding of himself or his emotional responses. Furthermore, he has no idea how to behave in this setting. When the French flight attendant wants to accompany him out of the airplane in Dublin, he insists on walking four feet behind her, because he is afraid to be seen next to a white woman. The flight attendant is as baffled and touched by such behavior as the few other French people on the airplane, all of whom display no racism at all and have nothing but friendly smiles for the young black American. At first glance, we could thus assume that Wright is setting up a simple confrontation between "bad" American and "good" French attitudes toward blacks. In 1959, however, when he was writing this novel, he had been living too long in France to believe in such easy dichotomies.

The French gaze in "Island of Hallucination" is by no means "good" or even neutral; rather, it expresses a set of attitudes and emotions that, for an African American like Fishbelly, is difficult to fully comprehend. As Rebecca Ruquist notes, "African Americans were welcomed by French intellectuals as symbols of unjust suffering under US capitalism, providing the French with unique opportunities to critique the United States . . . and highlight their philosophical tradition of antiracist universalist humanism" (285–286). Ironically, however, this did not stop them from racializing blacks themselves. In the French imagination of the time, explains Ruquist, black people stood for pureness, health, primitivity, and other "'positive' racial essentialisms" (294). Wright, she argues, "challenges this aspect of French culture," as the French in his novel clearly "project their own primitivity, irrationality, fear, and mysticism onto black male bodies" (294). Indeed, we repeatedly find references—especially by French women—to the "healthy" and friendly nature of black people, culminating in the smiling black face of jazz player Trombone Bailey on an advertisement in Paris, which Fishbelly and his friend Harrison ponder at the end of the novel. While being less derogatory and aggressive in their attitudes than American society, the French, too, construct blacks as irretrievably "other" and, in fact, inferior members of an out-group. Fishbelly, however, chooses to be blissfully ignorant of such realities for most of the story.

Within the first few chapters of "Island of Hallucination," Wright presents many of what will become the central themes of his novel, themes I have already introduced in my discussion of *The Stone Face* in chapter 3: the flight to France as an attempted escape from American racism for the black American; the conflict and confusion of the African American as he is confronted with a new racial ideology; and his inability to let go of learned fears and behavior patterns, on the one hand, and the friendly attitudes of French people toward blacks, which turn out to be not quite all that they seem, on the other. Wright makes clear, though, that a "perfect" and racism-free French society is not necessary for African Americans to start over. Like Smith, he seems to have appreciated the fact that French society was at least *less* racist than American society, thus allowing blacks to develop an identity that isn't as self-debilitating as the black identities we see in Bigger Thomas and Cross Damon. As in *Native Son* and *The Outsider*, his main concern in "Island" is with the choices that the black individual can or must make within (and often against) a given set of sociocultural determinants.

Another central theme is introduced only a little later in the novel: the many suspicions and animosities that—in Wright's version of black

Paris—poison the relationships between American expatriates, all of whom believe of one another that they are spying for the Stalinists, for the Trotskyites, or for the French or American government. Most of them actually do. Only one man, the African American Ned Harrison, seems to be above these games and betrayals.[24] The only one with a cosmopolitan (and also decidedly Marxist) outlook is Harrison, who represents the voice of wisdom in the novel and lectures Fishbelly—in an often highly didactic manner—on how he should act and live.

Like Max in *Native Son* and Ely Houston in *The Outsider*, Harrison is the moral compass of the tale, orienting not only the protagonist, but also the reader, toward the cosmopolitan worldview he shares with the author of the novel. Not only is Harrison quite unhappy about the fact that Fishbelly has, in his excitement about readily accessible white French women, become a pimp in Paris, he also criticizes Fishbelly's inability to let go of his American racial conditioning and his lack of empathy for others. But Fishbelly does not want to hear about morality in the handling of other people. He just greatly enjoys his new freedom and the fact that he can spend hours in French cafés without worrying about his skin color. Fishbelly experiences Paris as a kind of beautiful dream, and he wants it to remain a dream, a *hallucination*, in which he can live safely and freely, and care about nothing but making money and having sex with white women. In this view, he invites comparison with the protagonist of *The Stone Face*, but Smith's Simeon is not only older, but also much more pensive and indeed *sensitive*, than Fishbelly. At no point is he as detached and solipsistic as Wright's protagonist, who is much too concerned with his own needs and nightmares to engage openly and empathically with others, and therefore cannot be troubled by their distress.

Throughout much of the novel, Fishbelly retains this detached and uncaring attitude, understanding himself as a radically independent man. Again, we recognize not only Cross Damon in this attitude, but also the Richard Wright of *Pagan Spain*, who declares that he belongs nowhere and needs no attachments. And once again, we see this attitude fail in practice. No matter how much he likes to imagine himself as radically independent and self-sufficient, Fishbelly cannot leave America behind. Like all of his black compatriots, he proves incapable of letting go of emotional memories and habituated responses to American racism. As Harrison explains, this is the problem of all African Americans in Paris: Even as they live in France, they are so habituated to American patterns of racism that they continue to live with the dark emotions and pathological behaviors they have learned during their subjugation at home.

The character most affected by this American ideological conditioning is the main villain—and "black monster"—of the novel, Mechanical, who has become both mean and masochistic as a result of his experiences.[25] As Harrison explains to Fishbelly, "Mechanical *is* hate, defensive hate and fear" (215), and because of this dangerous mix of emotions, "He's going to *kill*" (215), although one cannot know whether he will kill himself or someone else. Once again, Wright confronts his readers with a human time bomb that is the product of American racial politics, but, as I mentioned earlier, this time they are allowed—and even invited—to keep their emotional distance. Disfigured by his scarred face, as well as by his shifty gaze and his robot-like movements, the always fearful, unattractive, and almost obscene bisexual character is not only an expression of Wright's considerable homophobia, but also of his conviction that life in the United States literally *destroyed* a black man. Mechanical, Harrison explains to Fishbelly, is "emotionally naked" (507), unable to relate to any other human being and feeling rejected by all of them. His traumatic experiences in the United States have filled him with so much self-loathing that he is now without a trace of moral consciousness. He makes his money as a double-crosser, posing as a Stalinist in front of the Communist community of Paris, when in reality he is a Trotskyite who denounces his Stalinist "comrades" to both the French and American governments. And we cannot even be entirely sure about his Trotskyism, because in the end, there is nothing in which Mechanical really believes.

As in the earlier novels, Wright suggests in "Island" that a man who does not believe in anything and who is disconnected from all others cannot survive. As Harrison points out earlier in the novel, such a man is destined to kill either others or himself, and with Mechanical, it is the latter. When, in the melodramatic ending of the novel, he is about to hang himself from one of the gargoyles of Notre Dame because his ruthless double-crossing has been exposed, he yells again and again a single phrase at the police, his compatriots, and the thousands of Parisians who have gathered underneath him: "YOU CAN'T UNDERSTAND!" (492). It is a phrase that is reminiscent of Cross Damon's desperate attempts to communicate to his lover why he has killed her husband and other human "insects," while facing her complete lack of understanding. Up on the roof of Notre Dame, Mechanical is in a similar situation. Nobody can understand his motivations or the excruciating pain that fills him, because in his French refuge, he has been living on an "island of hallucination," a dark private world filled with horrifying mental images from the past that is utterly disconnected from real life in France. Fishbelly nevertheless has a dim sense of Mechanical's pain. "Hot compassion flame[s] ragingly in him" (489), provoking an urge to somehow prevent the man from killing himself. At the same time, Fishbelly cognitively understands that this upsurge of compassion is exactly what Mechanical was trying to provoke. His public suicide is "a desperate claim upon the emotions of others, declaring, in the most cruel fashion, a kinship with the human family" (489). It is Mechanical's last claim before he dies.

Unlike in *Native Son* and *The Outsider*, it is a black antagonist who perishes at the end of the story and not the protagonist himself. And only after he is dead does Harrison tell us that Mechanical actually wasn't a machine but rather "a fantastically sensitive organism" (512). The sensitive African American male, Wright—like Smith—suggests here, is in a precarious situation because of his increased vulnerability, but when he shuts himself off to protect his vulnerable self, he is doomed to a nightmarish, lonely existence. Fishbelly, although in some ways in the same situation as Mechanical, is still young enough to learn. While he is neither as sympathetic as Smith's Simeon Brown, nor as darkly fascinating as Bigger Thomas and Cross Damon, he offers readers an opportunity to ponder once again the necessity of human connection. Harrison suggests that it is unlikely that Fishbelly will be able to survive in radical isolation because humans *need* sustaining roots and emotional ties to other humans (see 222). Importantly, however, nowhere does Harrison—who is clearly Wright's mouthpiece in the novel—suggest that these roots have to be in his native soil. What he asks Fishbelly to do is rather to live differently in Paris (or anywhere else), in a way that is connected to the lives of the people around him. In Harrison's eyes, this is the only way to finally get *beyond* the American nation emotionally in order to stop being constructed as an inferior black subject by its racist ideology.

Like *The Outsider*, "Island of Hallucination" thus ends with a Sartrean (and Gadamerian) affirmation of human connection and the absolute necessity of an "Other" for human (self-)understanding and development. Mechanical, who is unable to learn that lesson and hence unable to ever loosen his painful emotional attachment to American ideology, finds relief only in suicide. Fishbelly, on the other hand, might be able to escape such a terrible destiny because of the deep friendship he develops with Harrison. While romantic love plays only a minor role in "Island," emotional attachment is central for the protagonist's cosmopolitan development. Although he has come to understand that because of his "socially inherited black emotions" (256) of fear, anger, hate, and shame, he could never become French or even similar to the French, he no longer wants to remain caught in American ideology. At the end of Wright's 517-page-long manuscript, we still do not know for certain which way things will go for him, but it is clear that he now realizes that he needs to accept responsibility for his actions. If he wants to live a life worth living, Wright's last hero has come to realize, then he needs to engage in serious and responsible interaction with others. "Island of Hallucination" therefore offers more than simply interesting insights into Wright's view of the black expatriate community around him. It also pushes cosmopolitan thinking, already present in *The Outsider*, a step further, in that it envisions a solution for the African American individual that does not involve death. That solution, however, necessarily involves the abandonment of the American "home." Like Smith—whom he despised by the time he wrote this novel—Wright came to believe that it is only *outside* of the American nation where a black American can learn to create an identity that does not rely on any national, political, or racial ideology, but instead is critical toward all of them.

Wright finished "Island of Hallucination" only a few months before his premature death at the age of fifty-two. He was not very hopeful that American audiences would be kindly disposed toward such an "un-American" stance as was expressed in his novel. In a letter to his literary agent Paul Reynolds that accompanied the manuscript in early 1959, he writes that he "can readily think of a hundred reasons why Americans won't like this book. But the book is true" (quoted in Campbell, "Island"). And while it is not true, as Wright also claims in the same letter, that "Everything in the book happened," since he takes elements of real-life events, as well as physical and psychological traits of people he knew, and recombines them freely in order to create his fictional tale, the book seems to have been true to his own understanding of the world at the time. Both Fabre and Rowley have shown in great detail how much pressure Wright was under at the time. "We know now," Rowley writes, "and Wright knew at the time, that the spies employed within the black communities (even in Paris) were mostly black" ("The 'Exile'"). Wright was aware that the tentacles of American intelligence were reaching for him, and as a result, he decided that he could trust no one. He felt threatened from many sides, not least by the African American expatriates around him. He had had disagreements with James Baldwin and Chester Himes, both of whom had criticized him as a writer.[26] He was also angry at William Gardner Smith and Richard Gibson, believing both to be on the payroll of the CIA—spying on black American expatriates with Marxist leanings, such as him.[27] Therefore, "Island of Hallucination" is, among other things, a forceful expression of his manifold suspicions and fears in the Cold War climate of the late 1950s. The novel was never published, and to this day, it is not entirely clear how well-founded his allegations about his fellow expatriates were. The long files that both the CIA and the FBI accumulated on Wright over the years make quite clear that he was indeed under heavy surveillance, but who exactly was spying on him, and whether or not the CIA had something to do with his sudden and mysterious death, are still unclear.[28]

What is unambiguous, however, is that at the end of his life, Wright was a lonely outsider—despite his many calls for human connectedness. After all, his similarities with all of the groups he was affiliated with politically—the Pan-African intellectuals, as well as the French existentialists—only went so far: practically none of them was African American, and those who were did not share his cosmopolitan and transracial vision. In a letter to James Holness in 1959, he wrote not without bitterness that, as an "American Negro," he was completely "alone. I belong to no gang or clique or party or organization. If I'm attacked there is nobody to come to my aid or defense" (quoted in Rowley, *Richard*, 475). However, in the very same letter, he also wrote of his "right to fight for the Africans" in the way he "see[s] fit" (475), thus declaring his cosmopolitan solidarity with other humans and even with particular groups. This is again the same ambivalence that we find in *The Outsider*, "Island of Hallucination," and many of his nonfiction texts. The detached vision of the Cynic and the multi-attached vision of the Stoic cosmopolitan both stayed with Wright as ideals until the very end of his life, and the enormous tension between the two—finding expression in many of his writings—seems at times to have almost torn him apart.

CONCLUSION

In this chapter, I have examined the role of negative moral emotions, such as fear, anger, transgression guilt, and shame, in the development of cosmopolitan imaginations. Using the literary work of Richard Wright as an example, I have suggested that protracted forms of fear, anger, and shame can complicate the emergence of such imaginations because they inhibit an open-minded engagement with others. Wright's novels offer an excellent opportunity to think through these issues, because their rhetorical strategies invite readers to empathize with protagonists who are driven by fear and anger, and, as a result, commit morally transgressive acts. Such acts, Wright suggests, lead to feelings of transgression guilt and shame, but when actors feel incapable of alleviating the distress of those they have hurt, this might make them even more fearful, angry, and aggressive. *Native Son, The Outsider*, and "Island of Hallucination" encourage us to think critically about the role of the surrounding sociocultural conditions in the development of such protracted forms of negative emotions and related feelings of powerlessness. The *un*cosmopolitan sociocultural formation of the United States, Wright argues in all of these works, historically produced what he calls "socially inherited black emotions": protracted negative emotions that were fatal both for the individual experiencing the emotions and for the environment that was confronted with the resulting aggressive behavior. At the same time, however, we have to acknowledge that such "socially inherited black emotions" also helped produce the cosmopolitan worldviews of both Richard Wright and William Gardner Smith; had they been treated as full-fledged American citizens, they might never have stretched their imaginations beyond the nation in the way that they did. Although their cosmopolitan literary imaginations differ in various ways, they share a common history and an insistence on the importance of building transracial and transnational solidarities against oppression.

There is of course the question of whether Wright's somewhat atypical emplotment of cosmopolitanism was successful. For a long time, the dominant understanding of his overall development as a writer was as follows: working his way up from an illiterate farm boy to the most influential black writer in the world, he reached a zenith in the late 1930s and early-to-mid-1940s; after that, contemporaneous with his expatriation, he started his artistic and personal decline.[29] Wright's insistence on his radical independence has, in this context, often been understood as symptomatic of the identity crisis that necessarily resulted from his self-chosen exile. In an essay on Wright's travelogue *Black Power*, Appiah argues that the writer's trip to the Gold Coast was "yet another quest for a place of his own," a quest that failed miserably ("A Long," 188). In Appiah's understanding, Wright's rejection of "a racial explanation"—his unwillingness to commit to the idea of an essential Negritude—made it impossible for him to go to Africa on grounds of racial commonality. Without those grounds, he fell prey to a "paranoid hermeneutic" (Appiah, "A Long," 188): his Western arrogance, and the need to distance himself from the black "natives," ultimately led to his embracing the logic of his own oppressor. Between then and now, this outright dismissal of *Black Power* and later works by Wright has, of course, been challenged. Defenses date at least as far back as Cedric Robinson's 1983 *Black Marxism*, and since

Gilroy's decisive intervention in *The Black Atlantic*, critical judgment has slowly changed.[30] However, even if we do not embrace the racial essentialism that is implied in Appiah's criticism of *Black Power*, we must acknowledge that Wright indeed saw himself as a Western outsider on the Gold Coast who, throughout the text, defines himself as *American* by nationality and as *Western* by culture. In this, we see a Richard Wright who not only falls short in the eyes of critics like Appiah—and the many others for whom he had surrendered "racial authenticity"—but also fails utterly to follow through on his proclaimed radical independence and the severing of all attachments.

The fact that not only Wright's cosmopolitan imagination, but also that of Boyle and Buck—and to some degree even that of Smith—involved and included lifelong struggles with American ideas and ideals illustrates how difficult it is to transcend one's historical situatedness and the ideological baggage that comes along with it, the best of intentions notwithstanding. This Gadamerian situatedness is the inevitable dilemma of every cosmopolitan and indeed the dilemma of intercultural encounters in general, and no one explored the manifold physical and psychological dangers involved in such encounters more thoroughly than the American writer Paul Bowles, to whom I will turn in the next and final chapter of this book. Bowles's experiences as a long-term expatriate in Morocco allowed him to offer important insights into the interplay of complex and often contradictory emotions, such as curiosity, fascination, fear, disgust, contempt, and horror, in Western encounters with North Africa. Similar to the work of the authors I have discussed in this and earlier chapters, Bowles's novels and short stories confront their American protagonists with cultures that feel alien to them, but the outcomes of such encounters are often less than rewarding. Like Wright, Bowles liked to shock his American readers into awareness; however, rather than encouraging them to empathize with a monstrous member of the out-group, he confronted them with thoroughly dehumanized members of the in-group, thus triggering strong responses of horror and disgust.

CHAPTER 5

THE LIMITS OF COSMOPOLITANISM:
DISGUST AND INTERCULTURAL HORROR
IN THE FICTION OF PAUL BOWLES

PAUL BOWLES WAS ONLY NINETEEN YEARS OLD when he ran away from home and sailed to Europe in 1929. He first went to Paris and then, following the advice of Gertrude Stein, to North Africa, where he traveled throughout Morocco, the Sahara, Algeria, and Tunisia. The natural and cultural environment of the Maghreb made a deep impression on him, and in 1947, Bowles exchanged a quasi-nomadic life as a composer based in New York for a quasi-nomadic life as a writer based in Tangier, Morocco. With a fresh advance from Doubleday, he revisited the Sahara desert, which had impressed him deeply during his travels in the 1930s, and wrote his first novel, *The Sheltering Sky* (1949). And although Doubleday rejected the book on the grounds that it was "not a novel," Bowles had made his choice. For the rest of his life he would understand himself first and foremost as a writer because, as he once explained, "There are things that cannot be said with music. . . . Music is abstract and I wanted to be very specific in describing these things" (Bowles quoted in Alameda, 223). What Bowles wanted to be specific about was the nature of human relationships. In much of his fiction, these relationships are interracial, intercultural, and transnational, and more often than not, they are fraught with emotional turmoil and physical danger. Confronting his (mostly American) readers with fascinating and alien worlds, he invites them to simulate the experiences of characters who share their Western perspective and, partly because of their cultural arrogance and lack of sensitivity, get caught in life-threatening situations that resist intercultural decoding. Often, such situations evoke a powerful sense of shock. In their exploration of the ways in which emotions and judgments can operate in problematic and often harmful ways when people are confronted with out-group others whom they do not understand, Bowles's novels and short stories illustrate the *limits* of the cosmopolitan imagination.

Chapter 4 focused on the literary imagination of negative emotions, such as anger, fear, shame, and transgression guilt, and their effects on readers' empathy and sympathy. It also touched upon the emotion of moral *disgust*, both when considering reader responses to Richard Wright's violent and amoral protagonists and when discussing these protagonists' feelings of shame as a form of self-disgust. This chapter will look more closely at the role of disgust in our imagining of and interaction with out-group others, considering its relationship not only with related emotions, such as fear and contempt, but also with complementary emotions, such as curiosity, fascination, sexual desire, and attachment. Bowles's fiction offers an excellent opportunity to contemplate the complex interactions between these positive and negative emotions in moments of intercultural encounter. Moreover, his use of authorial strategic empathizing is of particular interest in my context here. Many of his short stories and novels invite readers to empathize with and (to a certain degree) have sympathy for American protagonists who start out as seemingly superior and morally transgressive perpetrators and end up as miserable victims of their own lack of understanding. Bowles's rhetorical strategy therefore differs from Wright's in that it first encourages readers' empathic alignment with a member of the *in-group* and then proceeds to defamiliarize that character beyond recognition, making "sympathetic allegiance" (M. Smith, 220) with that protagonist nearly impossible.[1] Whereas in the beginning these narratives tend to cue an exciting combination of curiosity, fascination, and (sometimes) sexual arousal in readers, the curiosity and/or sexual interest tend to die away swiftly, leaving the protagonist—and, in a different way, the reader—with a much less pleasurable mixture of fear, terror (or, in the reader's case, horror), and disgust toward the end of the story.

Although we will find no cosmopolitan didacticism in Bowles's fiction, the horrible fates encountered by most of his American protagonists serve as a sharp critique of Western cultural arrogance and racial supremacy. At the same time, however, Bowles's depiction of North Africans can be—and has been—taken to task for its participation in and reinforcement of Orientalist imaginaries. Arguably, the evocation of intercultural horror and disgust necessitates a certain degree of strategic essentialism, and we will therefore have to examine Bowles's fiction within the force field between cosmopolitan ethics and Orientalist essentialism. From Bowles's four novels and dozens of short stories, I have selected two narratives from the late 1940s that strike me as particularly interesting for a discussion of the emotions and narrative strategies that are at the center of this chapter: the often-anthologized short story "A Distant Episode" (1947) and Bowles's first and best-known novel, *The Sheltering Sky*, which was published two years later. In both narratives, Bowles explores the potential consequences of a *physical* immersion in a world of difference previously only imagined from a safe distance. In both cases, this immersion is related in ways that are increasingly likely to trigger responses of horror and disgust in readers, but the *object* of disgust changes in the course of the story, inviting readers to reflect critically on the emotions, attitudes, and behaviors of American (or more broadly Western) visitors to North Africa, as well as on their impact on intercultural understanding and interaction.

In the first section of the chapter, I consider the role of disgust in our reactions not only to inanimate objects that we perceive as threatening, but also in relation to the members of ethnic, national, or religious outgroups. In this context, I am particularly interested in the interaction between disgust and other negative and positive emotions and in the ways in which this interaction has been used by authors and filmmakers to provoke both parallel and complementary emotional responses in readers and viewers. A third concern in this first section is the meaning of disgust for the narrative emplotment of cosmopolitanism. While disgust responses may seem too aversive and hostile to be of any benefit for the cosmopolitan imagination, I will argue that certain forms of moral disgust may actually further the development of critical and reflexive modes of cosmopolitanism, especially if they can be experienced at a safe distance, as is the case when we read literature. The second section then turns to Bowles's short story "A Distant Episode" as a pertinent example of his strategic use of readers' disgust for a shocking revelation of the possibly horrific consequences of cultural ignorance and supremacist arrogance. It relates these insights to Bowles's personal experiences in North Africa and his deliberations on the fictionalization of intercultural encounters, thereby considering the charge of Orientalism. The third section offers a reading of *The Sheltering Sky* that demonstrates that the same rhetorical strategies that can be observed in the short story are also at work in some of Bowles's longer fiction, albeit in much more elaborate and complex form. I argue that *The Sheltering Sky* is yet another example of the romantic emplotment of critical cosmopolitanism, but one that produces highly uncomfortable emotions in readers as they mentally simulate the divergent fates of its three American travelers in the Sahara desert.

DISGUST, CONTEMPT, AND THE HORROR OF EXCITEMENT

Similar to fear and anger, disgust is a response to a perceived threat; and, as in the case of fear and anger, what seems to be a relatively simple response is in fact a very complex and elaborate emotion system. As psychologist Jonathan Haidt and colleagues point out, in the most general sense, "Disgust makes us step back, push away, or otherwise draw a protective line between the self and the threat" (127). Its principal evolutionary function is to keep our bodies safe from contaminants and disease,[2] but what we find disgusting is also the result of sociocultural factors. "For North Americans," explain psychologists Paul Rozin, Jonathan Haidt, and Clark McCauley, "elicitors of disgust come from nine domains: food, body products, animals, sexual behaviors, contact with death or corpses, violations of the exterior envelope of the body (including gore and deformity), poor hygiene, interpersonal contamination (contact with unsavory human beings) and certain moral offenses" (757). As we shall see in later sections of this chapter, all of these elicitors are present in Bowles's fiction, which treats readers to a full spectrum of the disgust response, including the last domain listed—"certain moral offenses"—which is obviously quite different from the first eight domains. We can easily see that the avoidance of spoiled food, body products such as feces, corpses, poor hygiene, and interpersonal contamination contribute to the maintenance of bodily health. It is also comprehensible that some sexual behaviors and the contact with violations of someone else's exterior envelope of the body (such as oozing wounds) should be avoided for the same reason. "Certain moral offenses," however, at first sight seem to have little to do with an urge to protect one's body from contamination. It cannot be the body alone that is at stake here. And indeed, Rozin, Haidt, and McCauley suggest that disgust is a complex "rejection system" that protects not only the body, but also "the soul[,] from the full range of elicitors listed above" (757). In this context, they differentiate among three different forms of disgust—"core disgust," "animal-reminder disgust," and "sociomoral disgust"—that over time have been shaped by evolutionary forces. Since all three are relevant for my discussion of Bowles's fiction, I will briefly summarize them here.

"Core disgust," according to the authors, is a category "of food rejection" (759) and relates to the first three domains on their list. As "an oral defense against harm from potential foods, or things that can easily contaminate foods such as body products and some animals" (761), it is a basic and evolutionarily early disgust response that helps us ensure that we do not touch or put into our mouths anything that can potentially harm us. "Animal-reminder disgust" concerns the next four domains on the list—inappropriate sexual behaviors, contact with death, violations of the exterior envelope of the body, and poor hygiene—in which "the focus of threat has spread from the mouth to the body in general," involving "potential sources of biological contagion and infection" (761). Rozin, Haidt, and McCauley call this "animal-reminder disgust" because confrontations with sexual behavior, death, uncleanliness, and injuries "are uncomfortable reminders of our animal vulnerability" (761). While I agree that a concern for the body as a whole rather than solely the ingestion of food is an important domain of disgust, I am not certain whether it is helpful to reduce these disgust responses to a (cognitive) unwillingness or even fear to recognize and acknowledge the animal in the human.[3] Carl Plantinga has suggested the more neutral term "physical disgust" (*Moving*, 206) as an umbrella term that encompasses both food-related "core" disgust responses and body-related "animal-reminder" disgust responses. Therefore, I will hereafter use this term when I refer to the first seven domains on Rozin, Haidt, and McCauley's list.

The remaining two domains—interpersonal contamination and moral offenses—trigger what the authors call "sociomoral disgust" (Rozin, Haidt, and McCauley, 762). As the most elaborate disgust response, it denotes the common practice of discussing moral and political issues in terms of disgust, establishing, as Plantinga has argued, "a clear connection between bodily reactions and ideology" (*Moving*, 203). While cultural variation demonstrates that all forms of disgust are modulated by sociocultural processes,[4] sociomoral disgust is largely a culture-specific social construction that is mapped onto physical disgust responses. As such, it can and often has been used to regulate social norms, becoming "a powerful form of negative socialization" (Rozin, Haidt, and McCauley, 771). This latter point is crucial in my context here because sociomoral disgust plays an important role in in-group/out-group relations. As Hogan explains in *Understanding Nationalism* (2009), "responses to outgroups are not confined to fear-related amygdala activation, but may include, for example, disgust-related insula activation" (32).[5] If the latter is the case, then the out-group will be considered as unsavory, decaying, and disease-bearing. In this context, we might remember the statement made by one of the white American soldiers in William Gardner Smith's novel *Last of the Conquerors* (1948) that "the colored man was dirty and very poor and had much sickness" (196). This racist slur, which I have discussed in chapter 3, is a typical example of the ways in which well-established disgust-eliciting qualities—in this case poor hygiene and disease and, interestingly, a lack of financial resources, which arguably is considered equally disgusting in an American context—are projected onto the members of an out-group in order to define the superiority of the projecting in-group.[6]

Psychologists Keith Oatley, Dacher Keltner, and Jennifer Jenkins have argued that in such cases, feelings of disgust are often integrated with the related emotion of *contempt*, which "is the emotion of rejection of members of out-groups" (254). Together, the two emotions make the "treatment of people as non-people, as things" possible (254). In order to understand the psychology behind phenomena such as war, genocide, or slavery, suggest Oatley, Keltner, and Jenkins, we must "think not just in terms of anger, though this may also be involved, but in terms of the emotions of disgust and contempt" (253).[7] Such an attitude toward others quite obviously runs counter to the ethics of cosmopolitanism, and thus it could be argued that sociomoral disgust is by definition an *un*cosmopolitan emotion. It should be remembered, however, that most people feel moral disgust when imagining the genocidal crimes of Hitler's Nazi Germany, the Hutu's 1994 massacre of the Tutsi minority in Rwanda, or the violent suppression of the political opposition in today's Syria. One could also make the argument that in Smith's novel *The Stone Face* (1963), which I have also discussed in chapter 3, the protagonist's moral disgust at the insensate and hateful stone face is an important motivation for his cosmopolitan development. As law scholar William Ian Miller has observed, "moral judgment seems almost to demand the idiom of disgust" (xi), and so it may be premature to condemn feelings of moral disgust wholeheartedly. Rather, we should ask ourselves about the exact role of disgust in cosmopolitan ethics.

Before we do so, however, I first want to give some thought to the interaction of disgust with other kinds of emotions that may operate in intercultural, interracial, and transnational encounters, as well as in the imagining of such encounters. Hogan reminds us that "an ethics of disgust often focuses on bodily functions, particularly the ejection of substance from the body—feces, semen—or the ingestion of substances into the body" (*What Literature*, 240). What we have here, then, is an interaction of sociomoral disgust with physical disgust in the policing of sexual conduct and other pleasure-seeking activities. In American history, such forms of disgust have been ideologically created in order to prevent, among other things, the "amoral" act of miscegenation between white-skinned European Americans and nonwhite individuals. As we have seen in chapters 2 and 3, the narrative strategies of the interracial love stories of Pearl S. Buck and William Gardner Smith are geared toward working *against* this ideologically circumscribed disgust response toward out-group others. "[A]ttachment," explains Hogan, "promotes proximity seeking . . . which is directly opposed to the actional outcomes of disgust" (45n8). The same is true for romantic love, which mixes attachment with sexual desire. Feelings of sympathy and compassion must be similarly expected to inhibit the disgust response. Therefore, when Buck and Smith use authorial strategic empathizing to invite their readers to sympathize with attractive and likeable fictional members of an out-group, they seek to minimize these readers' habituated disgust response in the hope that this will help change their cognitive understanding of similar out-group others in the real world.

As we will see, Bowles's use of authorial strategic empathizing is very different from the approach of Buck and Smith. It is also different from Wright's angry depictions of miscegenation and interracial murder, although Bowles shares an interest in existential terror with Wright. Unlike these previously discussed texts, Bowles's fiction frequently (though not always) features white and often American protagonists who are curious about and fascinated with nonwhite others whom they at the same time find intimidating and/or objectionable. The strength of Bowles's evocative writing is that it allows readers to vividly imagine these unfamiliar others, as well as the equally unfamiliar environments in which they live, thus evoking in readers positive emotions of curiosity and fascination *independent* of their empathic feelings for the protagonist.[8] Readers' curiosity and fascination might parallel those of the curious and fascinated protagonist, but they might also be present when the character feels complementary emotions, such as fear and disgust. As Plantinga points out, "In the realm of art, at least, the disgusting may also attract the viewer [or reader], creating a push and pull between curiosity and fascination on the one hand and aversion and repulsion on the other" (*Moving*, 212). This is true not only for stories of sexual transgression, in which the protagonist engages in sexual practices that viewers and readers consider morally transgressive, but also for moral transgressions that involve what Rozin, Haidt, and McCauley call "violations of the exterior envelope of the body" (757). As I have mentioned earlier, Bowles's stories often move from a protagonist's fascination with the vaguely fear-inducing but also attractive "Other" to situations in which the exterior envelope of either the protagonist's or the other person's body is violated, often in the most horrific ways. This brings us to another quality of Bowles's work, and to what the film scholar Noël Carroll has called the "paradox of horror" (11).

The paradox of horror is related to the "paradox of tragedy," which was at the center of my deliberations about sentimental cosmopolitanism in chapter 2, and refers to the seeming contradiction that (some) readers and viewers can enjoy themselves while watching or imagining scenes that induce strong negative emotions, in this case fear and disgust. Carroll's explanation for this phenomenon is that there is a tension between our negative feelings of fear and disgust, on the one hand, and our desire to learn more about the radically and potentially harmful "Other," on the other. "Horror attracts," he explains, "because anomalies command attention and elicit curiosity" (195); and this curiosity, or the desire to *know*, is what makes us endure the unpleasant feelings of fear and disgust to which we are subjected by horror narratives.

However, this is not the complete story. Although Carroll uses a strictly cognitive rather than a psychoanalytical approach, he acknowledges that a certain rebellion against socially prescribed forms of disgust also plays an important role in our enjoyment of horror films: "The paradox of horror can be explained by saying that the ambivalence felt toward the objects of horror derives from a deeper ambivalence about our most enduring psychosexual desires" (170). As an audiovisual medium, film has a great advantage over written literature in that it can present visually appealing (and appalling) representations of the objects of horror, which—as directly perceived objects—trigger immediate visceral responses in viewers. Ed Tan reminds us that "the major scenes in erotic and horror films are more than anything else a feast for the eyes" (175). While some of our emotional responses to horror are empathic in the sense that they are related to our concern for the suffering protagonist, other emotions, "such as enjoyment, excitement, horror, fear, and longing," may also be "nonempathetic, to the degree" that they focus "on the event itself, as a scene" (Tan, 175). In Tan's view, such "Nonempathetic interest might best be described as *fascination*: one is caught up in the spectacle" (175). The promise given by a horror film to the viewer, therefore, is "represented by the continuing or intensified enjoyment of the spectacle, rather than the prospect of increased understanding or any improvement in the chances of the protagonist" (Tan, 175). Although the protagonist is necessary for viewers' involvement in a horror film, their main source of enjoyment is the combination of their strong emotional responses to the horrific scenes that they witness and their cognitive awareness that there is no need for any actional outcomes (or indeed serious feelings of compassion), since what they see is fiction.

I would argue that something very similar is involved in the enjoyment of Bowles's stories of transcultural sociomoral transgression, except that the major scenes involved are not so much a feast for the eyes as they are a feast for the *imagination*. "Disgust in the movies," explains Plantinga, "results from the sensory stimulus put directly before the spectator" (*Moving*, 210), and while this direct sensory perception is of course not possible in the case of literature, Hogan's perceptual account of emotion suggests that this is in fact irrelevant for our emotional responses. What counts is the vividness of the images, and one of Bowles's great talents as a writer is that he is able to create such vivid imaginings in his readers' minds, allowing them to respond strongly to the fictional creations he puts before them. An excellent example of his mastery in the evocation of horror is "A Distant Episode," which is an early short story that portrays the potentially terrible knowledge acquired by the dislocated Western traveler through direct and embodied interaction with the North African environment.

Bowles drafted the story in 1945, and although he always insisted that it was based on actual occurrences he had learned about while traveling in the Sahara, it also seems to have been the imaginative outcome of his personal emotions. Not only has he made clear that many of his narratives served a "therapeutic purpose" in the more general sense (quoted in Stewart, 35), "A Distant Episode" was also born out of a very immediate, dentistry-related form of dread. According to his own account, Bowles wrote the story while on his way to the dentist, thinking he was going to have a tooth extracted. "[D]reading the experience," he believed that writing the story "would provide a counter-irritant, fight fire with fire," and so he began writing "feverishly because the moment of truth was approaching" (quoted in Stewart, 33). Whatever the immediate motivations behind his creation of "A Distant Episode," most commentators agree that it is a typical example of Bowles's tendency to render in cold, merciless prose the fate of Westerners who dare to venture too deeply into the North African desert, while arrogantly believing that they possess the necessary intercultural competence to converse with the Arabic "Other," without the slightest idea of what they are getting themselves into.

HORRIFIC OTHERS: DISGUST AND
DETACHMENT IN "A DISTANT EPISODE"

Less than twelve pages long, "A Distant Episode" is written with extreme economy. The protagonist of the story—a linguist who is only referred to as "the Professor," but who clearly is white and probably American[9]—travels by bus to the (fictitious) village of Aïn Tadouirt with "two small overnight bags full of maps, sun lotions, and medicines" (24). During the first half of the narrative, the Professor serves as focalizer, and so we learn that he plans to meet a man named Hassan Ramani, a café-keeper with whom he somewhat unreasonably believes he has "establish[ed] a fairly firm friendship" (24) during a three-day visit more than ten years ago. As the bus descends from the mountains at sunset, readers are confronted with the first sensuous impressions of what Bowles simply calls "the warm country" (24).[10] As the air is heating up, it begins "to smell of other things besides the endless ozone of the heights," among them the pleasant scent of "orange blossoms," as well as the decidedly disgusting smell of "sun-baked excrement [and] rotten fruit" (24). Surprisingly, this sensual assault does not disturb the Professor in the least. Instead, he for a moment lives "in a purely olfactory world" (24) that triggers memories of the past. While it is unclear to both the Professor and the reader what exactly the past is that is evoked by his olfactory perceptions, the smell of excrement and his reliance on senses other than the visual both foreshadow his later transformation into an animal-like being. Another moment of foreshadowing is provided by the chauffeur of the bus, who, when hearing that the Professor is making a survey of variations of the local Maghrebi language, suggests that he should "keep on going south," where he will "find some languages [he has] never heard before" (25). This encounter with the alien, and indeed the incomprehensible, is of course exactly what will happen to the Professor, who naïvely believes that his linguistic training allows him to safely navigate the unfamiliar terrain of the Sahara.

Once they arrive in Aïn Tadouirt, the Professor's demeanor with the natives is both arrogant and ignorant: He brusquely pushes away the boys who want to carry his bags, and when he arrives at Hassan Ramani's café later in the evening, he ignores the *qaouaji*'s suggestion that he sit at the table in the front room, and instead "walk[s] airily ahead into the back room," waiting to be served (25).[11] The *qaouaji* does not seem to appreciate this behavior, and when the Professor asks him in Maghrebi about Ramani, he answers curtly "in bad French" that the previous owner "is deceased" (25). This saddens the Professor, who now feels lonely in the remote desert town, but tells himself that such feelings are "ridiculous" (25). Perhaps because he is unable or unwilling to deal with his emotions, he offers the *qaouaji* an inappropriately large tip, expressing his wish to get some camel-udder boxes.[12] The *qaouaji* reacts with anger, telling the Professor that the Reguibat tribe makes and sells these boxes, and that they are unavailable in Aïn Tadouirt.[13] Undeterred by the man's increasing hostility and indignation, the Professor offers money for every box that he can procure and agrees when the *qaouaji* suddenly offers to lead him to an undisclosed place where he will "get camel-udder boxes if there are any" (26). This expository moment is followed by the Professor's—literal—descent into another state of being, as he embarks on what Allen Hibbard calls "one of those terrifying trips, characteristic in Bowles, where the character in an unknown landscape is escorted by a stranger whose intentions are unknown" ("Some Versions," 73). The harmful impact of the nocturnal trip on the Professor's physical well-being is signaled once again by the disgust-provoking "odor of human excrement" and "the sweet black odor of rotten meat" (Bowles, "A Distant," 27). However, nothing seems to be able to deter him from following the *qaouaji* into the pitch-black outskirts of the town.

Despite his unwavering determination, the Professor senses that what he is doing is potentially dangerous when his guide leads him to the edge of a dark abyss. Staring down into the blackness, he asks himself what it is he feels: "Indignation, curiosity, fear, perhaps, but most of all relief and the hope that this was not a trick" (28). This moment of self-analysis, in which the Professor cognitively monitors his own feelings, demonstrates his utter inability to develop any constructive action tendencies from his emotions. He is aware that the *qaouaji* may have an interest in harming him—either because he wants his money or because he wants to punish him for his obstinate behavior—and he reacts with the corresponding emotions of anxiety and fear. However, he seems unable to take any action that would lead him away from the danger zone. When he looks into the Arab's face, he is "terrified" because he notices "the most obvious registering of concentrated scheming" he has ever seen (28), but this act of mind-reading only strengthens his desire for the man to go away and leave him alone in the darkness. It is only when the *qaouaji* tells him that the money he has given him "is enough," because it was "an honor" to be his guide, that the Professor begins to sense that the true danger might lie elsewhere (29). He is "seized" by a "violent desire to run back to the road," but he once again suppresses the actional outcome of his fear and instead begins his "steady and steep downward climb" into the abyss (29).

During the Professor's slow descent to the bottom of the crevasse, Bowles continues to focus on his protagonist's emotions and on the rationalizing techniques he uses to inhibit his negative feelings and related actional outcomes. The Professor insists that the anxiety he feels must be due to his exhaustion from the strenuous trip, and when it "occur[s] to him that he ought to ask himself why he was doing this irrational thing," he brushes that off, too, considering it "not so important to probe for explanations at the moment" (29–30). And so he finally reaches the bottom of the abyss, still unable to reflect critically on his emotions and actions. Only seconds later, he is attacked by a dog and brutally mishandled by several men with guns. He recognizes that his attackers are Reguibat, and the sight of them instantly triggers memories of the maxims he has heard in shops and marketplaces throughout the Sahara, such as "The Reguibat is a cloud across the face of the sun" (30). Assuming the perspective of the objective scientist and good-willed cosmopolitan, the Professor decides that this is "An opportunity . . . of testing the accuracy of such statements" (30); but given the rampant aggression of his attackers, his goodwill seems ludicrous at best. They either disregard or do not understand the words he utters in Maghrebi, and in his fear and pain, the Professor adopts an increasingly detached, almost ironic stance toward his own fate. He is "scandalized" by the "breach of etiquette" when being attacked again by the Reguibat's dogs (30). After receiving a "terrific blow on the head," he is relieved that he will now "at least . . . lose consciousness" (31), and is puzzled when in his deplorable state, he continues to hear the voices of his tormentors, whose language he cannot understand, despite his linguistic training. "These people are not primitives" (29), he told himself earlier, but what the Reguibat really *are* remains incomprehensible. The only thing the Professor—and with him the reader—grasp is that they are deeply and unrelentingly hostile toward him.

The Professor survives the night on the ground next to the Reguibat's camels. Too scared to open his eyes, he once again exists in a world that is delineated by sound and smell, rather than by vision. His inability or unwillingness to *see* things—both literally and metaphorically—also marks the most horrific moment of the story, in which he finally opens his eyes, only to notice that he is being approached by one of the Reguibat:

> The man looked at him dispassionately in the gray morning light. With one hand he pinched together the Professor's nostrils. When the Professor opened his mouth to breathe, the man swiftly seized his tongue and pulled on it with all his might. The Professor was gagging and catching his breath; he did not see what was happening. He could not distinguish the pain of the brutal yanking from that of the sharp knife. Then there was an endless choking and spitting that went on automatically, as though he were scarcely part of it. (31)

The climactic violence in this key moment of the story is both sudden and well prepared. The reader knows enough about the Professor's dire situation at this point to expect nothing good from the Reguibat. Nevertheless, the monstrosity and callousness of the act are shocking. Readers who simulate the described events in their minds are likely to feel a pang of painful recognition when they understand what is actually happening to the

Professor. Although Bowles never mentions that his protagonist has had his tongue cut out, the idea of a blood-filled mouth of "choking and spitting" suggests a violation of the exterior envelope of the body, triggering the disgust response. In addition, readers are likely to feel a spurt of empathic pain, and this moment of empathic identification may further increase the disgust response.

There are additional emotional responses involved in the imagination of this passage, however. While the Professor, quite appropriately, feels "terror" (31) in response to the mutilation and thus an emotion of extreme fear that leads the subject to freeze, the reader is likely to respond with horror. According to Robert Solomon, "horror is a 'spectator' emotion," but this does not mean "that it is a detached or disinterested emotion. To the contrary, horror is usually an overwhelming emotional reaction" (*True*, 47) and one that, "like terror, differs from fear in that it leaves us utterly helpless" (46). Bowles cleverly—and quite deliberately—uses authorial strategic empathizing in this scene to evoke a combination of horror and disgust in the reader, leading to a sense of shock. "If there's anything to teach in 'A Distant Episode,'" Bowles explains in a 1971 interview with Oliver Evans, "it can only be taught through shock. Shock is a *sine qua non* to the story. You don't teach a thing like that unless you are able, in some way, to make the reader understand what the situation would be like to *him*. And that involves shock" (quoted in Evans, 49). Although we do not know any details of the dentist appointment that allegedly prompted Bowles to write "A Distant Episode," his imaginative anticipation of the bloodbath and resulting pain seems to have been very helpful in the creation of a shocking passage in which a linguist is robbed of his *lingua*.[14] The question, however, is *what* Bowles wanted to teach his American readers through his strategic use of authorial empathizing, and this question can only be answered by also considering the rest of the story, which is markedly different from the first part in that it assumes a different narrative perspective.

After the Professor has lost his tongue, the narrative ceases to use him as a focalizer, offering instead a more detached point of view that relates the linguist's subsequent career as a mute and pet-like companion for the Reguibat. One of the reasons why we no longer learn much about the Professor's thoughts and feelings is that he, quite literally, does not have any. When the Reguibat "adorn" him with "a series of curious belts made of the bottoms of tin cans strung together" and command him to dance for them, the Professor does as they say, but he is "no longer conscious" (Bowles, "A Distant," 32). He simply goes through the motions, causing "a good deal of merriment" among his captors (32). Whenever he is not performing, they put him "doubled-up into a sack" (31) so that they can more easily transport him as they move farther southeast. The narrative now moves along swiftly, jumping forward a whole year, after which, we learn, "the Professor was much better trained" (35). He can now "do a handspring" and "make a series of fearful growling noises which had, nevertheless, a certain element of humor" (35). The Professor has been thoroughly dehumanized by the Reguibat and now holds the position of a trained animal, comparable to a dancing bear or a similarly tortured creature. We could also conceptualize his state as a form of what Giorgio Agamben has called "bare life." As I have explained in chapter 1, the notion of bare life refers to someone who is still alive but who can be killed with impunity at any time (see Agamben, 23). Since there is no one in the huge expanse of the Sahara who would even know that the Reguibat are in possession of the Professor, he cannot count on anyone to defend his citizenship or human rights. Since he is completely at the mercy of a tribe that is portrayed as exceptionally cruel and contemptuous, the Professor's psychological strategy is to completely disengage from thought and emotion. Instead, he is "dancing, rolling on the ground . . . and finally rushing toward the group in feigned anger" (Bowles, "A Distant," 33). Curiously, what is left to him is the *feigning* of emotional expressions such as anger, but other than that, he is mercifully unaware of his predicament.

For the reader, the effect of the thorough dehumanization of the protagonist is an increased emotional distance, a distance that is encouraged by Bowles's narrative strategies. Unlike in Kay Boyle's novels, the reduction of a human being to bare life is not rendered in ways that evoke strong empathic emotions in readers. Not only do they no longer receive any information about the protagonist's thoughts and feelings, but the portrayal of his coping strategies also invites a mixture of pity, sociomoral disgust, and contempt, all of which lead to an urge to distance oneself from the perceived object. In addition, Bowles's descriptions of the Professor's bizarre performances and of the Reguibat's uncanny practice of treating a human exactly as one would treat a trained circus animal have an estranging but nevertheless vivid quality. Readers' mental simulations are therefore likely to produce the imaginative equivalent of what Tan calls "spectacle," with the resulting nonempathic emotions of curiosity and fascination.[15] While readers' empathic concern for the Professor must be expected to significantly decrease in the second half of the narrative, it is their curiosity about the ending of the story—and their fascination with the inconceivable horror of the spectacle that is presented to them—that keep them reading.

The story ends with the Professor's painful return to consciousness. Reaching the desert town of Fogara, the Reguibat sell him to one of the locals. When his new owner receives visitors, one of whom speaks in classical Arabic, the Professor, for the first time in over a year, is *"conscious of the sound"* of these familiar words (34). Coming back into consciousness, he not only feels pain again, but also other negative emotions, such as rage. As a result, he refuses to perform for the first time. On the final pages of the story, the Professor is able to free himself, but Bowles suggests that he has gone too far to ever become fully human again. Noticing a French calendar, he realizes that the "black objects" on "white paper" actually make "sounds in his head . . . *Juin. Lundi. Mardi. Mercredi"* (34), and his cognitive recognition of the French language triggers anger. With "his emotion [getting] no further than this one overwhelming desire" (35), the Professor starts smashing the interior of the house and then "gallops" toward the gateway of the town. A French solider sees him and, considering him "a holy maniac," shoots at him as he runs into the desert (35). The shot misses, but it is unlikely that the Professor will survive more than one day in the Sahara. Not only is he without food or water, his returned emotional memories and cognitive awareness of his condition are also more than he is able to bear.

What Bowles seems to have wanted to teach his American reader through this particular kind of shock therapy is that a lack of intercultural sensitivity and critical self-reflection can be fatal when exercised in the wrong kind of environment. As Hibbard points out, the Professor's "tragic end . . . comes because he does not realize that he does not understand, let alone consider the consequences of his misunderstanding" ("Some Versions," 74). The Gadamerian intercultural conversation depends on the goodwill of *both* participants, and Bowles's short story suggests that would-be cosmopolitans are well advised to critically reflect not only on their own limited understanding, but also on the possibility that their interlocutors might be hostile to their advances. Hibbard aptly describes this conundrum: "Had the arrogance of the Professor, and his host of mistaken assumptions, been met with more goodwill than his Moroccan interlocutors were prepared to offer, his fate may have been otherwise" (74). However, things might have also "had another conclusion had the Professor been less mesmerized and more attentive to the dangerous position he was in" (75). The tragedy of the Professor's fate is that the two crucial elements of critical cosmopolitanism—self-reflection and mutual goodwill—are *both* missing, with horrific results. In fact, one could easily argue that the Professor's fate is a case of *tragic excess*, since the Reguibat's merciless punishment is grossly disproportionate to the Professor's comparatively minor cultural insensitivity.[16]

Timothy Weiss calls "A Distant Episode" "A masterpiece of defamiliarization and horror" (41), and it is important to see that what is made unfamiliar in the narrative is the Western protagonist. Both the setting and the cultural codes and practices of everyone else in the story are unfamiliar to most American readers from beginning to end, but by depicting the protagonist in a way that triggers disgust and contempt in the second part of the narrative, Bowles invites (American) readers to develop a critical distance from him as well in order to morally judge his naïveté and his inability to reflect on his behavior and situation. What we might find problematic, however, is his treatment of the Reguibat, who are depicted as irretrievably, and even monstrously, "other." Bowles himself has insisted that the tribe's ethnic identity is unimportant, explaining that he "could have called them—*anything*" (quoted in Stewart, 35). However, the fact that he uses the name of an actually existing Sahrawi tribe, and one that is ethnically a mix of Arabs, Berbers, and black Africans, leaves his work open to the charge of Orientalism.

Orientalism, according to Edward Said's landmark study of the same title (1978), is the Western reduction of the Middle East to a set of essentializations and stereotypes that defame Islamic culture in order to assert the superiority of European culture.[17] In a 1980 article in *The Nation*, Said made clear that the United States shares this supremacist attitude, asserting that "Very little of the detail, the human density, the passion of Arab-Moslem life has entered the awareness of even those people whose profession it is to report the Arab world. What we have instead is a series of crude, essentialized caricatures of the Islamic world presented in such a way as to make that world vulnerable to military aggression" ("Islam"). A number of critics have chastised Bowles for his use of Orientalist stereotyping. Colm Tóibín, for example, writes that "Long before the sin of Orientalism was discovered . . . Bowles had frequently been guilty of it, in word, in thought and in deed" (30). Thinking back to "A Distant Episode," we might indeed wonder about the accuracy of Bowles's portrayal of the Reguibat and their inhumane acts of cruelty. While it is certainly the case that the narrative encourages readers to distance themselves increasingly from the Western protagonist, it is unlikely that they will engage in any positive way with the Reguibat. Their overall portrayal could easily be considered yet another version of the decidedly *un*cosmopolitan "essentialized caricatures" of the North African world that Said finds so problematic.

Timothy Weiss has defended Bowles against the accusations of Orientalism, arguing that the critics who make them (deliberately) misread his intentions. "[F]or Bowles," Weiss explains, "the orient is not an occasion for composing fictions that demonstrate or are imbued by a sense of western superiority," as would be the case in a typical Orientalist narrative; instead, "he was rebelling against and escaping from things North American and European" (39).[18] Not only does Bowles's work lack the imperialist attitude, argues Weiss, it purposely exposes "American and western arrogance as a cultural debility," showing "the weakness of the western viewpoint when confronted by an alien environment where the cultural and social props on which it depends vanish" (39).[19] Weiss certainly has a point; however, Bowles's lack of imperialist attitude does not change the fact that his reduction of a North African tribe to a monstrous and irrational "Other" that punishes a minor cultural insensitivity with brutal mutilation runs the danger of unwittingly perpetuating racist stereotypes and reinforcing Western hegemony.

DANGEROUS FEELINGS:
BOWLES'S THOUGHTS ABOUT EMOTION

Despite their sometimes problematic reliance on cultural binaries and Orientalist imaginaries, "A Distant Episode" and other works by Bowles are important because of the emotional challenge they present to Western feelings of superiority and American nationalist ideology. Bruce Robbins understands them as part of a "worldly" tradition of American literature that "sends characters not toward America but away from it," thus revising "the tradition of Hawthorne, James, and Fitzgerald, which made Europe a dangerous playground for the rich and aimless, by moving beyond Europe and playing up both the danger and the aimlessness" ("Worlding," 1100). And indeed, while European tours, too, have been dangerous to the physical and mental well-being of American protagonists,[20] Bowles's characters are, as a result of their contact with North African environments, infinitely more estranged from the emotions, beliefs, and values that used to define their American identities.

This profound estrangement mirrors Bowles's own attitude toward the land of his birth. If Boyle, Buck, and Wright (and, to some degree, Smith) had relationships to the United States that were marked by various and often unhappy combinations of attachment and anger, Bowles's feeling toward his homeland seems to have been predominantly one of disgust and contempt. Although he tended to downplay his aversions, stating simply that he "didn't find the United States particularly interesting" (quoted in Bailey, 115), he occasionally allowed himself a remark that suggests stronger emotions, as when he insisted that "the America of today is a country without values or 'culture': it is a huge monstrous 'non-culture,' a 'non-civilization' . . . It's an apocalypse" (quoted in Loshitzky, 130). The evocation of a "monstrous non-civilization" is an expression of both disgust and contempt, and so it makes sense that Bowles would try to distance himself from what he considered harmful (even apocalyptic), leaving the United States for good in 1947.

Hibbard might indeed be right when he declares, "No other American writer has committed himself so completely to a life elsewhere" (*Paul*, 10). Although Smith, too, distanced himself radically from the United States after his departure in 1951, his feelings of bystander guilt vis-à-vis the civil rights movement constituted a continual emotional tie that Bowles seems not to have had. Bowles embraced Morocco and the rest of North Africa not only because he was fascinated by the variety of landscapes and cultures, but also because these landscapes and cultures were so utterly different from the place he had grown up in, and he *needed* them to be as different as possible. As Brian Edwards notes, Bowles's departure from the United States was in many ways "a definitive rupture" (309). The only connections he retained were his emotional memories and his literary work, since he was well aware that despite what has often been called his "exile," his readership was mostly on the other side of the Atlantic. And so he seems to have developed an interesting habit of subjecting American characters to daunting experiences in North African landscapes, partially to shock his readers into awareness of their own "monstrosity" and partially because he, like Richard Wright, believed that writing would help him to purge himself of painful emotions.

It is remarkable how frequently readers and critics insist on a disconcerting *absence* of emotions in Bowles's fiction and nonfiction. "Paul Bowles's unsentimentality and cruel wit are not for everyone," declares Robert Stone in his Introduction to *The Stories of Paul Bowles* (2001). Quoting an acquaintance of his who insists that Bowles has "a piece missing," Stone speculates that "[o]rdinary human sympathy is the piece I think she means" (ix). Bowles himself has furthered the myth that his work lacks emotional texture. "I don't try to analyze the emotions of any of my characters," he explains in an interview. "I don't give them emotions. . . . You can explain a thought but not an emotion. You can't use emotions. There's nothing you can do with them" (quoted in Warnow and Weinreich, 215). As I hope to have shown in my discussion of "A Distant Episode," this statement does not really mirror the actual state of affairs. One could rather make the argument that the narrative focuses almost obsessively on the protagonist's emotions up to the point where he is brutally mutilated, the loss of tongue and speech coinciding with a general loss of emotion, of thought, of consciousness. Neuroscientist Antonio Damasio has argued that "human consciousness depends on feelings" (*The Feeling*, 314), and given that in his model emotions (and the feeling of those emotions) are responses to mental patterns he calls images, we should not be surprised that it is an aural image—triggered by the perception of a language he understands—that causes the Professor to feel *rage* and thus return to consciousness.

The question is, then, why Bowles insisted that he did not give his characters emotions when he so obviously did. Similarly, he claimed that emotional or empathic processes had nothing to do with the creation of these characters and their fictional fates. "My characters are the products of my thoughts," he declared in another interview. "Emotions can't give you protagonists, can't give you anything, it seems to me" (quoted in Warnow and Weinreich, 216). One reason for this ostentatious disavowal of emotion might be that an emphasis on feelings was not *en vogue* among modernist writers. As we have seen in chapters 1 and 2, both Boyle and Buck had to face the contempt of contemporary critics when they chose to write sentimental novels, and while Bowles certainly was in no danger of being perceived as a sentimentalist writer, his insistence on the utter uselessness of emotions in the creation of literature might nevertheless have been informed by modernist aesthetics. Another reason, however, might have been Bowles's conflicted relationship to his own emotions. Mitzi Hamovitch writes that "it is clear from [Bowles's] autobiography *Without Stopping* that he suffered at times from almost unbearable anxiety" (442), and while I do not share her psychoanalytic perspective, I agree with Hamovitch that a consideration of Bowles's early emotional experiences helps us better understand his creative production.[21] In *Without Stopping* (1972), he remembers his strict upbringing in a family that was dominated by his cold and authoritarian father, who believed "that pleasure was destructive, whereas engaging in an unappealing activity aided in character formation" (17).

The idea that pleasure is harmful to a person's (moral) well-being is, as Hogan reminds us, part of an ethics of disgust (see *What Literature,*

240–241). Given that Bowles was homosexual, we might at least speculate that, among many other things, his sexual preferences were firmly circumscribed by this ethics of disgust while growing up in New York. The
same was true for his love for music, art, and literature. Unsurprisingly,
this denigration of pleasure met with resistance. Not only did Bowles
learn to strongly dislike his father—his biographer Virginia Spencer Carr
even insists that he "hated his father" (1)—he also developed strategies to
evade paternal dominance:

> Very early I understood that I would always be kept from doing what I en-
> joyed and forced to do that which I did not. . . . Thus I became an expert
> in the practice of deceit, at least insofar as general mien and facial expres-
> sions were concerned. . . . I could feign enthusiasm for what I disliked and,
> even more essential, hide whatever enjoyment I felt. (Bowles, *Without*, 17)

Seen in the light of these early experiences, Bowles's later statement that
men tend "to hide what they feel" because showing themselves "to be
emotional and ever-changing seems embarrassing to them" (quoted in
Alameda, 225) reveals more than just a general cultural inclination. It
should also make us skeptical of Bowles's statements about the uselessness
of emotions in the creation of literary texts.

Curiously, *Without Stopping*, too, has often been considered a text
that lacks emotional charge. When it was published, many reviewers
complained about the fact that Bowles had only described a succession
of events, without offering any insight into his emotional experiences.[22]
Reading Bowles's autobiography, I found it difficult to understand these
complaints. Not only does it convey Bowles's feelings of resentment toward his father and American society as a whole, it also gives insight into
the peculiar combination of emotions that distinguishes his many horrific
tales of American encounters with the non-American "Other." At one
point he remembers how, during his childhood roamings in the woods,
he would deliberately look for the highly poisonous *Amanita* (Caesar's
mushroom): "I would seek out an *Amanita* and stand staring down at it
in fascination and terror. There at my feet grew death itself, only waiting
for the decisive contact" (*Without*, 19). This horrific moment of prolonged
and obsessive visual perception, the *staring* at an object that triggers emotions of disgust, fear, and fascination, as well as the suicidal desire to
touch that which must not be touched, is a driver of plot in Bowles's first
novel, *The Sheltering Sky*, to which I will now turn.

Written partially while Bowles was traveling in the Sahara, *The Shel-*

tering Sky is in some ways based on "A Distant Episode." Bowles later remembered that he did not really plan the novel before writing it: "I knew it was going to take place in the desert, and that it was going to be basically the story of the professor in 'A Distant Episode.' . . . [I]t described the same process in other terms" (quoted in Evans, 51, 54). Like "A Distant Episode," *The Sheltering Sky* is concerned with dangerous intercultural encounters and with what Richard Goldstone has called "the unbridgeable chasm which separates the European/American from the peoples of the North African–Moslem–Bedouin–Berber culture" (276). Unlike the short story, however, the novel divides its attention among three American protagonists who, shortly after World War II, lose themselves in the Sahara. According to Bowles, the Sahara must be understood as an agent in its own right, because it determines the fates of the human protagonists: "What I wanted to tell was the story of what the desert can do to us. That was all. The desert is the protagonist" (quoted in Evans, 54). I have written elsewhere about the material agency of the Sahara in the shaping of *The Sheltering Sky*;[23] my interest here lies more with the ways in which Bowles portrays his protagonists' emotional responses to the environment of North Africa, and with his use of authorial strategic empathizing to elicit fear and disgust, as well as curiosity and fascination, in his readers. As we will see, these emotional responses are crucial for the understanding of a novel that is somewhat less horrific and violent than "A Distant Episode" and also less brutal in its imagining of the limits of cosmopolitan engagement. Suggesting that in order to become truly worldly one must shed one's American identity completely, *The Sheltering Sky* confronts us with a rather remarkable version of the romantic emplotment of cosmopolitanism.

BODIES IN TRANSFER: (UN)COSMOPOLITAN ENCOUNTERS IN *THE SHELTERING SKY*

The Sheltering Sky opens with the description of an unnamed man's awakening in a room that "mean[s] very little to him" (3). Dislocated in space and time, he is only aware of his being "somewhere" and of the "certitude of an infinite sadness at the core of his consciousness" (3). The man is Port Moresby, one of the three American protagonists of the novel, who has traveled with his wife Kit and their friend Tunner to Algeria. Slowly realizing that it is late afternoon and that "On the other side of the window there would be air, the roofs, the town, the sea" (4), Port continues to lie "paralysed in the airless room" (4). His outlook on life, it is insinuated in these first lines of the narrative, is shaped by a protracted form of sadness, a mode of depression that gives him comfort because of its permanence. When he later sits next to Kit and Tunner in a local café, we learn that he is a thin man with "a slightly wry, distraught face" (5) and an obsession for maps. Whenever he sees a map, he studies it "passionately" and then "begin[s] to plan some new, impossible trip which sometimes eventually [becomes] a reality" (5). Port thinks of himself as a traveler, not a tourist, and thus as someone who, "belonging no more to one place than to the next, moves slowly, over periods of years, from one part of the earth to another. Indeed, he would have found it difficult to tell, among the many places he had lived, precisely where it was he had felt most at home" (5). Port's assertions of cosmopolitan rootlessness are reminiscent of Richard Wright's claim that he was perfectly able and happy to "make [him]self at home almost anywhere on this earth" (*White Man*, xxix). As in the case of Wright, Port is in fact not nearly as deracinated as he makes himself out to be. He likes North Africa, and the Sahara desert specifically, because in his understanding it is "nowhere," a "no-place" that is as far away as he can get from the consumerist American way of life, which he despises. It is its very remoteness from the comforts of American civilization that makes Algeria and the presumed "otherness" of its people so attractive for him. However, despite his fascination with North Africa, and his contempt for the American way of life, his outlook and attitude are profoundly American. As Edwards has shown, the novel compares Port and Kit's travels to the familiar American act of pioneering (see Edwards, 316). At one point, Port thinks of his great-grandparents' encounter with the American "wilderness" and takes satisfaction in the fact that "at present travellers are strongly advised not to undertake land trips into the interiors of French North Africa" (*Sheltering*, 107). His fantasized pioneering, however, is not the only reason why he likes the desert. He also believes that the "sun is a great purifier" (177) and perceives the Sahara as a vast, empty, and silent space where he—paradoxically—feels sheltered.

Port's wife Kit struggles with her husband's obsessive urge to be in constant movement, and her attitude is perhaps more easily understandable to the average reader. Her prime emotion in reaction to the Sahara is fear, mixed with some disgust whenever she is confronted with unclean sanitary facilities or spoiled food. Repeatedly, she begs Port to *stay* in one of the more pleasant places for a few weeks at least, but when he restlessly demands that they move on, she always gives in. It is her first journey to North Africa, and she is unprepared for its demanding environment. Partly this is the fault of her husband. We learn that Port withheld information from Kit, showing her "a carefully chosen collection of photographs he had brought from previous trips: views of oases and markets, as well as attractive vistas of the lobbies and gardens of hotels which no longer operated" (107). The North Africa that Kit expected upon her arrival was carefully constructed by her husband with the intention to mislead her about the actual state of affairs. It is thus unsurprising that, at least in the beginning, Kit is too intimidated and exhausted to share her husband's delight in their new surroundings. Port, who for some reason hopes that this new environment might heal his troubled and sexless marriage, reacts with disappointment, anger, and spite whenever it fails to do so. It is in part this disappointment that leads him to make the fateful trip—reminiscent of the one undertaken by the Professor in "A Distant Episode"—that will prove to be extremely harmful to his well-being. The difference is that rather than by some indistinct (and unexplained) curiosity, Port's trip into the unknown is motivated by his sexual desire for the exotic "Other."

Leaving the hotel for a late-night walk, Port exhibits the same airy attitude that also gets the Professor into trouble. Looking at the people around him, he decides that "What little energy they have is only the blind, mass desire to live" (13). And not only does he construct them as devoid of personality, he also doubts that they have any thoughts about him or that they would help him "if he were to have an accident" (13). Like the Professor, Port likes to cognitively monitor his emotions, and so he asks himself, "Why do I feel this way about them? Guilt at being well fed and healthy among them? But suffering is equally divided among all men" (13). Although, "Emotionally, he fe[els] that this last idea [is] untrue," Port decides that "at the moment it [is] a necessary belief" (*Sheltering*, 13), because it helps him to inhibit his feelings of what psychologist Martin Hoffman calls "guilt over affluence," which involves becoming "aware of the difference between [one's] advantaged life and the meager existence of others" (Hoffman, 184). Because it is "not always easy to support the stares of hungry people," Port can only carry on with his walk by pretending that "either he or the people did not exist" (*Sheltering*, 13). This decidedly *un*cosmopolitan suppression of empathy allows him to continue to enjoy himself, but it also leads to an emotional distance that is problematic not only in moral terms but also in terms of survival.

Once again, Bowles's readers are encouraged to simulate the thoughts and actions of a man who is out of touch with his environment. However, even as Port refuses to engage with the misery around him, the novel invites readers to become aware of the implied injustice. For Robbins, it is passages such as this one, in which the novel "manages not just to describe other places, but to describe the causal connections between those other places and ours" ("Worlding," 1102), that make *The Sheltering Sky* a worldly and cosmopolitan text, because reading them, an American reader can hardly avoid the feeling that, as Robbins puts it, "she or he may be a target of blame" (1103). Readers are encouraged to be disgusted by the protagonist's careless attitude while at the same time noticing their uncomfortable commonality with him. And as in the case of the short story, they are provided with a number of cues that alert them to the fact that this careless attitude will not go unpunished.

When Port notices that his feet are crushing the shells of large insects covering the street, he is "aware that ordinarily he would have experienced a thrill of disgust on contact with such a phenomenon," but instead he "unreasonably" feels "a childish triumph" (Bowles, *Sheltering*, 15). His egocentric excitement makes it impossible for him to respond in appropriate ways to the sight of the crushed insects, nor is he deterred by the increasingly stronger odors in the air, which all represent "filth of one sort or another" (15). And when he soon after is approached by a stranger, he, after some attempts at evasion, agrees to have tea with the man. This, of course, could be the beginning of a cosmopolitan conversation of the kind we find in Smith's *The Stone Face*, where the American protagonist befriends a young Algerian with whom he shares an increased empathic responsiveness. Bowles's protagonists, however, generally lack such sensitivity, and Port is no exception. After some preliminary talk, the man suggests taking him to a female "friend" of his, and Port is "perturbed to witness his own interior excitement" (22). Unable to resist, he follows the man out of town to the edge of a dark abyss, but unlike the Professor in "A Distant Episode," he indeed finds what he was hoping for after reaching the bottom of the trail. His guide leads him into a filthy tent and introduces him to a young woman with whom he cannot communicate but who nevertheless arouses his desire. The sexual act itself is not described in any detail, but what is remarkable is Bowles's suggestion that Port can only get "stimulated" in the disconcerting environment of the valley after imagining his wife as "a silent onlooker" (33).[24] Given that Port feels attached to Kit (he does) and that this mental image of her does not trigger the slightest amount of transgression guilt in him, we must assume that Port has inhibited his empathic responses toward those who are near and dear to him as thoroughly as those toward distressed strangers. As in the case of "A Distant Episode," this utter lack of sensitivity, and the related inability to reflect critically on his behavior, are what bring about the protagonist's downfall. Although Port's experience in the darkness of a secluded valley is not as terrifying as the Professor's, it will prove just as lethal. When he prevents the young prostitute from stealing his wallet, she alarms the community and he has to run for his life. He manages to escape, but what he does not yet know is that the girl has given him typhoid fever, which from now on will begin to manifest itself in his body and mind.

Port, however, is not the only one who is seeking sexual adventures. Kit gets involved with their traveling companion Tunner, the most stereotypically American character in the novel, and quite obviously the object of Port's contempt. Much more in touch with her emotions than her husband, Kit develops a strong sense of transgression guilt as a result of her affair, as well as anger at Port for his betrayal. Port responds to her emotional outbursts mostly with contempt, according to Oatley, Keltner, and Jenkins one of the "four toxic factors in intimate relationships" (239).[25] Since neither of them wants to talk about their mutual betrayals, their arguments tend to center on Port's obsession with the Sahara and his disdain for his wife's emotional dependence on her suitcases full of American "things." It soon becomes clear that what he calls Kit's "pathetic little fortress of Western culture" (Bowles, *Sheltering*, 167) is, indeed, pathetic. The deeper she follows Port into the Sahara, the less she is able to uphold her American identity.

Port's own relationship to the North African environment has from the beginning been marked by a substantial amount of psychological projection. Although he despises the stereotypical image of the tourist, he is exactly that: someone who comes to a place with an eye full of preconceptions and who then "consumes" the environment as well as the services of the locals, without ever truly engaging with them.[26] When his American passport gets stolen, however, everything changes for Port, because, as he puts it, "it's a very depressing thing in a place like this to have no proof of who you are" (164). The loss of his passport disrupts Port's identity and completely transforms his relationship to the environment around him. As Brian Edwards notes, "Port's experience of the Algerian landscape previously viewed from dominating vistas is now made 'senseless'" (318), and perceiving the awe-inspiring sights of the Sahara suddenly fills him with dread and terror. From now on he begins a steady decline, not only because of the typhoid germs in his body, but also because the climatic conditions of the actually existing desert, the one that he does not want to face, will worsen his malady and make it impossible for Kit to get him to a place where he can be treated by medical specialists. In the remote town of Sbâ, she is finally forced to watch her husband die a horrible death.

Port's final hours are related from both inside and outside his consciousness, allowing readers to share his terrifying feelings as he moves toward inevitable death.[27] Once again, he is in a room that means very little to him, but this time the room is "malignant" (Bowles, *Sheltering*, 240). Port is both delirious and in excruciating pain, hearing "a screaming sound in each ear" (241). Kit, who despite their eroded relationship still feels attached to her husband, overcomes her feelings of disgust in order to take care of his disintegrating and highly contagious body. As William Ian Miller has pointed out, "love (sexual and non-sexual) involve[s] a notable and non-trivial suspension of some, if not all, rules of disgust" (xi). It is this suspension that makes it possible for Kit to overcome the terror and repulsion she feels when she is confronted with Port's "monstrous groans of pain," and with the realization that "He's stopped being human," having been reduced "to his basic state: a cloaca in which the chemical processes continue. . . . It was the ultimate taboo stretched out there beside her, helpless and terrifying beyond all reason" (*Sheltering*, 226). Once again, we are reminded of the fate of the Professor in "A Distant Episode," but here the protagonist's dehumanized state is not the deed of monstrous human others, but of what Bowles considered the indifferent, uncaring, and unaware agency of nature (see Evans, 54). Port, who always projected his own thoughts and feelings onto the Sahara, refusing to engage with its unfamiliar environment or its inhabitants, is finally defeated and killed by an environment that does not care about his projections. Like the Professor, he is the victim of his own Western arrogance and self-centeredness, and here, too, the narrative does not invite the reader to feel much sympathy for the suffering American protagonist. The minute descriptions of Port's diseased body and mind—the vomiting, the spasms, the boundless pain—create mental images that trigger feelings of horror and disgust so profound that readers cannot help but distance themselves from what, as Kit suggests, is no longer "human."

Port's death opens up a new possibility of engagement for Kit. She leaves her American things behind with her husband's dead body and walks to a nearby oasis, where she undergoes a remarkable transformation: Feeling "a strange intensity being born within her" (Bowles, *Sheltering*, 263), she gradually loses her sense of time and self. If up to this point it was in many ways Port who mirrored the fate of the linguist in "A Distant Episode," it now is Kit who, like the Professor, relinquishes consciousness. While Tunner, who is desperately searching for her, begins to "hate the desert" because he feels that it has "deprived him of his friends" (268), Kit recovers an unconscious "joy of being" in the Sahara (265). She is picked up by Bedouins and travels with them across the desert, starting a sexual relationship with their leader Belqassim.

Although Bowles's portrayal of the Bedouins is much more sensitive than his depiction of the Reguibat in "A Distant Episode," Kit's enthusiasm for Belqassim's "friendly carnal presence," with its "perfect balance between gentleness and violence" (291–292), is disconcerting, and not only from a feminist perspective. For the next few months Kit lives as what some scholars have called a "sex slave" in a small room in the house of Belqassim, hidden from her lover's three wives. Although she is practically a prisoner, she is happy, feeling "sheltered" from her consciousness by the desert sky. It is only when Belqassim's wives force her to leave his house that she makes her way back to the U.S. consulate in Oran. However, like the Professor, she cannot, really, go back. Not only the English language, but human speech as such, have become strange to her, and the woman from the American embassy who tries to take care of her is wrong when she says that "The desert's a big place, but nothing really ever gets lost there" (339). Although, ironically, her American passport is the only worldly possession that Kit has left, she has lost her American identity for good and, according to most scholars, her sanity, too. "CANNOT GET BACK" (328), says the telegram she scribbles down after she has been found in the desert; but she does not remember whom she wanted to send it to, and in the end she disappears again in the streets of Oran, irretrievably estranged from Western civilization.

The Sheltering Sky is Bowles's best-known work, and although it too has disturbing and even horrific qualities at times, it is not difficult to see why it would be more easily digestible for American readers than "A Distant Episode." Not only is it less violent, it is also somewhat less cynical about the fate of the American traveler. While Port's insensitivity and self-centeredness condemn him to death, Kit's final fate is more ambiguous. Although some critics have interpreted her final decision as a descent into madness, this is not the only reading possible.[28] After all, Bowles does not describe her development in terms of madness, but rather suggests that because of her time in the Sahara, Kit has been able to recapture "a feeling of solid delight" that she wants to keep at all costs (264). Syrine Hout's interpretation, on the other hand, that "after two confining marriages" Kit can "perhaps like Bowles . . . find a compromise by settling in a new home in Oran or Tangier" (134), seems overly optimistic and also overly restrictive to me, since we must assume that Kit has developed a radically new identity and a new outlook on life as a result of her experiences in the North African desert.

In part, this is the doing of the ecological space of the Sahara. Facing the vastness and silence of the desert, writes Bowles in "The Baptism of Solitude" (1963), does "something very peculiar" to those who do not withdraw from it:

> Here in this wholly mineral landscape lighted by stars like flares, even memory disappears; nothing is left but your own breathing and the sound of your heart beating. The strange and by no means pleasant process of reintegration begins inside you and you have the choice of fighting against it and insisting on remaining the person you have always been or letting it take its course. (*Heads*, 134)

Kit clearly *does* let the process of reintegration take its course, and, as in the Professor's case, her new identity is devoid of all national, ethnic, or religious markers. However, she arrives at this new identity through a somewhat different process, and it is also described in much more positive terms. While the fact that Kit does not mind being "taken" by Belqassim and his Bedouin friend will be disturbing to many readers, leading (as in the case of the Professor) to a gradual disengagement from her and her fate, the novel suggests that this is what she wants. Unlike the Professor (and Port), Kit is not so much punished for her cultural insensitivities as she is enabled to engage with others in a profoundly different way. As Robbins has pointed out, the novel's evocation of transnational space "permits new forms of bonding" ("Worlding," 1100), and Kit in fact bonds not only with a member of an out-group, but also with the ecological space of the Sahara and something that Bowles simply calls "life" (Bowles, *Sheltering*, 265). While this somewhat peculiar love story might evoke sociomoral disgust and horror in many Western readers, it no doubt implies a radically cosmopolitan union, including both human and nonhuman others.

CONCLUSION

The evocation of horror and sociomoral disgust is a somewhat risky rhetorical strategy when it is employed with the aim of moving readers to adopt more cosmopolitan worldviews. While disgust is an important moral emotion that informs our cognitive judgments, its evocation for literary characters is not without problems and can easily lead to empathic inaccuracy. Furthermore, horror and disgust both involve an urge to distance oneself from the object of the emotions, which is perceived as threatening and harmful, and in the reading experience this can lead to (partial) disengagement. Both Wright and Bowles aim to evoke horror and disgust in readers, but they do so in very different ways. Wright's strategy is to confront the members of a chosen out-group with an angry, dangerous, and morally transgressive member of his in-group, thus partially confirming their negative prejudices. It nevertheless is a case of what Suzanne Keen has called "ambassadorial strategic empathy" ("Narrative," 71), since one of Wright's central aims was to make white American readers realize that his monstrous protagonists are the inevitable product of their own racist ideology. Because he despised the idea of evoking pity and compassion for African American protagonists, he made use of ambassadorial strategic empathizing in order to *shock* his readers into awareness. The risk involved in this strategy is that readers may be so horrified by the protagonist that they completely disengage from him and never get to the point where they would ask themselves why he acts in the way he does.

Bowles's narrative technique in "A Distant Episode" runs a similar risk. Evoking disgust and horror in American or Western readers for a protagonist who belongs to their own in-group may result in a sense of shock, but it also inhibits empathy and compassion. Given that in "A Distant Episode" the members of the out-group are also not necessarily portrayed in ways that trigger empathy, sympathy, or compassion in readers, we must expect that many of them engage with the story in the way that Ed Tan considers typical for the horror genre: While some of their emotional responses are empathic in the sense that they are related to the suffering protagonist, readers predominantly focus "on the event itself, as a scene," with the result that their reading experience is dominated by nonempathic emotions, such as "enjoyment, excitement, horror, fear," and disgust (Tan, 175). The well-being or goal-achievement of the protagonist becomes much less important to them than "the continuing or intensified enjoyment of the spectacle" (175). This is exactly the kind of emotional engagement that is cued by "A Distant Episode," though this is not to suggest that it is a piece of genre fiction. Although Bowles is different from all other writers discussed in this book in that he did not consider himself a politically engaged writer, he did make conscious rhetorical choices in order to change the minds of his readers. He once explained that "In certain sensitive people the awakening of the sensation of horror through reading can result in a temporary smearing of the lens of consciousness, as one might put it. . . . It's a dislocation, and if it's of short duration it provides the reader with a partially pleasurable shiver" (quoted in Halpern, 96). The effect of the evocation, however, does not end with this pleasurable moment. Bowles believed that "A good jolt of vicarious horror can cause a certain amount of questioning of values afterward" (96–97). It was this questioning of values that he was interested in, and given the popularity of some of his more shocking stories, we can only hope that he was right.

Although "A Distant Episode" is a particularly interesting text for an investigation of the role of disgust and related feelings in the cosmopolitan imagination, it should be mentioned that Bowles's literary oeuvre also includes countless narratives in which intercultural encounters, although fraught with miscommunication and misunderstanding, do not end with the death or disintegration of the Western protagonist. As I hope to have shown, *The Sheltering Sky* is already much more ambiguous than the short story on which it is based, suggesting that the embodied encounter with foreign environments and distant others can be ultimately liberating. The same is true for Bowles's other three novels, *Let It Come Down* (1952), *The Spider's House* (1955), and *Up Above the World* (1966). Later texts, such as the 1993 short story "Too Far from Home," are even more nuanced (and also much less horrific) in their evocation of American–North African relationships, portraying both Americans and Arabs in ways that invite empathic engagement and sympathy. Moreover, many of his stories include no American or Western character, depicting Moroccans interacting only with Moroccans. From the 1960s onward, his prolonged immersion in North African culture also led Bowles to seek what Brian Edwards calls an "intense collaboration with the Maghrebi" (326), transcribing and translating the oral tales of Mohammed Mrabet and other local artists.[29] After the death of his wife Jane—herself a well-respected writer—he continued to live in Morocco, never again returning to the United States.[30] When Bowles died in 1999, U.S. obituaries portrayed him as an American expatriate connected aesthetically to the writers of Euro-American modernism, despite what they saw as his self-imposed exile in Morocco. The central importance of Bowles's physical and intellectual immersion in North African culture was, as Edwards has noted, largely elided. However, it was this immersion that allowed him to write short stories and novels that, during the early Cold War period and afterward, offered his American readers a much-needed window onto the larger world. While much less optimistic about the potential outcome of intercultural encounters than any of the other writers discussed here, he confronted his readers with stories that were strange and shocking, but also fascinating in their evocative portrayal of foreign worlds.

(ECO-)COSMOPOLITAN FEELINGS?

IN THE PRECEDING CHAPTERS, I have tried to analyze from a cognitive perspective some of the ways in which cosmopolitan literary texts encourage readers to feel with others across national, ethnic, and religious boundaries. While the narrative emplotment of cosmopolitanism can be and has been approached from various perspectives, I believe that an increased attention to the rhetorical strategies and emotionalizing techniques of such narratives can add something valuable to the vigorous discourse already underway. Not only are emotions at the heart of our engagement with literary texts of all kinds, they also operate in our daily lives and crucially shape our imagining of and interaction with other humans within and beyond the nation. Cognitive theories of emotion are particularly helpful for an analysis of such engagements because they are rooted in the insights of contemporary neuroscience and psychology. As I hope to have shown, the important research undertaken in these disciplines, as well as in the emerging field of cognitive cultural studies, offers insights that are helpful not only for an analysis of the literary emplotment of cosmopolitanism, but also for a more general understanding of the role of empathic and emotional engagement in the development of cosmopolitan imaginations.

The study of affect and emotion in literary texts is still in its infancy and will no doubt develop rapidly within the coming years and decades. The important pioneering work of literary scholars such as Patrick Colm Hogan and Suzanne Keen demonstrates the enormous potential of this fascinating field of study. Related research in philosophy, film studies, and cultural studies offers a host of theoretical insights that, with some modulation, can also be brought to bear on literary texts, be they fiction or nonfiction. My hope is that this book contributes to that ongoing discussion by putting cognitive approaches to literary and film emotion in conversation with cosmopolitanism studies. As I hope to have shown in individual chapters, a theoretical approach that builds on Hogan's affective narratology and Keen's work on narrative empathy is extremely fruitful for an exploration of the narrative and rhetorical strategies used by a diverse set of American writers who during World War II and the early Cold War period wrote their literary texts with the aim of opening up the minds of their readers to the feelings, needs, and rights of out-group others. Moreover, it helps us better understand how these writers' own emotional engagements with such others led them to use their powers of empathetic projection in the narrative emplotment of cosmopolitanism. As we have seen, the diverse cosmopolitan imaginations of Kay Boyle, Pearl S. Buck, William Gardner Smith, Richard Wright, and Paul Bowles were the result of the experiences they had at home and abroad, and they critically depended on their emotional responses to the challenge of various non-American others.

The fact that none of these authors ever managed perfection in their open-minded engagement with and nonparochial care for others makes analysis of their respective literary texts all the more important for an understanding of critical and reflexive world citizenship. After all, one of the most consistent arguments *against* cosmopolitanism over the years has been that it is too difficult, too abstract, too altruistic—and thus simply too much against human nature—to ever be fully or perfectly achieved. In examining the trajectories and literary imaginations of five people whose lack of perfection itself played a role in their striving for cosmopolitan ideals in everyday life, we have seen that an imperfect and in many ways ambiguous cosmopolitanism *is* achievable and—regardless of occasional setbacks or even failures—desirable. It is desirable because a gradual broadening of intellectual and emotional concerns and attachments, which each of the five authors experienced, led in all cases to more open-mindedness and understanding. And led, in consequence, to a literary engagement with and for groups and individuals outside of their originary communities and/or nation.

Particularly interesting in this regard is my observation that all of the literary texts I have considered in this book rely in some way or another on the prototype of the romantic tragicomedy, which confirms Hogan's claim, made in *Understanding Nationalism* and elsewhere, that romantic emplotment has an intrinsic tendency toward internationalism and, ultimately, cosmopolitanism. At the same time, my analysis also provides a different theoretical perspective on Bruce Robbins's observation that "expatriate novels are often love stories of a sort," and his contention that "what they do with this novelistic convention may be their best claim to a more strenuous worldliness" ("The Worlding," 1100). As I have shown in the preceding chapters, such claims to worldliness can be strenuous indeed, and the novels also are not always successful in the sense of provoking the intended empathic responses in readers. Nevertheless, they are important modes of cosmopolitan *critique* in that they expose American (and non-American) readers to the needs and claims of non-national others, imbuing those needs and claims with emotional value.

I am aware that my focus on the emotional and "sentimental" aspects of the cosmopolitan imagination may cause some discomfort among scholars who, like Andrew Dobson, believe that empathy and compassion alone will not suffice to bring about more equity and justice in the world, and that what we need instead are rational, moral, and material engagements (see Dobson, 171). The fact, however, is that as human beings we cannot avoid our emotions; once we understand them as an integral part of our cognition, we realize that our rational and moral judgments, as well as our material engagements with the world, are necessarily informed and suffused by emotion. Once we accept this fact, supported as it is by a host of empirical research, it is easy to recognize that our cosmopolitan engagements with the actual world and with the imagined worlds of literary texts become comprehensible only through and because of our emotions. Psychologists Keith Oatley, Dacher Keltner, and Jennifer Jenkins have rightly observed that "if emotions are to some extent universal, then as well as separating people they can build links" (255). The role of empathy is particularly crucial in this context, since "emotional empathy for other people and other cultures can provide a foundation for an intercultural morality" (255). Emotional empathy is a capacity that is shared by human beings all over the world, and it is therefore one of the foundations of the cosmopolitan imagination. "If there were no universals of emotions," Oatley, Keltner, and Jenkins remind us, "there would be no basis for concerted world action on anything, no human sympathy for the oppressed, no outrage against tyranny, no passion for justice, no concern for protecting or sharing the world's limited resources" (255). Although the authors do not mention cosmopolitan ethics, this is exactly what they describe. And since there *are* universals of emotions—regardless of the important cultural differences and variations that I do not wish to deny—there *is* in fact a basis for concerted world action on many things, and those who would like to encourage such action do well to appeal to their constituencies' emotions.

Literary texts are one form in which such appeals can be made. If we are interested in helping students in the United States and elsewhere to become less ethnocentrically oriented and more worldly, the teaching of American cosmopolitan texts such as the ones I have discussed in this book might be an effective choice, exactly because they open up to the world while still actively wrestling with their own residual Americanness. Not only do such texts encourage the kind of imaginative engagement with world history and politics for which scholars in a number of disciplines, among them Martha Nussbaum, Domna Stanton, Martin Hoffman, and Bonnie Honig, have called, but they also promote critical discussion of American dreams and realities. Of course, the five authors I have considered here constitute only a very small selection of literature that might be interesting for such a project. Texts of other worldly-minded American writers come to mind (James Baldwin, for example, as well as Gary Snyder, Martha Gellhorn, and Paul Theroux), as do the literatures of border-crossing immigrants *into* the United States and of ethnic minority groups within the nation. These texts, I believe, are just as important for a cosmopolitan "education" in the field of literature as texts of other languages and cultures (as Stanton has suggested).[1] They invite meditation on and discussion of the inherent and inevitable *interdependency* of the United States with the rest of the world, something that still seems to be underappreciated by a good number of Americans. Conversely, for students of American literature in other parts of the world, the reading of such texts encourages a consideration of American literature in relation to their own or other cultures, and it offers them a different perspective on the entity that is called American literature. A good number of influential scholars in American Studies are already suggesting a reconceptualization of American literature as a transnational entity, among them Paula Moya, Ramón Saldívar, John Carlos Rowe, Jessica Berman, Amy Kaplan, Wai Chee Dimock, and Brent Hayes Edwards.[2] The work of these transnational critics certainly points in the right direction, and I see my own work also as part of the movement their efforts represent.

In "Patriotism and Cosmopolitanism," the essay that helped spark the reengagement with cosmopolitanism in the mid-1990s, Martha Nussbaum offers a rather compelling reason for why not only American students, but all of us, should care about this global interdependency, why it is important that we learn to be better citizens of the world. Nussbaum's rationale is to a large degree ecological, as she argues that "we live in a world in which the destinies of nations are closely intertwined with respect to basic goods and survival itself" (*For Love*, 12). It is because air and water pollution do not stop traveling at national boundaries that Nussbaum asserts that "any intelligent deliberation about ecology—as, also, about the food supply and population—requires global planning, global knowledge, and the recognition of a shared future" (12). While I do take issue with the nationalist undertone that Nussbaum's reasoning displays, here and elsewhere, she makes an important point. Recent ecological developments—such as the noticeable shrinkage of resources and the drastic effects of global climate change—have reminded us that capital is not the only transnational force. A renewed interest in world citizenship is not only ethically "nice," but materially *crucial*. This is why, in the end, cosmopolitan education, if we take it seriously, cannot stop with the academic study of literary texts of any kind. While I do believe that such imaginative engagement can be an important first or parallel step, an education that truly aims at making people better citizens of the world must necessarily go beyond literary studies or even the humanities. Raising awareness of the interconnectedness of political, social, economic, and environmental problems worldwide requires a transcending of traditional disciplinary boundaries. As Gro Harlem Brundtland already insisted in her 1987 Foreword to *Our Common Future*, the official report of the UN World Commission on Environment and Development, the challenges put before us "cut across the divides of national sovereignty, of limited strategies for economic gain, and of separated disciplines of science" (x). More than twenty years later, this imperative has not changed; only the challenges have become greater and that much more urgent.

A truly cosmopolitan education must prepare people to meet these global challenges, and it must thus work toward transcending narrow national imaginations, as well as disciplinary boundaries between the humanities and the social and natural sciences. It will not stop at engendering, as Nussbaum has requested, sympathetic *understanding* of other cultures, but also advocate, in the spirit of the Brundtland Commission, transnational and transracial *solidarity* for the sake of all, nonhuman animals and ecosystems included. Nevertheless, an empathic engagement with others, be it through embodied interaction, through literature, film, or other media channels, is a necessary *motivation* for the forms of solidarity called for in the Brundtland Report. As Oatley, Keltner, and Jenkins have noted, universals of emotions also provide the basis for a "concern for protecting or sharing the world's limited resources" (255). The fact that emotions are embodied and that they take place in constant interaction with our environments opens a wide field for further research in relation to the study of emotional response, and hopefully, some of this research will move beyond the anthropocentric concept of cosmopolitanism to the more inclusive imaginary of what ecocritic Ursula Heise has called "eco-cosmopolitanism" (10).[3] The development of an eco-cosmopolitan consciousness would allow those humans who evince it a deeper understanding of and connectedness with one another *and* with their natural environments. Eco-cosmopolitanism, therefore, seems to include what Lawrence Buell has called *ecoglobalist affects*, "a whole-earth way of thinking and feeling about environmentality" (227), which prompt us to think much more deeply about the role of emotion in our relationship not only to other humans, but also to our nonhuman environment.

One vision of lived eco-cosmopolitanism is what we find at the end of Paul Bowles's *The Sheltering Sky*, where his female protagonist lets go of her self-centered Americanness and begins to understand herself as part of a much larger form of life. As we have seen, it is a radical vision whose unfamiliar biocentrism can trigger aversive emotions of fear, disgust, and even horror. It is the power of fiction, however, that it can challenge us with such radical visions, as well as seduce us into feeling not only with human others but with nonhuman others also. My hope is that the emerging field of affective narratology will help us to understand such eco-cosmopolitan challenges and attractions as well.

INTRODUCTION

1. The common translation of *kosmopolitês* into "citizen of the world" is somewhat misleading, since the Greek word *"kosmos"* refers much more to the universe than to the "world" in its more limited sense.

2. Anderson has famously claimed that national culture is the domain of feeling (see 16). Barber suggests that "global citizenship demands of its patriots levels of abstraction and disembodiment most women and men will be unable or unwilling to muster" (34). Miller has similarly argued that national identity is a question of sentiment (see 38–40). Walzer believes that life would be easier for the impartialist if it weren't complicated by emotional entanglements (see 44).

3. Nussbaum has developed her appraisal account of emotion in several books, among them *Poetic Justice* (1995) and *Upheavals of Thought* (2001).

4. See Solomon, *The Passions: Emotions and the Meaning of Life* (1993); Frijda, *The Emotions* (1986); Oatley, *Best Laid Schemes* (1992). Solomon's edited volume *Thinking about Feeling: Contemporary Philosophers on Emotions* (2004) offers a good overview of contemporary theories of emotion.

5. Timothy Brennan's *At Home in the World* (1997), Amanda Anderson's *The Powers of Distance* (2001), Rebecca Walkowitz's *Cosmopolitan Style* (2006), Berthold Schoene's *The Cosmopolitan Novel* (2009), and Robert Spencer's *Cosmopolitan Criticism and Postcolonial Literature* (2011) are all concerned with either postcolonial or British literature. Jessica Berman's *Modernist Fiction, Cosmopolitanism, and the Politics of Community* (2001) analyzes the work of both British and American writers.

6. Ulf Hannerz has been even more radical in this regard, arguing that the figure *best placed* to develop a cosmopolitan perspective is the expatriate. He acknowledges, however, that expatriation does not guarantee cosmopolitanism (see 243).

7. For an overview of writings on political cosmopolitanism see Gillian Brock and Harry Brighouse's edited volume *The Political Philosophy of Cosmopolitanism* (2005) and Garrett Wallace Brown and David Held's *The Cosmopolitanism Reader* (2010).

8. Appiah's essay was initially published in Nussbaum's *For Love of Country* (1996), and then republished—in a revised and extended version—in Cheah and Robbins's *Cosmopolitics* (1998). I am quoting here from the latter book.

9. Other treatments of "rooted cosmopolitanism" include Mitchell Cohen, "Rooted Cosmopolitanism" (1992); Bruce Ackerman, "Rooted Cosmopolitanism" (1994); and Domna Stanton, "On Rooted Cosmopolitanism" (2006).

10. This specter of undemocratic, irresponsible, and egocentric world citizenship is of course closely related to the Cynic concept. Diogenes, after all, proclaimed that he owed no special obligations to Sinope, Athens, or any other polis. And, nevertheless, he lived in the streets of Athens, being sustained (in an ever so minimal way) by a citizenry he did not support. Such a "parasitic" existence was disagreeable to many proper Athenian citizens. If we further trace the career of "rootless" cosmopolitanism throughout history, we find that it often adhered to unwanted or possibly disruptive subjects. While Stalin famously used the term "rootless cosmopolitans" to denounce members

of the Jewish diaspora (which is, of course, anything but rootless), the idea of the Wandering Jew and the challenge or even threat that she poses to the well-ordered (ethnocentric) society has emerged in many other contexts.

11. See, for example, Solomon, *Not Passion's Slave* (2003) and *True to Our Feelings* (2007); Jenefer Robinson, *Deeper than Reason* (2005); Peter Goldie, *The Emotions* (2000); Ronald de Sousa, *The Rationality of Emotion* (1987) and *Emotional Truth* (2011).

12. While acknowledging the importance of culture for the development of an individual's emotions, Nussbaum argues that the social constructivist's assumption that "cultural forces leave no room for individual variety and freedom" goes too far (*Upheavals*, 169). In her view, the close relationship between cognition and emotion gives "societies and individuals . . . the freedom to make improvements. If we recognize the element of evaluation *in the emotions*, we also see that they can themselves be *evaluated*—and in some ways altered, if they fail to survive criticism" (172–173).

13. See Goldie, "Emotion, Feeling, and Knowledge of the World" (2004) and "Getting Feelings into Emotional Experience in the Right Way" (2009); de Sousa, *The Rationality of Emotion* (1987) and "Emotions: What I Know, What I'd Like to Think I Know, and What I'd Like to Think" (2004).

14. LeDoux has explained this process with neurological evidence that points to the existence of two pathways by which we process our perceptions: one of them, the "low road," goes directly from the sensory thalamus to the amygdala; the other one, the "high road," goes from the sensory thalamus to the sensory cortex and only then to the amygdala. Although the "low road" is a relatively crude system, "it has an important advantage over the cortical input pathway to the amygdala. That advantage is time. . . . It is a quick and dirty processing system" (163). The cortical input pathway, on the other hand, is slower, but much more precise. Depending on what it tells the amygdala, the initial "quick and dirty" perceptual emotion will either be decreased or increased.

15. For a cognitive approach to horror film, see Noël Carroll, *The Philosophy of Horror* (1990).

16. For an explanation of the nature of emotional memories, see Hogan, *What Literature Teaches Us about Emotion*, 51.

17. Craig Calhoun, for example, has noted that "there are a variety of ways in which people are joined to each other, within and across the boundaries of states and other polities" (99). But, Calhoun insists, we need to learn more about what exactly binds people to each other, and to foster those binding agents.

18. See Held, *Democracy and the Global Order* (1995) and *Cosmopolitanism: Ideals, Realities, and Deficits* (2010); Benhabib, *The Rights of Others* (2004) and *Another Cosmopolitanism* (2006). The dominant figure for this line of thought is John Rawls, who outlined his social contract theory in *A Theory of Justice* (1971). Rawls's liberal thought remains the focus of debate for many. Nussbaum and other cosmopolitan thinkers, however, take issue with Rawls's confinement of justice to the nation-state and have argued that we must expand our understanding of justice beyond that limited arena.

19. Long's term unhelpfully suggests an *excess* of emotion (the common definition of sentimentalism), while in truth representing a theoretical account of the complex role played by emotions in the development of cosmopolitan attitudes and practices.

20. In *The Mind and Its Stories*, Hogan develops a theory of literary universals, defining them as "properties and relations found across a range of literary traditions" (17).

21. See Foucault, *Discipline and Punish* (1975); Jameson, *The Political Unconscious* (1981).

22. Harold Bloom has similarly insisted that "the pleasures of reading indeed are selfish rather than social" and that we make a mistake if we "connect the pleasures of solitary reading to the public good" (22).

23. Jacques Derrida is one of the few poststructuralist thinkers who have concerned themselves with cosmopolitanism. In *On Cosmopolitanism and Forgiveness* (2001), he investigates, with recourse to Hannah Arendt, the question of why humans can act inhumanely to other humans and cautiously advocates a form of Kantian hospitality.

24. See Lévinas, *Totality and Infinity* (1969).

25. See Booth, *The Company We Keep* (1988).

26. Mar et al. (2006) report that "fiction print-exposure positively predicted measures of social ability. . . . The tendency to become absorbed in a story also predicted empathy scores" (694). In a follow-up study (Mar, Oatley, and Peterson, 2009) the researchers controlled for several personality traits to make their results more generally applicable. They found that "even after accounting for these variables, fiction exposure still predicted performance on an empathy task. Extending these results, we also found that exposure to fiction was positively correlated with social support" (407). See also Mar and Oatley (2008), Hakemulder (2000), Strange (2002), and Strange and Leung (1999).

27. Bracher's *Literature and Social Justice* (2013) explores the harmful impact of "faulty person-schemas" (xiii) and literature's potential to change such problematic cognitive structures. Taking three influential protest novels—Upton Sinclair's *The Jungle*, John Steinbeck's *Grapes of Wrath*, and Richard Wright's *Native Son*—as examples, Bracher argues for these texts' ability to "replace the misleading exemplars, prototypes, and information-processing routines of the four faulty person-schemas with more adequate counterparts" (xiv).

28. As Dromi and Illouz note, our opinions are subject to influence by stories even when we consciously agree that these stories are not reliable references (see 353). Strange (2002) has shown that this influence can take place even when we explicitly try to avoid it.

29. David Hollinger has argued that "the continuity and degree of separation of the black people as a group have been heavily influenced, historically, by the manifest refusal of the whites to accept black people as equals" ("Not Universalists," 237). Feminist and queer readings of culture have discerned similar patterns—though of course differently manifested—of marginalization of women and homosexuals.

CHAPTER ONE

1. For a lucid treatment of the role of our mind-reading abilities in the enjoyment of literature, see Lisa Zunshine's influential study *Why We Read Fiction* (2006).

2. Goldman has admitted that recent neuroscientific research by Iacoboni and his team suggests that "even reconstructive empathy is mediated by neurons with mirroring properties" (44), but insists that this discovery does not necessarily undercut

his distinction between automatic mirroring and complex reconstructive processes. Rather, it suggests that "neurons with mirror properties might also participate in such an effortful process as imagination" (Goldman, 44).

3. Spivak's concept of "strategic essentializing" is based on the insight that for postcolonial subjects and groups it is sometimes advantageous to temporarily "essentialize" themselves, regardless of their actually existing differences and diversity in identity, in order to achieve certain political goals (see Spivak, 214).

4. See, for example, Marjorie Taylor, Sara D. Hodges, and Adèle Kohányi, "The Illusion of Independent Agency" (2002–2003).

5. Malcolm Cowley famously described the modernist expatriate generation (which included himself) as "cosmopolitan" in *Exile's Return* (1934). Many among this group, though, fell more than a little short of the sort of critical intercultural solidarities that make cosmopolitanism more than just a pretty, empty title.

6. Such cliquishness did not come without a certain disdain for nonmembers, even if those nonmembers happened to be the sought-out hosts themselves. F. Scott Fitzgerald, for example, one of the most prominent members of the Lost Generation, tended to display questionable intercultural (in)sensibilities, as we learn from Ernest Hemingway's famous chronicle of the Parisian 1920s, *A Moveable Feast* (1964).

7. Austenfeld refers to Boyle's style of expatriation as "deep expatriation" because "her emotional involvement with Europe is deeper than that of any other expatriate author I am familiar with, and her political observations about Europe between the wars show unparalleled perspicacity, especially to readers reared in a European background" (*American Women*, 45). While I agree with Austenfeld's assessment, I disagree that the depth of Boyle's emotional involvement was unparalleled. Smith, Buck, and Bowles had similarly deep relationships with the various worlds in which they lived, and the list presumably is much longer. Austenfeld in fact mentions Bowles as a possible candidate for "deep expatriatism" in a footnote.

8. Used synonymously with terms like "well-traveled," "sophisticated," "knowledgeable," and "refined," modernist cosmopolitanism evokes images of a bohemian life in foreign metropolises. However, the majority of the modernist American expatriates in Paris preferred to remain among themselves and generally did little to understand or engage with their host culture, let alone allow their own understanding of the world to be dramatically questioned or changed.

9. Boyle was one of the signers of Eugène Jolas's "The Revolution of the Word"—a modernist manifesto that appeared in 1929 in Jolas's literary journal *Transition* (http://www.davidson.edu/academic/english/Little_Magazines/transition/manifesto.html [accessed February 14, 2013]). The manifesto states that "The revolution in the English language is an accomplished fact," and that "The writer expresses. He does not communicate."

10. In her introduction to the 2001 edition, Sandra Spanier explains that the manuscript for *Process* got lost in 1928, when Boyle gave her only copy away to a publishing house and never saw it again. Spanier found the manuscript when conducting research in the New York Public Library. Spanier emphasizes the importance of *Process* for Boyle scholars, as its modernist style corresponds to Boyle's highly acclaimed poetry of the time. For a detailed discussion of the stylistic elements of *Process*, see Anne Reynes-Delobel, "'Calculating the Leap from Void to Absence': Abstraction in the Writing of Kay Boyle" (2008).

11. Kay Boyle in a letter to her sister Joan, quoted in Sandra Spanier's introduction to *Process* (2001), p. xviii.

12. For a detailed discussion of these issues in Boyle's early novels, see my essay "The Wandering Woman: The Challenges of Cosmopolitanism in Kay Boyle's Early Novels" (2008).

13. For a detailed discussion of *Death of a Man*, see Weik, "The Wandering Woman" (2008). See also Jennifer L. Barker's "Double Exposure" (2008).

14. *365 Days* has remarkable structure and intent. Composed of 365 stories, each of three hundred words or less, and written by 116 different authors (among them Nancy Cunard, Robert McAlmon, Emanuel Carnevali, Hilaire Hiler, Charles Henry Ford, Langston Hughes, and Henry Miller), it was intended as a fictional record of recent events and of individual lives all over the world on each day in the year 1934. While most of the contributors wrote only one piece for the collection, Boyle herself wrote 96, many of which are concerned with social injustice and racial discrimination.

15. Boyle herself was heavily involved in her lover's rescue, but it was her husband and his mother who pulled most of the strings to get the ex-Austrian out of the internment camp and eventually into a plane to America (see Spanier, 149).

16. Davis had selected the place not only because it had been declared international territory—which was helpful, since he no longer was in possession of a French visa— but also because it allowed him to voice his concerns in an international forum. On November 19, 1948, Davis interrupted a session of the UN General Assembly at the Palais de Chaillot, calling for "One government for one world" (Davis, 62). Understanding the needs of the nation-state, he later resorted to creating his own "world passport" and—in a story almost too good to be true—has managed in the past fifty years to get this world passport recognized in 150 countries "on a de facto basis" (he has, however, also been imprisoned thirty-four times for not having appropriate papers). He also founded the International Registry of World Citizens in Paris in January 1949, which—according to his own record—has registered over 750,000 individuals. See Davis's website: http://www.garrydavis.org/index.html.

17. Walter Mignolo criticizes Kant's Eurocentrism in "The Many Faces of Cosmopolis" (2000). David Harvey notes, in "Cosmopolitanism and the Banality of Geographical Evils" (2000), that Kant's vision of world citizenship is compromised by his *Geography* (1802), a text that, in Harvey's view, "is nothing short of an intellectual and political embarrassment" (532). While acknowledging that the text was compiled from notes of Kant's students, leaving certain doubts as to its accuracy, Harvey argues that the sometimes rampant racism expressed in *Geography* nevertheless has serious implications for Kant's cosmopolitan project. In "Kant's Second Thoughts on Race" (2007), philosopher Pauline Kleingeld agrees with Harvey that "probably until at least 1792, [Kant's] disturbing views on race contradicted his own moral universalism" (592). In her analysis, however, Kant was able to resolve this contradiction "during the mid-1790s, at the latest during the writing of the manuscript for *Toward Perpetual Peace*," a change of mind she finds expressed not only "in his explicit strengthening . . . of the status of non-Europeans," but also in his "harsh criticism of the injustice perpetrated by the European colonial powers" (592). For a critical assessment of Kant's *Geography*, see also Stuart Elden and Eduardo Mendieta's *Reading Kant's Geography* (2011).

18. For works of political cosmopolitanism that engage critically with Kant's leg-

acy, see David Held, *Democracy and the Global Order* (1995) and *Cosmopolitanism: Ideals, Realities, and Deficits* (2010), as well as Seyla Benhabib, *The Rights of Others* (2004) and *Another Cosmopolitanism* (2006). See also Garrett Wallace Brown and David Held, eds., *The Cosmopolitanism Reader* (2010).

19. Arendt had herself been a Jewish refugee during the war, and Jaspers had lost his university post in Nazi Germany on grounds of his wife's Jewish identity.

20. For a contemporary critique of human rights vocabulary, see Slavoj Žižek, "Against Human Rights" (2005). For a poststructuralist account of the capitalist aspects of globalization that criticizes both cosmopolitanism and human rights discourses, see Pheng Cheah's *Inhuman Conditions* (2006).

21. Arendt experienced firsthand what it means to be a stateless and multiply displaced individual. As a Jewish German, she had been confronted with many acts of discrimination even before she fled her native country for France in 1933, after having been temporarily arrested by the Nazis in Berlin. In 1937, her German citizenship was revoked. She continued to live in Paris, helping and supporting Jewish refugees. In 1940, after the German invasion of France, Arendt was arrested and put for five weeks into a concentration camp. In January 1941 she escaped with her mother and her second husband Heinrich Blücher to Lisbon, where she lived as a stateless refugee, waiting for her passage to the United States. She and Blücher arrived in New York in May 1941, her mother shortly thereafter. In 1951, Arendt became a naturalized American.

22. In Schmitt's understanding, a power is sovereign when it is in a position to declare the state of exception, a state which involves the suspension of all normal legality. See *Politische Theologie* (1922).

23. Agamben takes his term from ancient Roman law, in which *homo sacer* referred to an outlawed person: somebody who was not (yet) dead, but could be killed with impunity. Such a person had no legal signification; he was a cipher before laws that nonetheless prevented him from acting freely.

24. In "Against Human Rights" (2005), Žižek further explains the relationship between Agamben's concept of bare life and the basic problem of human rights: "It is precisely when a human being is deprived of the particular socio-political identity that accounts for his determinate citizenship that—in one and the same move—he ceases to be recognized or treated as human. Paradoxically, I am deprived of human rights at the very moment at which I am reduced to a human being 'in general,' and thus become the ideal bearer of those 'universal human rights'" (127). We might state this paradox differently by noting that human rights cease to be useful to the individual at the precise moment when he or she needs them as a pure individual.

25. While Arendt and Agamben disagree on the nature of the concentration camp with regard to the political—for Arendt, the camp is the site where the political is negated; for Agamben, by contrast, it is the place where politics as the sovereign decision over life reveals itself in its purest form—they both understand it as the prime example of total deprivation of rights.

26. See the front and back flaps of the dust jacket of the first hardcover edition of *1939*.

27. While Sepp von Horneck is a thinly disguised fictionalization of Joseph von Franckenstein, Wolfgang shares many characteristics with Kurt Wick, who was, for a while, Boyle's lover. Spanier quotes a letter she received from Boyle, in which Boyle makes clear that it is Sepp who represents Franckenstein, not Wolfgang. "He, that

other Austrian," she writes, meaning Kurt Wick, "went voluntarily . . . into the Foreign Legion, while Joseph, refusing to apply for a Nazi passport, chose to remain in internment camp" (Boyle quoted in Spanier, 159).

28. Here, incidentally, we also see how varied cosmopolitan attachments can complicate one's original attachments. Many of Boyle's heroines, including Phyl, understand themselves as French—even those who are not so by birth.

29. *Avalanche* appeared first as a serialized novel in the *Saturday Evening Post*, a circumstance that has, among other things, noticeable effects on the plot structure of the book.

30. Suzanne Clark has dedicated a chapter to the political dimensions of Boyle's use of sentimental techniques in *Sentimental Modernism* (1991).

31. This tension corresponds with the notion of the "double gesture," as political theorist Bonnie Honig theorized in the context of cosmopolitanism (see 107).

32. In her piece "Report from Lock-up," published in *Four Visions of America*, Boyle portrays her time in the California detention center to which she had been committed after her arrest at an antiwar sit-in at the Army Induction Center in Oakland in 1968.

33. Heins explains that Arendt's "prime example of the subversion of an abstract idea by a boundless emotion is the corruption of solidarity and interpersonal compassion by 'pity'" (723). Pity, in this definition, "arises not from an immediate encounter but is the product of public speeches and public images that depict the misfortune of a great number of people that are 'depersonalized' and 'lumped . . . together' as objects of a public fantasy" (723). The very private experience of reading a novel about the fate of specific people is, supposedly, a very different experience, and it may thus, in Arendt's terms, lead to interpersonal compassion rather than to pity.

34. See Richard Posner, "Against Ethical Criticism" (1997) and Raymond Williams, *Culture and Society, 1780–1950* (1983).

35. See the Oprah Book Club's *Your Guide to* The Good Earth, http://www.oprah .com/oprahsbookclub/Pearl-S-Bucks-The-Good-Earth-at-a-Glance/2 (accessed January 12, 2012).

CHAPTER TWO

1. The term "China hand" denotes a China expert who has lived in the country and is thus well informed about its language, culture, and people. Originally, the term referenced nineteenth-century merchants in the Chinese treaty ports, but during the first half of the twentieth century, it also came to denote American civil service officers. Faulkner's use of the term in reference to Buck is more than just a little mocking.

2. Buck's literary work is infrequently taught at the college level, and few academics are familiar with her books, other than *The Good Earth*. At the same time, however, she is one of the best-known American authors to the general world public. A UNESCO survey conducted in 1970 tells us that Buck's work has been translated into 145 foreign languages—surpassing any other American writer (see Liao, 3).

3. For an introduction to the Chinese novel, see Chih-tsing Hsia, *The Classic Chinese Novel* (1996).

4. Hume explores the paradox of tragedy in his "Of Tragedy" (1793).

5. Mary Beth Oliver, "Exploring the Paradox of Sad Films" (1993).

6. Scheff's neo-Freudian view of catharsis suggests that the engagement with dramatic literature "is an attempt to relive, and therefore resolve, earlier painful experiences which were unfinished" (13) and that such reliving can be cathartic in the sense that it leads to a "repeated emotional discharge" (79) and thus to a purging of negative emotions that were "bottled up" inside the reader.

7. The legal scholar Richard Posner has, like Baldwin before him, advanced the view that the stylistic deficits of *Uncle Tom's Cabin* are directly related to the fact that it is what Baldwin called a "protest novel" (*Notes*, 13). Like Baldwin, Posner draws a direct line from *Uncle Tom's Cabin* to Richard Wright's *Native Son*, claiming that "When political criteria are imposed on literature," the resulting works are "preachy, dreary, banal, sentimental, implausible, [and] poorly written" (*Public*, 239).

8. The term "third culture" was originally coined in the 1950s by social scientists John and Ruth Hill Useem, who used it with reference to Americans who lived in closely circumscribed expatriate communities. In their view, American expatriates living in these communities—which were nevertheless informed by the surrounding host culture—developed a common "third culture" that fully reproduced neither American culture nor the host culture, but that was shared by nearly all subjects in the community. See John and Ruth Hill Useem, *The Western-Educated Man in India* (1955).

9. Pollock and Van Reken actually explicitly mention Buck as one of "the first ATCKs who recorded in words the world they had known as children growing up in China" (93).

10. On the difference between episodic memories and emotional memories, see Hogan, *What Literature*, 51.

11. Pollock and Van Reken write that "TCKs are often sadly ignorant of national, local, and even family history" (96).

12. Pollock and Van Reken argue that "confused loyalties" (90) and a feeling of "chronic rootlessness" (126) are typical for the Third Culture Kid experience.

13. The Nanking Incident occurred in March 1927, when several foreign residents of the city were robbed, injured, or killed in a turmoil that was caused by fights between troops of the Chinese Nationalist Party and the troops of the Chinese warlord Zhang Zongchang. Although Western and Japanese troops tried to stop the assault, the majority of foreign residents saw themselves as forced to flee.

14. Conn maintains that this feminist awakening in Buck (who, like Boyle, always insisted that she was not a feminist, while writing decidedly feminist texts all along) was furthered considerably by her undergraduate training at Randolph-Macon Woman's College (see 51).

15. Buck's speech was later published as *Is There a Case for Foreign Missions?* (1932).

16. Shaffer's article "Women and International Relations" (1999) similarly stresses the fact that Buck's view on American and world politics was a decidedly (and consciously) gendered one.

17. The biographies of Buck's parents are *The Exile* (1936) and *Fighting Angel* (1936).

18. Buck's translation of *All Men Are Brothers* became a best seller in the United States, but it was also severely criticized by Chinese scholars for containing a number of inaccuracies and mistranslations. More recent publications in Chinese translation studies, however, take into account Buck's transcultural background and consider her translation a complex hybrid text that is interesting in its own right.

19. In her 1930 review for the *New Republic*, Isidore Schneider calls Buck's first novel, *East Wind: West Wind*, an "ordinary, quite mechanical novel, full of plot and sentiment, but empty of any lifelikeness in its characters or significance in its thesis—the clash between modern and traditional China" (24). Mary McGrory, reviewing *Pavilion of Women* for the *New York Times Book Review* in 1946, wrote that "the novel is a searching, adult study of women written with high seriousness and sympathy, which should find a multitude of women readers" (6). These two reviews can be considered symptomatic for the way that reviewers—even the more sympathetic ones—tended to see Buck's novels.

20. Buck also makes clear that the traditional Chinese novels tended to have several authors, which allowed them to change and evolve over time. Her emphasizing, in her Nobel lecture, that she would rather have her stories published in magazines "read by the million" than in "magazines read only by a few" is an obvious side blow to those modernist contemporaries who preferred to publish their pieces in small journals like *transition* or *This Quarter*, which were predominantly read by other modernist artists and critics.

21. Buck's concern for the masses was clearly influenced by the aesthetic of China's New Culture Movement, to which she had been exposed during her final years in China. Scholars often locate the origins of the New Culture Movement in 1915, when Peking University professor Chen Duxiu founded the *New Youth* journal. The movement was influenced by Western philosophical ideas (most prominently American pragmatism) and promoted individual freedom, science, democracy, the emancipation of women, and the introduction of Vernacular Chinese. The latter was meant to allow people with little education to read articles and books.

22. After the attack on Pearl Harbor, approximately 120,000 Americans considered to be ethnically Japanese were arrested on order of the American government and put into internment camps called "War Relocation Centers" on the West Coast. Only in December 1944 did the Supreme Court rule the detainment unconstitutional and did the government begin clearing the camps. Many of the internees, however, suffered, in spite of the 1948 American Japanese Claims Act, significant property losses.

23. Hilary Spurling writes in her biography of Buck that *The Hidden Flower* was published "largely as propaganda for the Welcome House Adoption Agency" (240). In 1949 Buck and Walsh founded Welcome House, the first international, interracial adoption agency in the United States, with the goal of finding adoptive families for biracial children (in the beginning predominantly the children of Asian mothers and American GI fathers) who were considered unadoptable because of their ethnic status. She laid out her argument for such adoptions also in nonfictional form in *Children for Adoption* (1964).

24. It should not be denied, though, that her strong political and humanitarian agenda often also significantly weakened Buck's novels aesthetically. Kang Liao suggests in his generally very positive critique of Buck's fictional work that "the historical, cultural and cognitive values she pursued more deliberately after 1942 . . . caused her novels to go downhill. . . . Different from her efforts in founding and running the East and West Association from 1941 to 1951, the same wish and effort in literature brought an inevitable artistic sacrifice" (132—133).

25. White middle-class women also played a significant role in the abolition of slavery in the United States. Stowe's *Uncle Tom's Cabin* was credited with influencing the accompanying political processes by no less a personage than Abraham Lincoln.

26. The main character of the series is an American engineer who travels the world and, in the process, not only learns to understand and appreciate the culture of other countries and people, but also fights racial and national prejudice wherever he finds it. Most of the initial stories in *World's Finest* were written by Jack Schiff, with art by John Daly.

27. In addition, Shaffer informs us, the East and West Association "also printed hundreds of thousands of copies of these comic strip series on its own for use by school districts" ("Pearl," 19).

28. Buck did not shy away from publishing many of her novels in serial form in popular women's magazines such as *Cosmopolitan* and *The Women's Home Companion*—where they could be read by people who would not buy or could not afford books.

29. Mari Yoshihara partially agrees with Leong's critical standpoint when she notes, in *Embracing the East* (2003), that Buck's position vis-à-vis China was, because of her transcultural upbringing, a complex one that was nevertheless "embedded in . . . the unequal power relations between the West and China" (154).

30. Buck's choice to ignore the upper and middle social strata of Chinese society in *The Good Earth*, and to concentrate instead on poor peasants and on people who had fallen into despair, was very much counter to Chinese novelistic practice at the time, and thus brought on her the ire of many contemporary Chinese critics. Kiang Kang-Hu, for example, at the time head of the Chinese Studies Department at McGill University in Montreal, criticized Buck in his 1932 review of *The Good Earth* for selectively revealing "a particular phase of the darker side of Chinese life" (370). He attributed what he considered an inaccurate portrayal of Chinese society to Buck's dependence on the accounts of Chinese "coolies" and "amahs," because she herself, so he believed, was not able to read original texts of Chinese classical literature. Buck did not leave such criticism unanswered. In a 1933 piece, she writes that she is "less interested in tradition than in actuality. . . . I have lived with the common people, and for the past fifteen years I have lived among the intellectuals, and I know whereof I speak" ("Critical Excerpts," 372).

31. The German-born Jewish intellectual Horace Kallen argued, in "Democracy versus the Melting Pot" (1915), that cultural diversity and national pride were compatible with each other, and that an embrace of ethnic diversity and a respect for difference—what he termed "cultural pluralism"—would in fact strengthen American democracy. He believed that the United States was already "in the process of becoming a true federal state . . . a great republic consisting of a federation or commonwealth of nationalities" (Kallen). Randolph Bourne, who was influenced by Kallen, similarly saw huge potential in the cultural diversity of American immigrants. In "Trans-National America" (1916), he insisted that the United States was "already the world-federation in miniature, the continent where for the first time in history has been achieved that miracle of hope, the peaceful living side by side, with character substantially preserved, of the most heterogeneous peoples under the sun" (63). For Bourne, America was a sort of microcosm of the world, and its social development a testing ground for global cosmopolitan cohabitation.

32. Buck expressed her criticism of American internal and foreign policy in countless articles and nonfiction books. See, for example, "On Discovering America" (1937), "Democracy and the Negro" (1941), "American Imperialism in the Making" (1945),

and *American Unity and Asia* (1942). David Buck has argued that while American-Asian relations were still part of Buck's concern during the 1940s and '50s, her primary effort "became to proselytize Americans about her own liberal, democratic, and Protestant Christian principles" (29).

33. *The Good Earth*, of course, is a naturalist much more than a sentimental novel. Nevertheless, in its sympathetic depiction of the life of poor peasants, and especially the fate of women, the novel appealed to the compassion and sympathetic understanding of its audience.

34. This recent resurgence is discussed, for example, in Liu Haiping, "Pearl S. Buck's Reception in China Reconsidered" (1994); Choi Won-Shik, "West Goes East: Pearl Buck's *The Good Earth*" (2001); and Sheila Melvin, "Pearl's Great Price" (2006).

35. Shaffer quotes "one Chicago woman" who was so impressed with one of Buck's speeches that she sent to no less an authority than President Harry Truman a telegram that read: "Pearl Buck addressed 2,000 here tonight. Her message is tremendous. She understands the Orient and their leaders. I beg you to request her to come to see you and address your Cabinet members at once" (quoted in Shaffer, "Women," 155). The American government did indeed occasionally make use of Buck's texts. Leong tells us that "government officials could ignore neither Buck's status as a China authority nor her prolific output of commentary. Chester Kerr, the chief of the Office of War Information's Book Division, considered [Buck's nonfiction book] *American Unity and Asia* so important that he circulated a report throughout government offices suggesting it to others" (50).

36. The Chinese Exclusion Act of 1882 was an American federal law that served (very much like the exclusion acts for South Asians in 1917, Japanese and Koreans in 1924, and Filipinos in 1934) to bar Chinese immigrants from the political sphere of the United States. Later legislation, such as the Immigration Act of 1924, restricted Chinese and other Asian immigration even further. Buck was one of the public supporters of the Magnuson Act (also known as the Chinese Exclusion Repeal Act), which, in 1943, permitted a yearly quota of 105 Chinese immigrants to the United States and allowed (male) Chinese nationals already residing in the U.S. to become naturalized citizens.

CHAPTER THREE

1. So far, Hodges's 1985 biography of Smith (springing from his dissertation, directed by Michel Fabre) is the only book-length treatment of Smith's work.

2. Fabre writes in *From Harlem to Paris* (1991) that the novel "deserves close attention as one of the few works of fiction genuinely inspired by Afro-American expatriate experience" (245). Gilroy discusses two of Smith's novels in *Against Race* (2000), lauding them for approaching "complex and important questions that have a direct bearing upon the problems of identity, belonging, and nonraciological justice that concern us today" (308). Stovall has repeatedly noted that *The Stone Face* has much to offer students of race and colonialism in both France and America ("Preface," 310).

3. Drawing on Gadamer's notion of the "fusion of horizons" (*Horizontverschmelzung*), Delanty argues that "the cosmopolitan . . . is constituted in shifts in self-understanding that arise when both Self and Other are transformed" (11).

4. Hoffman explains that "when innocent bystanders view themselves as allowing

the victim's distress to happen or continue because of their inaction, guilt may be produced. That is, the self-blame attribution transforms the observer's empathic distress into a feeling of guilt" (102).

5. Linklater, in fact, supports such a thin conception of cosmopolitanism, which (much like Martha Nussbaum's concept) aims at "expanding [the] circle of human sympathy" (*The Transformation*, 79). Dobson, however, doubts that such sympathetic expansion will lead to any tangible results.

6. For a critical discussion of the differences between shame and guilt, see also Stephen Parker and Rebecca Thomas (2009).

7. See Mignolo, "The Many Faces of Cosmo-polis" (2000); Posnock, "The Dream of Deracination" (2002); and Kurasawa, "Critical Cosmopolitanism" (2011).

8. Black U.S. soldiers were also known to be especially generous with their seemingly endless supplies of food and of goods difficult to acquire in postwar Germany: coffee, sugar, chocolate, and cigarettes.

9. See, for example, two articles by Smith that were published in the *Pittsburgh Courier*: "Found Freedom in Germany: Few GIs Eager to Return to States" (February 1947) and "Keeping the Peace: American Prejudice Rampant in Germany" (March 1947).

10. For postwar relations between black American GIs and the German population, see Larry A. Greene and Anke Ortlepp's edited volume *Germans and African Americans: Two Centuries of Exchange* (2011). See also Heide Fehrenbach, *Race after Hitler* (2005), and Maria Höhn's "Heimat in Turmoil" (2001).

11. The fact that Smith's portrait of segregation in the American occupation forces is journalistically accurate has been stressed by both Smith's contemporaries and later critics; see, for example, Carl Milton Hughes (99–101) or Hodges (14). Leon C. Standifer gives a firsthand account of the life of black GIs in southern Germany in his memoir *Binding Up the Wounds* (1997), and his observations correlate closely with Smith's accounts in both fictional and nonfiction texts.

12. Fehrenbach explains that sexual competition between white and black American soldiers over German women greatly intensified already existing hostilities between black and white GIs in Germany (see 44–45).

13. Smith also wrote about this scandal in the U.S. Army as a journalist for the *Pittsburgh Courier*.

14. Van Vechten to Farrar, October 12, 1948, Farrar, Straus & Giroux, Inc., records, Manuscripts and Archives Division, New York Public Library, Astor, Lenox, and Tilden Foundations. Van Vechten was so excited about Smith's work that he expressed his desire to photograph him for the James Weldon Johnson Collection of Negro Arts and Letters, which he did a few months later in New York. Van Vechten's photographs of Smith are part of the James Weldon Johnson Collection in the Beinecke Rare Book and Manuscript Library at Yale University.

15. Jack Conroy sounds less enthusiastic than Van Vechten, but still approves of the novel, when he stresses in a 1948 review for the *Chicago Sun Times* that Smith's writing is "for the most part . . . strong, simple, and lively," and literary critic Carl Milton Hughes even writes in his 1953 *The Negro Novelist* that "*Last of the Conquerors* is outstanding for the quality of its style" (Hughes, 102).

16. For a discussion of *Last of the Conquerors* as a cosmopolitan text, see also chapter 4 of Stephanie Brown's *The Postwar African American Novel* (2011).

17. If German antiblack racism is addressed at all in the novel, it is done through references to the past, mainly through the mention of Hitler's commentaries on blacks.

18. Fehrenbach maintains that "interracial fraternization between black GIs and white German women was treated as an unbearable provocation by numerous white American soldiers and officers and by white German men more generally" (45). If women like Ilse were called "nigger lovers" by white Americans, the German population called them *Negerhuren* (nigger whores), suggesting that only the lowest forms of white femininity—namely, prostitutes or the pathologically promiscuous—would be willing to associate with black men (see Fehrenbach, 45–46).

19. Black women might have responded with a different kind of anger, since many of them did not overly appreciate what they perceived as black men's misguided attraction to white women.

20. Arguably, such idealization is much more problematic in a realist novel such as Smith's, which claims to be a truthful portrait of a certain historical situation, than it is in a sentimental novel such as Buck's.

21. In a 1949 letter to the publisher's marketing specialist, Carolyn Wolfe, Smith explains that he "did not originally plan to write novels directly about Negroes; for this would reach only a certain, limited audience. I planned, rather, to write stories about white people, bringing in the racial theme only indirectly." Smith to Wolfe, April 8, 1949, Farrar, Straus & Giroux, Inc., records, Manuscripts and Archives Division, New York Public Library, Astor, Lenox, and Tilden Foundations.

22. I am taking the term "white life novels" from Matthew Wilson, who defines them as novels that are written by African American authors but "contain only incidental African American characters and that concentrate on depictions of white experience" (xv). As Wilson makes clear in his discussion of Charles W. Chesnutt's white life novels, the common assumption among white publishers (and often readers) was that black authors were not really able to render an "authentic" depiction of white life because of their limited experience.

23. Smith to Farrar, undated letter (probably June 1949), Farrar, Straus & Giroux, Inc., records, Manuscripts and Archives Division, New York Public Library, Astor, Lenox, and Tilden Foundations.

24. *Anger at Innocence* not only presents too many unmotivated turns of action but also suffers from flat or inconsistent characters and a sometimes rather melodramatic plot. Hodges also finds fault with the fact that all of the white characters in the novel "speak Negro slang" (31).

25. Smith had intended *South Street* to be the first part of a trilogy, but not only did Farrar, Straus and Young turn down the second part, "Simeon," as that manuscript was entitled, also got lost in the mail on its way back to him; since he had not been able to afford a carbon copy, it was lost entirely. Unbelievably, the same thing happened to the completed third part of the trilogy, "The Gangsters," which disappeared somewhere en route between Farrar, Straus and Young and its author.

26. Smith himself stresses just this in a letter to his mother in November 1951: "I don't feel like a stranger at all," he explains there, "I feel at home in Paris." Smith to Edith Earle, November 1, 1951.

27. Smith to Edith Earle, February 21, 1953.

28. "*How did one fight to gain social acceptance?*" Smith has Claude ask himself in *South Street.* "*How did one, out of bitterness and a sense of injustice, struggle, not*

to overthrow the dominant group, but to be embraced by it?" (245; emphasis in original). These were questions that Smith asked himself, too, one of the reasons why he was highly skeptical about the potential of the civil rights movement.

29. Smith to Edith Earle, October 20, 1953.

30. On the history of the Algerian War and the Algerian question in France, see Charles-Robert Ageron, *Modern Algeria* (1991); James D. Le Sueur, *Uncivil War* (2001); and Jim House and Neil MacMaster, *Paris 1961* (2006).

31. Stovall had the seven-page section of *The Stone Face* that depicts the 1961 massacre of Algerians in Paris translated into French in 2004, and made both the excerpt of the original text and the translation part of his "Preface to *The Stone Face*" (2004).

32. Hodges mentions that the young Smith read and admired the literary craft of Richard Wright and Ernest Hemingway (see 6).

33. Hogan explains that attachment stories differ from love stories in that the element of sexual desire is missing in them (see *Affective*, 199–200). While attachment stories are often concerned with parent-child relationships, the one in *The Stone Face* focuses on the friendship between two men.

34. A detailed description of the historical massacre and Smith's authentic account of it can be found in Stovall's "Preface to *The Stone Face*" (2004).

35. Smith to Phyllis Ford, February 17, 1964.

36. In the letter to Roger Straus, Smith mentions in a postscript that "if the Negro movement had reached this point before I wrote the book, 'The Stone Face' would probably have had a different ending, with the hero returning to the States" (Smith to Straus, July 11, 1963). The implication of this is not that Smith maintained a sort of primary allegiance to the United States, but that he—like James Baldwin—wanted most of all to participate in a movement that stood a realistic chance of success. John Farrar's reply that "it would be enormously better for THE STONE FACE if you were to return Simeon to the United States" suggests the importance of financial concerns in the novel's new ending. Farrar continues, "We were able to call back the proofs, and if you do agree with us that this change should be made, if you can do it quickly, we do not need to postpone too much. We will, of course, fix the jacket also." Farrar to Smith, July 24, 1963, Farrar, Straus & Giroux, Inc., records, Manuscripts and Archives Division, New York Public Library, Astor, Lenox, and Tilden Foundations.

37. Contemporary reviewers also were quite excited about the content and literary quality of Smith's fourth novel. Nick Aaron Ford, in his 1964 review for *Phylon*, asserted that *The Stone Face* "establishes Smith as a serious contender for a place in the first rank of contemporary writers" (124) and went on to compare Smith with Ralph Ellison. He calls *The Stone Face* "a powerfully moving experience revealing the author's own bitterness toward racial bigotry and hate wherever they appear" (125). Joseph Friedman, the reviewer for the *New York Times*, even dared to read Smith as a worthy contemporary of nonblack writers. "Among the most worthy younger writers, Negro or white," he writes, "count this one" (BR27).

38. It is certainly interesting to view Smith's sensitive heroes in the context of bell hooks's *We Real Cool* (2004). Here, hooks argues that black American men have experienced a crisis of masculinity as a result of the patriarchal imperialism they were subjected to in U.S. society. Black men, hooks maintains, have been taught to "solve" problems with violence. Their greatest desires, according to hooks, are an ability to engage with intimacy and a longing for intersubjective love. Smith's heroes are inter-

esting in this context because they do exactly what hooks calls for: they engage emotionally not only with women, but also with their own roles as black males in a white-dominated patriarchal society.

CHAPTER FOUR

1. All of the citations in the following refer to the manuscript of "Island of Hallucination" held at the Beinecke Rare Book and Manuscript Library at Yale University as part of the Richard Wright Papers.

2. LeDoux reminds us that "for the existential philosophers (like Kierkegaard, Heidegger, and Sartre) dread, angst, and anguish are at the core of human existence" (129).

3. Wright believed that he "recognized familiar emotional patterns" ("How 'Bigger,'" xviii) in the growing fascist movement in Germany, and feared that this is what American society was headed for if it didn't pay attention.

4. In the case of failure of narrative empathy, the author's empathetic imagining of a fictional world does not *transmit to readers without interference*," with the result that elements of the story evoke empathy in readers in ways that are against the author's "apparent or proclaimed representational goals" (Keen, "Narrative," 81). In the case of falsity, "narrative empathy short-circuits the impulse to act compassionately or to respond with political engagement" (81).

5. The startle response is a rapid and involuntary reflex to a sudden and unexpected stimulus, such as a loud noise. It can be modulated by ongoing emotional states. As psychologists Lang, Bradley, and Cuthbert explain, "the startle reflex to a sudden loud noise is . . . an aversive or defensive response and would be augmented if it occurred in the context of an ongoing aversive emotion" (377).

6. Most negative criticism has tended to center on the weak third part of the book, entitled "Fate," which changes both tone and pace when Bigger's Communist attorney Max gives long and highly abstract speeches about socioeconomic inequality and the importance of class struggle.

7. William Gardner Smith reported about Wright's life in Paris in a 1953 piece for *Ebony* entitled "Black Boy in France." He wrote again about Wright after the latter's death in 1960, arguing that his black skin color was like an open "wound" within a racist American society (see "Richard Wright (1908–1960): The Compensation," 67).

8. The GI Bill was a law that provided a number of benefits (including low-cost mortgages and business loans) as compensation for returning World War II veterans. These benefits also included cash payments of tuition and living expenses to attend college or high school.

9. James Baldwin's term, taken from the title of an article he wrote for *Esquire*: "The New Lost Generation" (1961).

10. Rowley argues that this general insistence on Wright's being "in exile" in France has been hypocritical. After all, for writers such as Wright, as we learn from his literature of the 1930s and '40s, "exile begins at home" ("The 'Exile'"). It is important to note, though, that Wright himself repeatedly insisted on his being in exile.

11. Sartre gave the lecture "Existentialism Is a Humanism" ("*L'existentialisme est un humanisme*") in Club Maintenant in Paris on October 29, 1945. It was later the basis for his book *Existentialism and Humanism* (1947).

12. In her Introduction to *The Outsider*, Maryemma Graham reminds us of

Wright's long-standing interest in psychoanalysis, explaining that he was especially interested in "the psychology of oppression and violence" (xviii).

13. For a cogent example, see Claudia Tate's "Christian Existentialism in Richard Wright's *The Outsider*" (1982).

14. For a detailed discussion of *Black Power* and its meaning for Wright's critical cosmopolitanism, see my article "'The Uses and Hazards of Expatriation': Richard Wright's Cosmopolitanism in Process" in the *African American Review* (2007).

15. Despite all the problems that the travelogue exhibits, the Malian writer Manthia Diawara has called *Black Power* a "magnificent book," lauding Wright's vulnerable self-exposure of his conflicting emotions of "identification and estrangement, love and hate" toward the Africans as well as toward his own background (72).

16. Virginia Whatley Smith describes this process as a movement "from old to new, narrow to broad, American to Western intellectual that would culminate in the self-description he would later append as a 'Western Man of Color' in *White Man Listen!*" (190).

17. The final sentence of the *Communist Manifesto*—"Proletarier aller Länder, vereinigt Euch!" (Proletarians of all countries unite)—certainly implies a form of cosmopolitanism of its own. Although the Leninist tradition tended to use "cosmopolitan" as a derogatory term, it continued the transnational tendency of the *Communist Manifesto* in its proclamation of proletarian internationalism, if not necessarily in its practice.

18. This should not be confused with the oft-heard argument that America's melting-pot policy equals a micro-cosmopolitanism, as it can be found, for example, in Benjamin Barber's "Constitutional Faith" (1996) and Michael McConnell's "Don't Neglect the Little Platoons" (1996).

19. This is the tricky nature of historical situatedness: it cannot be fully renounced or left behind, because it shapes the way we see and think, and even the way we imagine a different way of seeing or thinking. This is why, as James T. Campbell has noted, "Innumerable African American travelers in Africa have experienced . . . moments of disillusionment, moments bringing them face-to-face with Africa's unfamiliarity and their own painful Americanness" (211).

20. His reliance on American distribution channels made Wright vulnerable to American domestic politics. One need only recall the remarkable preface that Harper made him write for *Black Power* before it would publish the book. "From 1932 to 1944 I was a member of the Communist Party of the United States of America," he writes there. "Today I am no longer a member of that party or a subscriber to its aims," because "Marxist Communism, though it was changing the world, was changing that world in a manner that granted me even less freedom than I had possessed before" (xxxv–xxxvi). This was written in 1954, over ten years after Wright left the CPUSA, but Harper had made it clear to him that without yet another renunciation of Communism it would not be able to publish his book in the United States.

21. Paul Robeson learned in 1950 that he would not receive a new passport to travel from the State Department, and that a "stop notice" had been issued at all ports, meaning his effectual confinement to the United States. He had repeatedly expressed his sympathies toward the Soviet Union, although he never was a member of the CPUSA. Only in 1956, six years after the initial revocation, was he allowed again to leave the United States. W. E. B. Du Bois also lost his American passport in 1950, af-

ter being acquitted as an agent of the Soviet Union. The State Department returned his passport in 1958, only to revoke it again in 1959, when he arrived at the U.S. border after visiting the USSR. Eventually, Du Bois renounced his U.S. citizenship and, shortly before his death, became a citizen of Ghana.

22. For accounts of the Gibson Affair see James Campbell, "The Island Affair" (2006), and Richard Gibson, "Richard Wright's 'Island of Hallucination' and the 'Gibson Affair'" (2005).

23. *The Long Dream* is set in the United States and concerned with the childhood and adolescence of Rex "Fishbelly" Tucker in the Jim Crow South.

24. Wright scholars are not entirely in agreement about which real-life person or persons are depicted in the character of Ned Harrison. Rowley writes that "Harrison is clearly based on Ollie Harrington" (*Richard*, 488). James Campbell seems to agree with her that Harrison is partly modeled after Harrington. Fabre, however, sees Wright himself in many of Harrison's traits and convictions, and Gibson, who finds himself partially depicted in the novel, argues that Harrison is "probably based . . . more on Noel Torres, who was an African American lawyer working for the US Army at its logistics base in Chateauroux, than on Ollie Harrington or Wright himself" (905).

25. Mechanical is thought by most scholars to be some kind of unhappy fictional composite of James Baldwin and William Gardner Smith.

26. Baldwin's "Everybody's Protest Novel" (originally published in the *Partisan Review* in June 1949, later collected in *Notes of a Native Son*) was, as I have mentioned in chapter 2, mainly targeted at Stowe's *Uncle Tom's Cabin*, but it was also an attack on so-called "protest novels" in contemporary African American literature, which, in his eyes, were so focused on social protest that they became uninteresting as fiction. The prime example for such a novel was, according to Baldwin, Wright's *Native Son*. Wright was never able to forgive Baldwin, to whom he had been a mentor and friend.

27. Rowley even goes so far as to call Smith "Wright's archenemy" (*Richard*, 499).

28. Rowley has written extensively about this aspect of Wright's life. Wright himself, though, met with similar allegations. As we learn from Rowley, he did repeatedly work with the American embassy to "offset Communist influence" (Wright quoted in Rowley, *Richard*, 474). In 1956, he met with officials at the American embassy to prevent the attendance of the "Communist faction" of the executive committee of the "Second Bandung" conference. This "Communist faction" seems to have included Paul Robeson and W. E. B. Du Bois, who both were unable to attend the conference because they could not get passports from the American authorities.

29. As Rowley reminds us, Wright continues to be most frequently associated with the three books he wrote in his thirties, before he left the United States for France in 1946: *Uncle Tom's Children*, *Black Boy*, and *Native Son* (see "The 'Exile'").

30. Of those critics who have discussed Wright's later work with appreciation, many build on Gilroy's assertion that Wright was a major thinker of Western modernity, seeking "complex answers to the questions which racial and national identities could only obscure" (*Black*, 173). Kevin Gaines, for instance, reconsiders Wright from the perspective of diaspora. In his *African Americans in Ghana* (2006), he asks us to see Wright as a proponent of a black diaspora that does not follow the more "conventional usage" of "describing a state of alienation resulting from a physical exile or displacement from an ancestral homeland" (54). In an earlier article, Gaines suggests that Wright's discussion of anticolonialism in *Black Power* and *The Color Curtain* (1956)

"recasts diaspora as the mobilization of black modernity toward a transnational and transracial community of struggle" ("Revisiting," 76). Although stressing, like Gilroy, the transnational and transracial aspects of Wright's thinking, Gaines does not take up Gilroy's claim that Wright's outlook was cosmopolitan, preferring instead, with Brent Edwards, the concept of black diaspora.

CHAPTER FIVE

1. I have explained the difference between alignment and allegiance in chapter 4 with reference to the work of Murray Smith. See in particular his essay "Gangsters, Cannibals, Aesthetes, or Apparently Perverse Allegiances" (1999).

2. See, for example, Paul Rozin and April E. Fallon, "A Perspective on Disgust" (1987); Megan Oaten, Richard Stevenson, and Trevor I. Case, "Disgust as a Disease-Avoidance Mechanism" (2009); and Valerie Curtis, Mícheál de Barra, and Robert Aunger, "Disgust as an Adaptive System for Disease Avoidance Behaviour" (2011).

3. As Patrick Colm Hogan has noted, we do not seem to feel disgusted by *all* attributes we share with animals. We are usually not disgusted by our eyes or hair, although we share both of them with many animals, and we are generally not disgusted by the fact that, like animals, we need food, water, and sleep, or that we care for our offspring. The central point of disgust, Hogan insists, is the (often quite visceral) urge to avoid perceived contaminants, and not a cognitive appraisal of our potential animality (see *What Literature*, 241n9).

4. Rozin, Haidt, and McCauley explain that there tends to be some variation across cultures with respect to what food is considered disgusting, but claim that "it is primarily in the last two steps of the expansion of disgust—interpersonal and moral disgust—that cultural differences seem to be greatest" (766). They name Hindu India as an example of a culture in which these forms of disgust "appear to be particularly elaborated" (766).

5. The insula, often also called the insular cortex or insulary cortex, is a portion of the human brain's cerebral cortex. Neuroscientists locate in the insular cortex the processing of many social emotions, among them disgust, pride, and guilt.

6. For a helpful treatment of disgust as an impediment to compassion in in-group/out-group relations, see also Martha Nussbaum, *Upheavals of Thought* (2001). Nussbaum writes that "throughout history, certain disgust properties—sliminess, bad smell, stickiness, decay, foulness—have repeatedly and monotonously been associated with, indeed projected onto, groups by reference to whom privileged groups seek to define their superior human status" (347).

7. Oatley, Keltner, and Jenkins draw on Primo Levi's autobiographical account of his life as a concentration camp prisoner in Auschwitz, *If This Is a Man* (1958), for evidence of the dehumanization of Jews that happened in German concentration camps. Such dehumanization techniques are of course also implied in Giorgio Agamben's concept of "bare life," which I discuss in chapter 1.

8. In the context of literary and film reception, curiosity and fascination are both what Plantinga calls "direct emotions" (*Moving*, 139), meaning that the viewer or reader can experience them independently from the emotional experience of a fictional character.

9. Bowles does not give any definite indication of the Professor's nationality in the

story. Most scholars assume that he is American; others have argued that his strong emotional response to the French calendar at the end of the story suggests that he is French. Of course, we must consider that, as a linguist, he has studied the language and might respond strongly to it even though it is not his mother tongue.

10. Because of the fictitious town names, the exact location of the "warm country" is unclear, but it is probably somewhere in southern Morocco or Algeria.

11. *Qaouaji* is a waiter at a coffee or tea shop.

12. Lawrence Stewart explains that the camel-udder boxes mentioned in the stories "are traditionally used by women for keeping kohl, the native cosmetic" (31). The fact that it is an item that is associated with Arab women helps explain the *qaouaji*'s angry reaction.

13. The Reguibat are a Sahrawi tribe that has historically dominated large areas of the Sahara desert and fervently resisted colonial rule by Spain and France.

14. *Lingua* is the Latin expression for both tongue and language.

15. One of the best-known treatments of the nature of the spectacle is Guy Debord's *The Society of the Spectacle* (1967).

16. I am grateful to Patrick Colm Hogan for turning my attention to the fact that the Professor's fate at the hands of the Reguibat is a case of tragic excess.

17. As we have seen in chapter 2, scholars such as Karen Leong have also used the term Orientalism to speak about essentializing imaginaries of Asia. See Leong, *The China Mystique* (2005).

18. Weiss quite deliberately uses a lower-case "o" when referring to Bowles's mode of Orientalism, explaining that he uses "the terms 'Orientalist' and 'Orientalism' to refer to western literary treatments of North African and Euro-Asian cultures and societies which are demonstrably racist or imperialist, and the terms 'orientalist' and 'orientalism' to refer to treatments which can not be readily classified and may, in fact, be quite mixed in their effects or have little or nothing to do with racist sentiment and imperialist attitudes" (38). Arguably, though, Bowles's lower-case "orientalism" in "A Distant Episode" still shares some central features with Orientalism, such as the essentializing portrayal of non-Europeans and the affirmation that the latter are fundamentally "other" and devoid of human compassion.

19. Bowles has explained that to him, America and Europe "are really the same. Western Europe becomes America a few years later. America does it first and Western Europe becomes . . . quickly imitates it. But it's all one thing as far as I'm concerned" (quoted in Alenier, Geraci, and Pottiger, 169).

20. In Hawthorne's *The Marble Faun* (1860), the more innocent American protagonists (Hilda and Kenyon) are confronted with a horrible murder that threatens to darken their souls. In James's *Daisy Miller* (1878), the heroine dies as a result of what the American expatriate community in Rome considers her moral transgressions (among them her nocturnal visit to the Colosseum). In Fitzgerald's *Tender Is the Night* (1934), the young Rosemary Hoyt visits the Riviera, only to end up with a corpse in her bed. Dick Diver's fate also does not suggest that living abroad is particularly healthy for Americans.

21. In Hamovitch's view, "Anger and fear" are what "characterize many of Bowles's memories of his childhood, the seedbed for the terrifying stories he has written" (445). I believe that this is true, but would want to add the emotions of disgust, contempt, and probably shame as formative emotional experiences.

22. Bowles has also insisted on the uselessness of emotions in relation to his auto-biography. Weinreich remembers that after reading *Without Stopping*, "one thing puzzled me. Now I knew what had happened to him, but not how he felt" (271). When she asked Bowles why he didn't disclose his feelings more, he "looked shocked, 'Well, that is what I intended. Why should I write about my feelings? I don't think they should be written about. What difference does it make?'" (271).

23. See my article "Encountering the Sahara: Embodiment, Emotion, and Material Agency in Paul Bowles's *The Sheltering Sky*" in *Interdisciplinary Studies in Literature and Environment* (2013). Some of what I discuss in this chapter parallels what I have discussed in that earlier article.

24. It is unclear whether this disappointment of reader expectations is calculated or a result of the fact that Bowles found both love and sex disgusting. To him, he once explained in an interview, love was "something abstract," and he was uncertain whether it had "anything to do with sex" (quoted in Alameda, 224). But he also rather unambiguously relates his cognitive understanding of love to feelings of sociomoral disgust when he adds that, because of his repressive upbringing, he "always thought about love as something that is prohibited by society [and] by the world," something that is "obscene" (224).

25. The other three toxic factors listed by Oatley, Keltner, and Jenkins are criticism, defensiveness, and stonewalling (see 239).

26. Scholars like John Urry and Chris Rojek have developed several typologies of tourists, as well as different modes of tourist experiences (see Urry, *The Tourist Gaze* [1990], and Rojek and Urry, *Touring Cultures* [1997]). Port's behavior and attitude, his need to escape American-style consumerism only to then consume the Sahara landscape, fit surprisingly well Christopher Tilley's description of the typical consumerist tourist in search of the new and different. This kind of tourist, Tilley argues, "goes on holiday to seek solace, to find sources of cultural heritage and identity that modernity has destroyed, another world. . . . Tourism becomes a kind of . . . rite of passage in which the old self is lost to find the new and the tourist is a semiotician of difference attempting to decode and read the signs of Otherness" (16). See also Yosefa Loshitzky's "The Tourist/Traveler Gaze: Bertolucci and Bowles's *The Sheltering Sky*" (1993).

27. Bowles has explained repeatedly that he was under the influence of drugs when writing these highly disturbing scenes. Hibbard remembers how Bowles once told him "that he had conceived of the death scene in *The Sheltering Sky* after eating a lot of majoun. The drug opened the writer up to imaginative possibilities outside the realm of sober, rational thought" (*Paul*, 87).

28. A number of critics have interpreted Kit's behavior in the final part of the novel as a descent into madness. See, for example, Richard Patteson (70), Steven Olson (338–339), Yosefa Loshitzky (118–119), and Wayne Pounds (*Paul*, 7).

29. Mrabet was illiterate, and since Bowles spoke Maghrebi, he was able to write his stories down and translate them into English. Regina Weinreich has described the unusual nature of this literary collaboration as follows: "Mrabet barely reads or writes even in his own Maghrebi. Instead he recites into a tape recorder and Bowles translates his stories without editing them" (270).

30. Jane Bowles published only one novel during her short life, *Two Serious Ladies* (1943). She, too, was homosexual, and there has been much speculation about the exact nature of the Bowleses' marriage. Jane Bowles suffered from alcoholism and had a

stroke in 1957 at age forty. After more than a decade of suffering and treatments, she died in a clinic in Málaga in 1973.

CONCLUSION

1. Stanton makes this suggestion in her 2005 MLA presidential address entitled "Rooted Cosmopolitanism."

2. See Paula Moya and Ramón Saldívar, "Fictions of the Trans-American Imaginary" (2003); John Carlos Rowe, *Post-Nationalist American Studies* (2000) and *Afterlives of Modernism* (2011); Jessica Berman, *Modernist Commitments* (2011); Amy Kaplan, *The Anarchy of Empire in the Making of U.S. Culture* (2002); Wai Chee Dimock, *Through Other Continents* (2006); and Brent Hayes Edwards, *The Practice of Diaspora* (2003). See also Dimock and Lawrence Buell's edited volume *Shades of the Planet: American Literature as World Literature* (2007), which assembles a valuable collection of essays on the topic.

3. Heise's concept of eco-cosmopolitanism, as it is developed in her *Sense of Place and Sense of Planet* (2008), differs from cosmopolitanism in that it is not "circumscribed by human social experience" (60). Instead, it "reaches toward what some environmental writers and philosophers have called the 'more-than-human world'—the realm of non-human species, but also that of connectedness with both animate and inanimate networks of influence and exchange" (61).

Ackerman, Bruce. "Rooted Cosmopolitanism." *Ethics* 104 (April 1994): 516–535.

Agamben, Giorgio. *Homo Sacer: Sovereign Power and Bare Life.* Translated by Daniel Heller-Roazen. Stanford, CA: Stanford University Press, 1998.

Ageron, Charles-Robert. *Modern Algeria: A History from 1830 to the Present.* Translated by Michael Brett. London: Hurst, 1991.

Alameda, Soledad. "Paul Bowles: Touched by Magic." In *Conversations with Paul Bowles*, ed. Gena Dagel Caponi, pp. 218–226. Jackson: University Press of Mississippi, 1993.

Alenier, Karren LaLonde, Francine Geraci, and Ken Pottiger. "An Interview with Paul Bowles." In *Conversations with Paul Bowles*, ed. Gena Dagel Caponi, pp. 157–179. Jackson: University Press of Mississippi, 1993.

Alexander, Jeffrey C. *The Civil Sphere.* New York: Oxford University Press, 2006.

Anderson, Amanda. *The Powers of Distance: Cosmopolitanism and the Cultivation of Detachment.* Princeton, NJ: Princeton University Press, 2001.

Anderson, Benedict. *Imagined Communities: Reflections on the Origin and Spread of Nationalism.* London and New York: Verso, 1991.

Appiah, Kwame Anthony. *Cosmopolitanism: Ethics in a World of Strangers.* New York: Norton, 2006.

———. "Cosmopolitan Patriots." In *Cosmopolitics: Thinking and Feeling beyond the Nation*, ed. Pheng Cheah and Bruce Robbins, pp. 91–114. Minneapolis and London: University of Minnesota Press, 1998.

———. "A Long Way from Home: Richard Wright in the Gold Coast." In *Richard Wright*, ed. Harold Bloom, pp. 173–190. New York: Chelsea House Publishers, 1987.

Arendt, Hannah. *The Origins of Totalitarianism.* Orig. 1951; New York: Harcourt, 1973.

Austenfeld, Thomas Carl. *American Women Writers and the Nazis: Ethics and Politics in Boyle, Porter, Stafford, and Hellman.* Charlottesville: University Press of Virginia, 2001.

Austenfeld, Thomas Carl, ed. *Kay Boyle for the Twenty-First Century: New Essays.* Trier, Germany: Wissenschaftlicher Verlag, Trier, 2008.

Bailey, Jeffrey. "The Art of Fiction LXVII: Paul Bowles." In *Conversations with Paul Bowles*, ed. Gena Dagel Caponi, pp. 111–134. Jackson: University Press of Mississippi, 1993.

Baldwin, James. "The New Lost Generation." *Esquire*, July 1961, pp. 113–114.

———. *Nobody Knows My Name: More Notes of a Native Son.* Orig. 1961; New York: Penguin, 1991.

———. *Notes of a Native Son.* Orig. 1955; Boston: Beacon Press, 1957.

Barber, Benjamin. "Constitutional Faith." In *For Love of Country: Debating the Limits of Patriotism*, Martha C. Nussbaum, ed. Joshua Cohen, pp. 30–37. Boston: Beacon Press, 1996.

Barker, Jennifer L. "Double Exposure: De-composing the 'Nazi Idyll' in Kay Boyle's

Death of a Man." In *Kay Boyle for the Twenty-First Century: New Essays*, ed. Thomas Austenfeld, pp. 43–61. Trier, Germany: Wissenschaftlicher Verlag, Trier, 2008.

Bayoumi, Moustafa. "October 17, 1961." In *On the Edges of Development: Cultural Interventions*, ed. Kum-Kum Bhavnani, John Foran, Priya A. Kurian, and Debashish Munshi, pp. 13–21. London: Routledge, 2009.

Bell, Bernard W. *The Afro-American Novel and Its Tradition*. Amherst: University of Massachusetts Press, 1987.

Bell, Michael. *Sentimentalism, Ethics, and the Culture of Feeling*. New York: Palgrave Macmillan, 2000.

Benhabib, Seyla. *Another Cosmopolitanism*. Edited by Robert Post. Oxford and New York: Oxford University Press, 2006.

———. *The Rights of Others: Aliens, Residents, and Citizens*. Cambridge, UK, and New York: Cambridge University Press, 2004.

Berman, Jessica. *Modernist Commitments: Ethics, Politics, and Transnational Modernism*. New York: Columbia University Press, 2011.

———. *Modernist Fiction, Cosmopolitanism, and the Politics of Community*. Cambridge, UK, and New York: Cambridge University Press, 2001.

Bloom, Harold. *How to Read and Why*. New York: Touchstone, 2001.

Bone, Robert. *Richard Wright*. Minneapolis: University of Minnesota Press, 1969.

Bontemps, Arna. Review of *The Outsider*. *Saturday Review*, March 28, 1953, pp. 15–16.

Booth, Wayne C. *The Company We Keep: An Ethics of Fiction*. Berkeley: University of California Press, 1988.

Bourne, Randolph S. "Trans-National America." In *In Search of a Democratic America: The Writings of Randolph S. Bourne*, ed. Martin S. Sheffer, pp. 55–68. Boston: Lexington Books, 2002.

Bowles, Jane. *Two Serious Ladies*. Orig. 1943; New York: Dutton, 1984.

Bowles, Paul. "A Distant Episode." In *The Stories of Paul Bowles*, pp. 24–35. New York: Ecco Press, 2001.

———. *Let It Come Down*. Orig. 1952; New York: Ecco Press, 2002.

———. *The Sheltering Sky*. Orig. 1949; London: Penguin, 2006.

———. *The Spider's House*. Orig. 1955; New York: Ecco Press, 2002.

———. *Their Heads Are Green and Their Hands Are Blue: Scenes from the Non-Christian World*. Orig. 1963; New York: Harper Perennial, 2006.

———. "Too Far from Home." In *The Stories of Paul Bowles*, pp. 624–657. New York: Ecco Press, 2001.

———. *Up Above the World: A Novel*. Orig. 1966; New York: Harper Perennial, 2006.

———. *Without Stopping: An Autobiography*. Orig. 1972; New York: Harper Perennial, 2006.

Boyle, Kay. *Avalanche*. New York: Simon and Schuster, 1944.

———. *Death of a Man*. New York: Harcourt, 1936.

———. *A Frenchman Must Die*. New York: Simon and Schuster, 1946.

———. *The Long Walk at San Francisco State*. New York: Grove Press, 1970.

———. *My Next Bride*. New York: Harcourt, 1934.

———. *1939*. New York: Simon and Schuster, 1948.

——. *Plagued by the Nightingale.* Orig. 1931; Carbondale: Southern Illinois University Press, 1966.

——. *Primer for Combat.* New York: Simon and Schuster, 1942.

——. *Process: A Novel.* Urbana: University of Illinois Press, 2001.

——. *The Underground Woman.* Garden City, NY: Doubleday, 1975.

——. *Year before Last.* New York: Greenberg, 1932.

Boyle, Kay, Erica Jong, Thomas Sanchez, and Henry Miller. *Four Visions of America.* Santa Barbara, CA: Capra Press, 1977.

Boyle, Kay, Laurence Vail, and Nina Conarain, eds. *365 Days.* New York: Harcourt, Brace and Co., 1936.

Bracher, Mark. *Literature and Social Justice.* Austin: University of Texas Press, 2013.

Brennan, Timothy. *At Home in the World: Cosmopolitanism Now.* Cambridge, MA: Harvard University Press, 1997.

——. "Cosmo-Theory." *South Atlantic Quarterly* 100.3 (Summer 2001): 659–691.

Brock, Gillian, and Harry Brighouse, eds. *The Political Philosophy of Cosmopolitanism.* Cambridge, UK, and New York: Cambridge University Press, 2005.

Brown, Garrett Wallace, and David Held, eds. *The Cosmopolitanism Reader.* Cambridge, UK, and Malden, MA: Polity Press, 2010.

Brown, Stephanie. *The Postwar African American Novel: Protest and Discontent, 1945–1950.* Jackson: University Press of Mississippi, 2011.

Brundtland, Gro Harlem. Foreword to *Our Common Future*, World Commission on Environment and Development, pp. ix–xv. Oxford and New York: Oxford University Press, 1987.

Buck, David D. "Pearl S. Buck in Search of America." In *The Several Worlds of Pearl S. Buck: Essays Presented at a Centennial Symposium. Randolph-Macon Woman's College, March 26–28, 1992*, ed. E. Lipscomb, F. Webb, and P. Conn, pp. 29–44. Westport, CT, and London: Greenwood Press, 1994.

Buck, Pearl S. *American Unity and Asia.* New York: John Day, 1942.

——. "Breaking the Barriers of Race Prejudice." *Journal of Negro Education* 11.4 (October 1942): 444–453.

——. *Children for Adoption.* New York: Random House, 1964.

——. *China Sky.* New York: John Day, 1941.

——. *The Chinese Novel.* New York: John Day, 1939.

——. *Come, My Beloved.* New York: John Day, 1953.

——. "Critical Excerpts." In *The Good Earth*, Pearl S. Buck, pp. 371–372. New York: Washington Square Press, 1994.

——. "Democracy and the Negro." *Crisis* 48 (December 1941): 376–377.

——. *East Wind: West Wind.* New York: John Day, 1930.

——. *The Exile.* New York: P. F. Collier and Son, 1936.

——. *Fighting Angel: Portrait of a Soul.* New York: John Day, 1936.

——. *The Good Earth.* Orig. 1931; Kingston, RI, and Lancaster, GB: Moyer Bell, 2004.

——. *The Hidden Flower.* Orig. 1952; New York: Pocket Books, 1960.

——. *Is There a Case for Foreign Missions?* New York: John Day Pamphlet Series 18, 1932.

——. *Letter from Peking.* Orig. 1957; New York: Pocket Books, 1964.

——. *My Several Worlds: A Personal Record.* New York: John Day, 1954.

————. "On Discovering America." *Survey Graphic* 26.6 (June 1937): 313–315, 353, 355.

————. *Pavilion of Women*. Orig. 1946; Kingston, RI, and Lancaster, GB: Moyer Bell, 1990.

————. *The Promise*. Orig. 1943; Kingston, RI, and Lancaster, GB: Moyer Bell, 1997.

Buck, Pearl S., and Eslanda Goode Robeson. *American Argument*. New York: John Day, 1949.

Buell, Lawrence. "Ecoglobalist Affects: The Emergence of U.S. Environmental Imagination on a Global Scale." In *Shades of the Planet: American Literature as World Literature*, ed. Wai Chee Dimock and Lawrence Buell, pp. 227–248. Princeton, NJ: Princeton University Press, 2007.

Calhoun, Craig J. "The Class Consciousness of Frequent Travellers: Towards a Critique of Actually Existing Cosmopolitanism." In *Debating Cosmopolitics*, ed. Daniele Archibugi, pp. 86–116. London and New York: Verso, 2003.

Campbell, James. *Exiled in Paris: Richard Wright, James Baldwin, Samuel Beckett and Others on the Left Bank*. New York: Scribner, 1995.

————. "The Island Affair." *The Guardian*, January 7, 2006. http://www.guardian.co.uk/books/2006/jan/07/featuresreviews.guardianreview25 (accessed February 25, 2013).

Campbell, James T. *Middle Passages: African American Journeys to Africa, 1787–2005*. New York: Penguin Press, 2006.

Caponi, Gena Dagel, ed. *Conversations with Paul Bowles*. Jackson: University Press of Mississippi, 1993.

Carr, Virginia Spencer. *Paul Bowles: A Life*. New York: Scribner, 2004.

Carroll, Noël. *The Philosophy of Horror*. New York and London: Routledge, 1990.

Cheah, Pheng. *Inhuman Conditions: On Cosmopolitanism and Human Rights*. Cambridge, MA: Harvard University Press, 2006.

Cheah, Pheng, and Bruce Robbins, eds. *Cosmopolitics: Feeling and Thinking beyond the Nation*. Minneapolis: University of Minnesota Press, 1998.

Clark, Suzanne. *Sentimental Modernism: Woman Writers and the Revolution of the Word*. Bloomington: Indiana University Press, 1991.

Cohen, Mitchell. "Rooted Cosmopolitanism: Thoughts on the Left, Nationalism and Multiculturalism." *Dissent* 39.4 (1992): 478–483.

Conn, Peter. *Pearl S. Buck: A Cultural Biography*. Cambridge, UK, and New York: Cambridge University Press, 1996.

Conroy, Jack. "Negro Soldier and Fraulein." *Chicago Sun Times*, August 17, 1948, p. 11.

Cowley, Malcolm. *Exile's Return: A Literary Odyssey of the 1920s*. Orig. 1934; London and New York: Penguin Books, 1994.

Curthoys, Ned. "The Émigré Sensibility of 'World-Literature': Historicizing Hannah Arendt and Karl Jaspers' Cosmopolitan Intent." *Theory & Event* 8.3 (2005).

Curtis, Valerie, Mícheál de Barra, and Robert Aunger. "Disgust as an Adaptive System for Disease Avoidance Behaviour." *Philosophical Transactions of the Royal Society B: Biological Sciences* 366.1563 (2011): 389–401.

Dadlez, Eva M. *What's Hecuba to Him? Fictional Events and Actual Emotions*. University Park: Pennsylvania State University Press, 1997.

Damasio, Antonio. *Descartes' Error: Emotion, Reason, and the Human Brain*. Orig. 1994; London: Vintage, 2006.

―――. *The Feeling of What Happens: Body and Emotion in the Making of Consciousness*. New York: Harcourt Brace, 1999.

―――. *Self Comes to Mind: Constructing the Conscious Brain*. New York: Pantheon, 2010.

Davis, Garry. *The World Is My Country: The Autobiography of Garry Davis*. New York: Putnam, 1961.

Debord, Guy. *The Society of the Spectacle*. Translated by Donald Nicholson-Smith. Orig. 1967; New York: Zone Books, 1994.

Delanty, Gerard. *The Cosmopolitan Imagination: The Renewal of Critical Social Theory*. Cambridge, UK, and New York: Cambridge University Press, 2009.

Derrida, Jacques. *On Cosmopolitanism and Forgiveness*. Translated by Mark Dooley and Michael Hughes. Orig. 1997; London and New York: Routledge, 2001.

de Sousa, Ronald. *Emotional Truth*. Oxford and New York: Oxford University Press, 2011.

―――. "Emotions: What I Know, What I'd Like to Think I Know, and What I'd Like to Think." In *Thinking about Feeling: Contemporary Philosophers on Emotions*, ed. Robert C. Solomon, pp. 61–75. Oxford and New York: Oxford University Press, 2004.

―――. *The Rationality of Emotion*. Orig. 1987; Cambridge, MA: MIT Press, 1990.

Diawara, Manthia. *In Search of Africa*. Cambridge, MA: Harvard University Press, 1998.

Dimock, Wai Chee. *Through Other Continents: American Literature across Deep Time*. Princeton, NJ, and Oxford: Princeton University Press, 2006.

Dimock, Wai Chee, and Lawrence Buell, eds. *Shades of the Planet: American Literature as World Literature*. Princeton, NJ: Princeton University Press, 2007.

Dobson, Andrew. "Thick Cosmopolitanism." *Political Studies* 54.1 (2006): 165–184.

Dobson, Joanne. "Reclaiming Sentimental Literature." *American Literature* 69.2 (June 1997): 263–288.

Dromi, Shai M., and Eva Illouz. "Recovering Morality: Pragmatic Sociology and Literary Studies." *New Literary History* 41.2 (Spring 2010): 351–369.

Du Bois, W. E. B. "The War for Race Equality." *Phylon* 3 (1942): 321–322.

Edwards, Brent Hayes. *The Practice of Diaspora: Literature, Translation, and the Rise of Black Internationalism*. Cambridge, MA: Harvard University Press, 2003.

Edwards, Brian T. "Sheltering Screens: Paul Bowles and Foreign Relations." *American Literary History* 17.2 (2005): 307–334.

Elden, Stuart, and Eduardo Mendieta. *Reading Kant's Geography*. Albany, NY: SUNY Press, 2011.

Evans, Oliver. "An Interview with Paul Bowles." 1971. In *Conversations with Paul Bowles*, ed. Gena Dagel Caponi, pp. 38–58. Jackson: University Press of Mississippi, 1993.

Fabre, Michel. *From Harlem to Paris: Black American Writers in France, 1840–1980*. Urbana: University of Illinois Press, 1991.

―――. *The World of Richard Wright*. Jackson: University Press of Mississippi, 1985.

Fehrenbach, Heide. *Race after Hitler: Black Occupation Children in Postwar Germany and America*. Princeton, NJ: Princeton University Press, 2005.

Fisher, Philip. *Hard Facts: Setting and Form in the American Novel*. New York: Oxford University Press, 1985.

Fitzgerald, F. Scott. *Tender Is the Night*. Orig. 1934; New York: Scribner, 1996.

Flanner, Janet. "The Expatriate Tradition: Then and Now." Interview with Virgil Thompson, Maria Jolas, Man Ray, John Levee, James Jones, and William Gardner Smith. *Paris Review* 33 (Winter–Spring 1965): 158–170.

Ford, Nick Aaron. "The Fire Next Time? A Critical Survey of Belles Lettres by and about Negroes Published in 1963." *Phylon* 25.2 (Summer 1964): 123–134.

Foucault, Michel. *Discipline and Punish: The Birth of the Prison.* Translated by Alan Sheridan. Orig. 1975; New York: Vintage Books, 1995.

Friedman, Joseph. "The Unvarying Visage of Hatred." *New York Times,* November 17, 1963, p. BR27.

Frijda, Nico. *The Emotions.* Cambridge and Paris: Cambridge University Press and Editions de la Maison des Sciences de l'Homme, 1986.

Gadamer, Hans-Georg. *Truth and Method.* Translated by Joel Weinsheimer. Orig. 1960; New York and London: Continuum, 2004.

Gaines, Kevin. *American Africans in Ghana: Black Expatriates and the Civil Rights Era.* Chapel Hill: University of North Carolina Press, 2006.

———. "Revisiting Richard Wright in Ghana: Black Radicalism and the Dialectics of Diaspora." *Social Text* 19.2 (Summer 2001): 75–101.

Garber, Marjorie, Beatrice Hanssen, and Rebecca L. Walkowitz. "Introduction: The Turn to Ethics." In *The Turn to Ethics,* ed. Marjorie Garber, Beatrice Hanssen, and Rebecca L. Walkowitz, pp. vii–xx. New York and London: Routledge, 2000.

Gibson, Richard. "Richard Wright's 'Island of Hallucination' and the 'Gibson Affair.'" *Modern Fiction Studies* 51.4 (2005): 896–920.

Gilroy, Paul. *Against Race: Imagining Political Culture beyond the Color Line.* Cambridge, MA: Harvard University Press, 2000.

———. *The Black Atlantic.* Cambridge, MA: Harvard University Press, 1993.

———. *Postcolonial Melancholia.* New York: Columbia University Press, 2005.

Goldie, Peter. "Emotion, Feeling, and Knowledge of the World." In *Thinking about Feeling: Contemporary Philosophers on Emotions,* ed. Robert C. Solomon, pp. 91–106. Oxford and New York: Oxford University Press, 2004.

———. *The Emotions: A Philosophical Exploration.* Oxford: Oxford University Press, 2000.

———. "Getting Feelings into Emotional Experience in the Right Way." *Emotion Review* 1.3 (2009): 232–239.

Goldman, Alvin. "Two Routes to Empathy: Insights from Cognitive Neuroscience." In *Empathy: Philosophical and Psychological Perspectives,* ed. Amy Coplan and Peter Goldie, pp. 31–44. Oxford and New York: Oxford University Press, 2011.

Goldstone, Richard H. Contribution to "Aspects of Self: A Bowles Collage." *Twentieth Century Literature* 32.3/4 (Autumn–Winter 1986): 274–279.

Gould, Carol C. "Transnational Solidarities." *Journal of Social Philosophy* 38.1 (Spring 2007): 148–164.

Graham, Maryemma. Introduction to *The Outsider,* Richard Wright, pp. xi–xxix. New York: Harper Perennial, 2003.

Greene, Larry A., and Anke Ortlepp. *Germans and African Americans: Two Centuries of Exchange.* Jackson: University Press of Mississippi, 2011.

Haidt, Jonathan, Paul Rozin, Clark R. McCauley, and Sumio Imada. "Body, Psyche, and Culture: The Relationship between Disgust and Morality." *Psychology and Developing Society* 9 (March 1997): 107–131.

Haiping, Liu. "Pearl S. Buck's Reception in China Reconsidered." In *The Several Worlds of Pearl S. Buck: Essays Presented at a Centennial Symposium, Randolph-Macon Woman's College, March 26–28, 1992,* ed. Elizabeth Lipscomb, Frances E. Webb, and Peter Conn, pp. 55–67. Westport, CT, and London: Greenwood Press, 1994.

Hakemulder, Jèmeljan. *The Moral Laboratory: Experiments Examining the Effects of Reading Literature on Social Perception and Moral Self-Concept.* Utrecht Publications in General and Comparative Literature 34. Amsterdam: John Benjamins, 2000.

Hallström, Per. "The Nobel Prize in Literature 1938 Presentation Speech." In *Nobel Lectures, Literature 1901–1967,* ed. Horst Frenz, pp. 310–314. Amsterdam: Elsevier Publishing Company, 1969.

Halpern, Daniel. "Interview with Paul Bowles." In *Conversations with Paul Bowles,* ed. Gena Dagel Caponi, pp. 86–101. Jackson: University Press of Mississippi, 1993.

Hamovitch, Mitzi Berger. "Release from Torment: The Fragmented Double in Bowles's *Let It Come Down.*" *Twentieth Century Literature* 32.3/4 (Autumn–Winter 1986): 440–450.

Hannerz, Ulf. "Cosmopolitans and Locals in World Culture." In *Global Culture: Nationalism, Globalization and Modernity,* ed. Mike Featherstone, pp. 237–251. London; Newbury Park, CA; and Delhi: Sage Publications, 1990.

Harvey, David. "Cosmopolitanism and the Banality of Geographical Evils." *Public Culture* 12.2 (2000): 529–564.

Harvey, Jean. "Moral Solidarity and Empathetic Understanding: The Moral Value and Scope of the Relationship." *Journal of Social Philosophy* 38.1 (Spring 2007): 22–37.

Hawthorne, Nathaniel. *The Marble Faun.* Orig. 1860; Oxford and New York: Oxford World's Classics, 2002.

Heins, Volker. "Reasons of the Heart: Weber and Arendt on Emotion in Politics." *European Legacy* 12.6 (2007): 715–728.

Heise, Ursula. *Sense of Place and Sense of Planet: The Environmental Imagination of the Global.* New York: Oxford University Press, 2008.

Held, David. *Cosmopolitanism: Ideals, Realities, and Deficits.* Cambridge, UK, and Malden, MA: Polity Press, 2010.

———. *Democracy and the Global Order: From the Modern State to Cosmopolitan Governance.* Stanford, CA: Stanford University Press, 1995.

Hemingway, Ernest. *A Moveable Feast.* Orig. 1964; New York: Scribner, 2003.

Hendler, Glenn. *Public Sentiments: Structures of Feeling in Nineteenth-Century American Literature.* Chapel Hill: University of North Carolina Press, 2001.

Hibbard, Allen. *Paul Bowles: Magic & Morocco.* San Francisco: Cadmus Editions, 2004.

———. "Some Versions of Ironic (Mis)Interpretation: The American Abroad." *Alif: Journal of Comparative Poetics* 8 (Spring 1988): 66–87.

Hodges, LeRoy. *Portrait of an Expatriate: William Gardner Smith, Writer.* Westport, CT: Greenwood Press, 1985.

Hoffman, Martin. *Empathy and Moral Development: Implications for Caring and Justice.* Cambridge, UK, and New York: Cambridge University Press, 2000.

Hogan, Patrick Colm. *Affective Narratology: The Emotional Structures of Stories.* Lincoln: University of Nebraska Press, 2011.

————. *The Mind and Its Stories: Narrative Universals and Human Emotion.* Cambridge, UK, and New York: Cambridge University Press, 2003.

————. *Understanding Nationalism: On Narrative, Cognitive Science, and Identity.* Columbus: Ohio State University Press, 2009.

————. *What Literature Teaches Us about Emotion.* Cambridge, UK, and New York: Cambridge University Press, 2011.

Höhn, Maria. *GIs and Fräuleins: The German-American Encounter in 1950s West Germany.* Chapel Hill: University of North Carolina Press, 2002.

————. "Heimat in Turmoil: African-American GIs in 1950s Western Germany." In *The Miracle Years: A Cultural History of West Germany, 1949–1968,* ed. Hanna Schissler, pp. 145–163. Princeton, NJ: Princeton University Press, 2001.

Hollinger, David. *Cosmopolitanism and Solidarity: Studies in Ethnoracial, Religious, and Professional Affiliation in the United States.* Madison: University of Wisconsin Press, 2006.

————. "Not Universalists, Not Pluralists: The New Cosmopolitans Find Their Own Way." In *Conceiving Cosmopolitanism: Theory, Context and Practice,* ed. Steven Vertovec and Robin Cohen, pp. 227–239. New York: Oxford University Press, 2002.

Honig, Bonnie. "Another Cosmopolitanism? Law and Politics in the New Europe." Response to Seyla Benhabib. In *Another Cosmopolitanism,* ed. Robert Post, pp. 102–127. Oxford and New York: Oxford University Press, 2006.

hooks, bell. *We Real Cool: Black Men and Masculinity.* New York: Routledge, 2004.

House, Jim, and Neil MacMaster. *Paris 1961: Algerians, State Terror, and Memory.* Oxford and New York: Oxford University Press, 2006.

Hout, Syrine C. "Grains of Utopia: The Desert as Literary Oasis in Paul Bowles's *The Sheltering Sky* and Wilfred Thesiger's *Arabian Sands.*" *Utopian Studies* 11.2 (Spring 2000): 112–136.

Hsia, Chih-tsing. *The Classic Chinese Novel: A Critical Introduction.* Ithaca, NY: Cornell University East Asia Program, 1996.

Hughes, Carl Milton. *The Negro Novelist: A Discussion of the Writings of American Negro Novelists, 1940–1950.* New York: Citadel Press, 1953.

Hughes, Langston. *The Big Sea.* Orig. 1940; New York: Hill and Wang, 1993.

Hume, David. *An Enquiry Concerning the Principles of Morals.* Orig. 1751; Radford, VA: Wilder Publications, 2008.

————. "Of Tragedy." In *Of the Standard of Taste and Other Essays,* ed. John W. Lenz, pp. 29–37. Indianapolis and New York: Bobbs-Merrill, 1965.

Iacoboni, Marco. *Mirroring People: The Science of Empathy and How We Connect with Others.* New York: Picador, 2009.

James, Henry. *Daisy Miller.* Orig. 1878; Oxford and New York: Oxford World's Classics, 2009.

James, Susan. "Passion and Politics." In *Philosophy and the Emotions,* ed. Anthony Hatzimoysis, pp. 221–234. New York: Cambridge University Press, 2003.

Jameson, Fredric. *The Political Unconscious: Narrative as a Socially Symbolic Act.* Ithaca, NY: Cornell University Press, 1981.

Johnson, Marcia K. Foreword to *Narrative Impact: Social and Cognitive Foundations,* ed. Melanie C. Green, Jeffrey J. Strange, and Timothy C. Brock, pp. xi–xii. Mahwah, NJ: Erlbaum, 2002.

Kallen, Horace. "Democracy versus the Melting Pot." *The Nation*, February 25, 1915. http://www.expo98.msu.edu/people/Kallen.htm (accessed February 5, 2012).

Kang-Hu, Kiang. "Critical Excerpts." In *The Good Earth*, Pearl Buck, p. 370. New York: Washington Square Press, 1994.

Kant, Immanuel. *Perpetual Peace*. Translated by H. B. Nisbet. Orig. 1795; New York: Filiquarian Pub., 2007.

Kaplan, Amy. *The Anarchy of Empire in the Making of U.S. Culture*. Cambridge, MA: Harvard University Press, 2002.

Kaplan, Caren. *Questions of Travel: Postmodern Discourses of Displacement*. Durham, NC: Duke University Press, 1996.

Kappelhoff, Hermann. "Träneneseelingkeit: Das Sentimentale Geniessen und das Melodramatische Kino." In *Kinogefühle: Emotionalität und Film*, ed. Matthias Brütsch, Vinzenz Hediger, Ursula von Keitz, Alexandra Schneider, and Margrit Tröhler, pp. 33–55. Marburg, Germany: Schüren Verlag, 2005.

Keen, Suzanne. *Empathy and the Novel*. Oxford and New York: Oxford University Press, 2007.

———. "Narrative Empathy." In *Toward a Cognitive Theory of Narrative Acts*, ed. Frederick Luis Aldama, pp. 61–94. Austin: University of Texas Press, 2010.

Kendall, Gavin, Ian Woodward, and Zlatko Skrbis. *The Sociology of Cosmopolitanism: Globalization, Identity, Culture and Government*. New York: Palgrave Macmillan, 2009.

Keniston, Kenneth. *Young Radicals: Notes on Committed Youth*. New York: Harcourt, 1968.

Kim, Sue J. "Anger, Temporality, and the Politics of Reading *The Woman Warrior*." In *Analyzing World Fiction: New Horizons in Narrative Theory*, ed. Frederick Luis Aldama, pp. 93–108. Austin: University of Texas Press, 2011.

Kleingeld, Pauline. "Kant's Second Thoughts on Race." *Philosophical Quarterly* 57.229 (October 2007): 573–592.

Kleingeld, Pauline, and Eric Brown. "Cosmopolitanism." *Stanford Encyclopedia of Philosophy*. http://plato.stanford.edu/entries/cosmopolitanism (accessed February 12, 2013).

Kurasawa, Fuyuki. "Critical Cosmopolitanism." In *The Ashgate Research Companion to Cosmopolitanism*, ed. Maria Rovisco and Magdalena Nowicka, pp. 279–294. Farnham, Surrey, UK: Ashgate, 2011.

Lang, Peter J., Margaret M. Bradley, and Bruce N. Cuthbert. "Emotion, Attention, and the Startle Reflex." *Psychological Review* 97.3 (1990): 377–395.

LeDoux, Joseph. *The Emotional Brain: The Mysterious Underpinnings of Emotional Life*. New York: Simon and Schuster, 1996.

Lee, Henry. "Pearl S. Buck: Spiritual Descendant of Tom Paine." *Saturday Review of Literature* 25 (December 5, 1942): 16–18.

Leong, Karen J. *The China Mystique: Pearl S. Buck, Anna May Wong, Mayling Soong, and the Transformation of American Orientalism*. Berkeley: University of California Press, 2005.

Le Sueur, James D. *Uncivil War: Intellectuals and Identity Politics during the Decolonization of Algeria*. Philadelphia: University of Pennsylvania Press, 2001.

Levi, Primo. *If This Is a Man*. Translated by Stuart Woolf. Orig. 1958; London: Sphere, 1987.

Lévinas, Emmanuel. *Totality and Infinity: An Essay on Exteriority.* Translated by Alphonso Lingis. Orig. 1961; Pittsburgh: Duquesne University Press, 1969.

Liao, Kang. *Pearl S. Buck: A Cultural Bridge across the Pacific.* Westport, CT, and London: Greenwood Press, 1997.

Linklater, Andrew. "Cosmopolitan Citizenship." *Citizenship Studies* 2.1 (1998): 23–41.

———. *The Transformation of Political Community: Ethical Foundations of the Post-Westphalian Era.* Cambridge, UK: Polity Press, 1998.

Lipset, Seymour Martin. *American Exceptionalism: A Double-Edged Sword.* New York: Norton, 1996.

Long, Graham. "Moral and Sentimental Cosmopolitanism." *Journal of Social Philosophy* 40.3 (Fall 2009): 317–342.

Loshitzky, Yosefa. "The Tourist/Traveler Gaze: Bertolucci and Bowles's *The Sheltering Sky.*" *East-West Film Journal* 7.2 (1993): 111–137.

McAlmon, Robert. *Being Geniuses Together.* Revised with Supplementary Chapters and an Afterword by Kay Boyle. 1968. Baltimore: Johns Hopkins University Press, 1997.

McConnell, Michael W. "Don't Neglect the Little Platoons." In *For Love of Country: Debating the Limits of Patriotism*, Martha Nussbaum, ed. Joshua Cohen, pp. 78–84. Boston: Beacon Press, 1996.

McGrory, Mary. "Review of *Pavilion of Women.*" *New York Times Book Review*, November 24, 1946, p. 6.

Mar, Raymond A., and Keith Oatley. "The Function of Fiction Is the Abstraction and Simulation of Social Experience." *Perspectives on Psychological Science* 3.3 (2008): 173–192.

Mar, Raymond A., Keith Oatley, Maja Djikic, and Justin Mullin. "Emotion and Narrative Fiction: Interactive Influences before, during, and after Reading." *Cognition & Emotion* 25.5 (2011): 818–833.

Mar, Raymond A., Keith Oatley, Jacob Hirsh, Jennifer dela Paz, and Jordan B. Peterson. "Bookworms versus Nerds: Exposure to Fiction versus Non-fiction, Divergent Associations with Social Ability, and the Simulation of Fictional Social Worlds." *Journal of Research in Personality* 40 (2006): 694–712.

Mar, Raymond A., Keith Oatley, and Jordan B. Peterson. "Exploring the Link between Reading Fiction and Empathy: Ruling Out Individual Differences and Examining Outcomes." *Communications: The European Journal of Communication* 34 (2009): 407–428.

Melvin, Sheila. "Pearl's Great Price." *Wilson Quarterly* 30.2 (Spring 2006): 24–30.

Mignolo, Walter. "The Many Faces of Cosmo-polis: Border Thinking and Critical Cosmopolitanism." *Public Culture* 12.3 (Fall 2000): 721–748.

Miller, David. *Citizenship and National Identity.* Cambridge, UK: Polity Press, 2000.

Miller, William Ian. *The Anatomy of Disgust.* Cambridge, MA: Harvard University Press, 1997.

Moya, Paula M. L., and Ramón Saldívar. "Fictions of the Trans-American Imaginary." *Modern Fiction Studies* 49.1 (2003): 1–18.

Nussbaum, Martha. "The Capabilities Approach and Ethical Cosmopolitanism: The Challenge of Political Liberalism." In *The Ashgate Research Companion to Cos-*

mopolitanism, ed. Maria Rovisco and Magdalena Nowicka, pp. 403–410. Farnham, Surrey, UK: Ashgate, 2011.

———. "Compassion and Terror." In *The Many Faces of Patriotism*, ed. Philip Abbott, pp. 15–35. Lanham, MD: Rowman and Littlefield Publishers, 2007.

———. *Cultivating Humanity: A Classical Defense of Reform in Liberal Education*. Cambridge, MA: Harvard University Press, 1997.

———. *Poetic Justice: The Literary Imagination and Public Life*. Boston: Beacon Press, 1995.

———. *Upheavals of Thought: The Intelligence of Emotions*. Cambridge, UK, and New York: Cambridge University Press, 2001.

———. *For Love of Country: Debating the Limits of Patriotism*, ed. Joshua Cohen. Boston: Beacon Press, 1996.

Oaten, Megan, Richard Stevenson, and Trevor I. Case. "Disgust as a Disease-Avoidance Mechanism." *Psychological Bulletin* 135.2 (2009): 303–321.

Oatley, Keith. *Best Laid Schemes: The Psychology of Emotions*. Cambridge, UK, and New York: Cambridge University Press, 1992.

———. "Communications to Self and Others: Emotional Experience and Its Skills." *Emotion Review* 1.3 (2009): 206–213.

———. "Emotions and the Story Worlds of Fiction." In *Narrative Impact: Social and Cognitive Foundations*, ed. Melanie C. Green, Jeffrey J. Strange, and Timothy C. Brock, pp. 39–69. Mahwah, NJ: Erlbaum, 2002.

———. *Such Stuff as Dreams: The Psychology of Fiction*. Chichester, UK, and Malden, MA: Wiley-Blackwell, 2011.

———. "Why Fiction May Be Twice as True as Fact: Fiction as Cognitive and Emotional Simulation." *Review of General Psychology* 3.2 (1999): 101–117.

Oatley, Keith, Dacher Keltner, and Jennifer M. Jenkins. *Understanding Emotions*. Malden, MA, and Oxford: Blackwell Publishing, 2006.

Oliner, Samuel P., and Pearl M. Oliner. *The Altruistic Personality: Rescuers of Jews in Nazi Europe*. New York: Free Press, 1988.

Oliver, Mary Beth. "Exploring the Paradox of Sad Films." *Human Communication Research* 19.3 (1993): 315–342.

Olson, Steven E. "Alien Terrain: Paul Bowles's Filial Landscapes." *Twentieth Century Literature* 32.3/4, Paul Bowles Issue (Autumn–Winter 1986): 334–349.

Parker, Stephen, and Rebecca Thomas. "Psychological Differences in Shame vs. Guilt: Implications for Mental Health Counselors." *Journal of Mental Health Counseling* 31.3 (July 2009): 213–224.

Patteson, Richard F. *A World Outside: The Fiction of Paul Bowles*. Austin: University of Texas Press, 1987.

Plantinga, Carl. *Moving Viewers: American Film and the Spectator's Experience*. Berkeley: University of California Press, 2009.

———. "The Scene of Empathy and the Human Face on Film." In *Passionate Views: Film, Cognition, and Emotion*, ed. Carl Plantinga and Greg M. Smith, pp. 239–255. Baltimore and London: Johns Hopkins University Press, 1999.

Pogge, Thomas. "Cosmopolitanism and Sovereignty." *Ethics* 103.1 (1992): 48–75.

Pollock, David C., and Ruth Van Reken. *Third Culture Kids: Growing Up among Worlds*. Rev. ed. Boston and London: Nicholas Brealey Publishing, 2009.

Posner, Richard A. "Against Ethical Criticism." *Philosophy and Literature* 21.1 (April 1997): 1–27.

———. *Public Intellectuals: A Study of Decline.* Cambridge, MA: Harvard University Press, 2001.

Posnock, Ross. "The Dream of Deracination: The Uses of Cosmopolitanism." *American Literary History* 12.4 (Winter 2000): 802–818.

Pounds, Wayne. *Paul Bowles: The Inner Geography.* Bern, Switzerland, and New York: Peter Lang, 1985.

Radway, Janice A. *Reading the Romance: Women, Patriarchy, and Popular Literature.* Chapel Hill: University of North Carolina Press, 1991.

Rancière, Jacques. "Who Is the Subject of the Rights of Man?" *South Atlantic Quarterly* 103.2/3 (Spring/Summer 2004): 297–310.

Rawls, John. *A Theory of Justice.* Cambridge, MA: Belknap Press of Harvard University Press, 1971.

Reilly, John M. Afterword to *Native Son*, Richard Wright, pp. 393–397. New York: Harper Perennial, 2001.

———. *Richard Wright: The Critical Reception.* New York: Burt Franklin, 1978.

Reynes-Delobel, Anne. "'Calculating the Leap from Void to Absence': Abstraction in the Writing of Kay Boyle." In *Kay Boyle for the Twenty-First Century: New Essays*, ed. Thomas Austenfeld, pp. 9–22. Trier, Germany: Wissenschaftlicher Verlag, Trier, 2008.

Richardson, Brian. "U.S. Ethnic and Postcolonial Fiction: Toward a Poetics of Collective Narratives." In *Analyzing World Fiction: New Horizons in Narrative Theory*, ed. Frederick Luis Aldama, pp. 3–16. Austin: University of Texas Press, 2011.

Rizzolatti, Giacomo, and Corrado Sinigaglia. *Mirrors in the Brain: How Our Minds Share Actions and Emotions.* Translated by Frances Anderson. Oxford and New York: Oxford University Press, 2008.

Robbins, Bruce. "Actually Existing Cosmopolitanism." In *Cosmopolitics: Feeling and Thinking beyond the Nation*, ed. Peng Cheah and Bruce Robbins, pp. 1–19. Minneapolis: University of Minnesota Press, 1998.

———. *Feeling Global: Internationalism in Distress.* New York and London: New York University Press, 1999.

———. "The Weird Heights: On Cosmopolitanism, Feeling, and Power." *differences* 7.1 (1995): 165–187.

———. "The Worlding of the American Novel." In *The Cambridge History of the American Novel*, ed. Leonard Cassuto, Clare Virginia Eby, and Benjamin Reiss, pp. 1096–1106. Cambridge Histories Online. Cambridge, UK, and New York: Cambridge University Press, 2011.

Robinson, Cedric. *Black Marxism: The Making of the Black Radical Tradition.* London: Zed Press; Totowa, NJ: Biblio Distribution Center, 1983.

Robinson, Jenefer. *Deeper than Reason: Emotion and Its Role in Literature, Music, and Art.* Oxford and New York: Oxford University Press, 2005.

Rojek, Chris, and John Urry. *Touring Cultures: Transformations of Travel and Theory.* London and New York: Routledge, 1997.

Ross, Kristin. *May '68 and Its Afterlives.* Chicago and London: University of Chicago Press, 2002.

Rovisco, Maria, and Magdalena Nowicka, eds. *The Ashgate Research Companion to Cosmopolitanism*. Farnham, Surrey, UK: Ashgate, 2011.

Rowe, John Carlos. *Afterlives of Modernism: Liberalism, Transnationalism, and Political Critique*. Hanover, NH: Dartmouth College Press, 2011.

———. *Post-Nationalist American Studies*. Berkeley: University of California Press, 2000.

Rowley, Hazel. "The 'Exile' Years? How the '50s Culture Wars Destroyed Richard Wright." *Bookforum*, December/January 2006. http://www.bookforum.com /archive/dec_05/rowley.html (accessed February 24, 2013).

———. *Richard Wright: The Life and Times*. New York: Henry Holt and Co., 2001.

Rozin, Paul, and April E. Fallon. "A Perspective on Disgust." *Psychological Review* 94.1 (1987): 23–41.

Rozin, Paul, Jonathan Haidt, and Clark R. McCauley. "Disgust." In *Handbook of Emotions*, 3rd ed., ed. Michael Lewis, Jeanette M. Haviland-Jones, and Lisa Feldman Barrett, pp. 757–776. New York: Guilford, 2010.

Ruquist, Rebecca. "Non, Nous Ne Jouons Pas la Trompette: Richard Wright in Paris." *Contemporary French and Francophone Studies* 8.3 (Summer 2004): 285–303.

Said, Edward. "Islam through Western Eyes." *The Nation*, April 26, 1980. http:// www.thenation.com/article/islam-through-western-eyes# (accessed May 12, 2012).

———. *Orientalism*. Orig. 1978; New York: Vintage Books, 1994.

Samuels, Shirley, ed. *The Culture of Sentiment: Race, Gender, and Sentimentality in Nineteenth-Century America*. New York: Oxford University Press, 1992.

Sartre, Jean-Paul. *Essays in Existentialism*. Edited by Wade Baskin. New York: Kensington Publishing, 1993.

———. *Existentialism and Humanism*. Orig. 1945; New York: Philosophical Library, 1947.

Scarry, Elaine. "The Difficulty of Imagining Other People." In *For Love of Country: Debating the Limits of Patriotism*, Martha C. Nussbaum, ed. Joshua Cohen, pp. 98–110. Boston: Beacon Press, 1996.

———. *Dreaming by the Book*. Princeton, NJ: Princeton University Press, 2001.

Scheff, Thomas J. *Catharsis in Healing, Ritual and Drama*. Berkeley: University of California Press, 1979.

Scheffler, Samuel. "Conceptions of Cosmopolitanism." *Utilitas* 11.3 (1999): 255–276.

Schmitt, Carl. *Politische Theologie*. Berlin: Duncker und Humblot, 1922.

Schmundt-Thomas, Georg. "America's Germany: National Self and Cultural Other after World War II." PhD diss., Northwestern University, 1992.

Schneider, Isidore. Review of *East Wind: West Wind* by Pearl Buck. *New Republic* 63 (May 21, 1930): 24.

Schneider, Ryan. *The Public Intellectualism of Ralph Waldo Emerson and W. E. B. Du Bois: Emotional Dimensions of Race and Reform*. New York: Palgrave Macmillan, 2010.

Schoene, Berthold. *The Cosmopolitan Novel*. Edinburgh: Edinburgh University Press, 2009.

Sellars, John. *Stoicism*. Berkeley: University of California Press, 2006.

Shaffer, Robert. "Pearl S. Buck and the East and West Association: The Trajectory and Fate of 'Critical Internationalism.'" *Peace & Change* 28.1 (January 2003): 1–36.

———. "Women and International Relations: Pearl S. Buck's Critique of the Cold War." *Journal of Women's History* 11.3 (1999): 151–175.

Sherk, Warren. *Pearl S. Buck: Good Earth Mother.* Philomath, OR: Drift Creek Press, 1992.

Shui Hu Chuan. *All Men Are Brothers.* Translated by Pearl S. Buck. New York: Grove Press, 1937.

Skrbis, Zlatko, Gavin Kendall, and Ian Woodward. "Locating Cosmopolitanism: Between Humanist Ideal and Grounded Social Category." *Theory, Culture & Society* 21.6 (2004): 115–136.

Slote, Michael. *Moral Sentimentalism.* Oxford and New York: Oxford University Press, 2010.

Smith, Adam. *The Theory of Moral Sentiments.* Edited by Knud Haakonssen. Orig. 1759; Cambridge, UK, and New York: Cambridge University Press, 2002.

Smith, Anthony D. *The Ethnic Origins of Nations.* Oxford and New York: Blackwell, 1986.

Smith, Greg M. *Film Structure and the Emotion System.* Cambridge, UK, and New York: Cambridge University Press, 2003.

Smith, Murray. "Gangsters, Cannibals, Aesthetes, or Apparently Perverse Allegiances." In *Passionate Views: Film, Cognition, and Emotion,* ed. Carl Plantinga and Greg M. Smith, pp. 217–237. Baltimore: Johns Hopkins University Press, 1999.

Smith, Virginia Whatley. "French West Africa: Behind the Scenes with Richard Wright, the Travel Writer." In *Richard Wright's Travel Writings: New Reflections,* ed. Virginia Whatley Smith, pp. 179–214. Jackson: University Press of Mississippi, 2001.

Smith, William Gardner. *Anger at Innocence.* New York: Farrar, Straus and Company, 1950.

———. "Black Boy in France." *Ebony* 8.9 (July 1953): 32–36, 38–42.

———. "Found Freedom in Germany: Few GIs Eager to Return to States." *Pittsburgh Courier,* February 22, 1947, pp. 1, 4.

———. "Keeping the Peace: American Prejudice Rampant in Germany." *Pittsburgh Courier,* March 1, 1947, p. 13.

———. *Last of the Conquerors.* New York: Farrar, Straus and Company, 1948.

———. "The Negro Writer: Pitfalls and Compensation." *Phylon* 11.4 (Fourth Quarter 1950): 297–303.

———. *Return to Black America.* Englewood Cliffs, NJ: Prentice-Hall, 1970.

———. "Richard Wright (1908–1960): The Compensation for the Wound." *Two Cities* 6 (Summer 1961): 67–69.

———. *South Street.* New York: Farrar, Straus and Young, 1954.

———. *The Stone Face.* New York: Farrar, Straus and Company, 1963.

———. "Through Dark Eyes." Unpublished, undated manuscript. Farrar, Straus & Giroux, Inc., records, Manuscripts and Archives Division, New York Public Library, Astor, Lenox, and Tilden Foundations.

Solomon, Robert C. "Emotions, Thoughts, and Feelings: Emotions as Engagements with the World." In *Thinking about Feeling: Contemporary Philosophers on Emotions,* ed. Robert C. Solomon, pp. 76–88. New York: Oxford University Press, 2004.

———. *Not Passion's Slave: Emotions and Choice.* Oxford and New York: Oxford University Press, 2003.

————. *The Passions: Emotions and the Meaning of Life*. Indianapolis: Hackett, 1993.

————. *True to Our Feelings: What Our Emotions Are Really Telling Us*. Oxford and New York: Oxford University Press, 2007.

Solomon, Robert C., ed. *Thinking about Feeling: Contemporary Philosophers on Emotions*. New York: Oxford University Press, 2004.

Sommer, Doris. "Irresistible Romance: The Foundational Fictions of Latin America." In *Nation and Narration*, ed. Homi K. Bhabha, pp. 71–98. London and New York: Routledge, 1990.

Spanier, Sandra Whipple. *Kay Boyle: Artist and Activist*. Carbondale: Southern Illinois University Press, 1986.

Spencer, Robert. *Cosmopolitan Criticism and Postcolonial Literature*. New York: Palgrave Macmillan, 2011.

Spivak, Gayatri Chakravorty. "Subaltern Studies: Deconstructing Historiography." In *The Spivak Reader: Selected Works of Gayatri Chakravorty Spivak*, ed. Donna Landry and Gerald MacLean, pp. 203–235. New York and London: Routledge, 1996.

Spurling, Hilary. *Pearl Buck in China: Journey to* The Good Earth. New York: Simon and Schuster, 2010.

Standifer, Leon C. *Binding Up the Wounds: An American Soldier in Occupied Germany, 1945–1946*. Baton Rouge: Louisiana State University Press, 1997.

Stanton, Domna C. "Presidential Address 2005: On Rooted Cosmopolitanism." *PMLA* 121.3 (May 2006): 627–640.

Sterne, Laurence. *A Sentimental Journey through France and Italy*. Orig. 1768; London and New York: Penguin, 2005.

Stewart, Lawrence D. *Paul Bowles: The Illumination of North Africa*. Carbondale: Southern Illinois University Press, 1974.

Stirling, Nora. *Pearl Buck: A Woman in Conflict*. Piscataway, NJ: New Century Publishers, 1983.

Stone, Robert. Introduction to *The Stories of Paul Bowles*, pp. ix–xii. New York: Ecco, 2001.

Stovall, Tyler. "The Fire This Time: Black American Expatriates and the Algerian War." *Yale French Studies* 98 (Fall 2000): 182–200.

————. "Harlem-Sur-Seine: Building an African American Diasporic Community in Paris." *Stanford Humanities Review* 5.2 (1997). http://www.stanford.edu/group /SHR/5-2/stoval.html (accessed February 20, 2013).

————. "Preface to *The Stone Face*." *Contemporary French and Francophone Studies* 8.3 (2004): 305–327.

Stowe, Harriet Beecher. *Uncle Tom's Cabin*. Orig. 1852; Oxford and New York: Oxford University Press, 1998.

Strange, Jeffrey J. "How Fictional Tales Wag Real-World Beliefs." In *Narrative Impact: Social and Cognitive Foundations*, ed. Melanie C. Green, Jeffrey J. Strange, and Timothy C. Brock, pp. 263–286. Mahwah, NJ: Erlbaum, 2002.

Strange, Jeffrey J., and Cynthia C. Leung. "How Anecdotal Accounts in News and in Fiction Can Influence Judgments of a Social Problem's Urgency, Causes, and Cures." *Personality and Social Psychology Bulletin* 25.4 (1999): 436–449.

Stueber, Karsten R. *Rediscovering Empathy: Agency, Folk Psychology, and the Human Sciences*. Cambridge, MA, and London: MIT Press, 2006.

Tan, Ed S. *Emotion and the Structure of Narrative Film: Film as an Emotion Machine.* Mahwah, NJ: Lawrence Erlbaum Associates, 1996.

Tan, Ed S., and Nico H. Frijda. "Sentiment in Film Viewing." In *Passionate Views: Film, Cognition, and Emotion,* ed. Carl Plantinga and Greg M. Smith, pp. 48–63. Baltimore and London: Johns Hopkins University Press, 1999.

Tangney, June P. "Moral Affect: The Good, the Bad, and the Ugly." *Journal of Personality and Social Psychology* 61.4 (October 1991): 598–607.

Tate, Claudia. "Christian Existentialism in Richard Wright's *The Outsider.*" *College Language Association Journal* 25 (June 1982): 371–395.

Taylor, Marjorie, Sara D. Hodges, and Adèle Kohányi. "The Illusion of Independent Agency: Do Adult Fiction Writers Experience Their Characters as Having Minds of Their Own?" *Imagination, Cognition & Personality* 22.4 (2002–2003): 361–380.

Thompson, Dody W. "Pearl S. Buck." In *American Winners of the Nobel Literary Prize,* ed. Warren G. French and Walter E. Kidd, pp. 85–110. Norman: University of Oklahoma Press, 1968.

Tilley, Christopher. "Introduction: Identity, Place, Landscape and Heritage." *Journal of Material Culture* 11.1 (2006): 7–32.

Tóibín, Colm. "Avoid the Orient." *London Review of Books* 29 (January 4, 2007): 30–34.

Tompkins, Jane. *Sensational Designs: The Cultural Work of American Fiction, 1790–1860.* New York: Oxford University Press, 1985.

Tuan, Yi-Fu. *Cosmos and Hearth: A Cosmopolite's Viewpoint.* Minneapolis: University of Minnesota Press, 1996.

Turner, Jonathan. *On the Origins of Human Emotions: A Sociological Inquiry into the Evolution of Human Affect.* Stanford, CA: Stanford University Press, 2000.

Urry, John. *The Tourist Gaze.* Orig. 1990; London; Thousand Oaks, CA: Sage, 2002.

Useem, John, and Ruth Hill Useem. *The Western-Educated Man in India: A Study of His Social Roles and Influences.* New York: Dryden Press, 1955.

Vertovec, Steven, and Robin Cohen, eds. *Conceiving Cosmopolitanism: Theory, Context and Practice.* New York: Oxford University Press, 2002.

Walkowitz, Rebecca. *Cosmopolitan Style: Modernism beyond the Nation.* New York: Columbia University Press, 2006.

Walzer, Michael. *Arguing about War.* New Haven, CT: Yale University Press, 2004.

Warnow, Catherine, and Regina Weinreich. "Paul Bowles: The Complete Outsider." In *Conversations with Paul Bowles,* ed. Gena Dagel Caponi, pp. 210–217. Jackson: University Press of Mississippi, 1993.

Weik, Alexa. "'The Uses and Hazards of Expatriation': Richard Wright's Cosmopolitanism in Process." *African American Review* 41.3 (Fall 2007): 459–475.

———. "The Wandering Woman: The Challenges of Cosmopolitanism in Kay Boyle's Early Novels." In *Kay Boyle for the Twenty-First Century: New Essays,* ed. Thomas Austenfeld, pp. 151–167. Trier, Germany: Wissenschaftlicher Verlag, Trier, 2008.

Weik von Mossner, Alexa. "Confronting *The Stone Face*: The Critical Cosmopolitanism of William Gardner Smith." *African American Review* 45.1–2 (Spring/Summer 2012): 167–182.

———. "Encountering the Sahara: Embodiment, Emotion, and Material Agency in Paul Bowles's *The Sheltering Sky.*" *Interdisciplinary Studies in Literature and Environment* 20.2 (Spring 2013), in press.

Weinreich, Regina. Contribution to "Aspects of Self: A Bowles Collage." *Twentieth Century Literature* 32.3/4 (Autumn–Winter 1986): 267–274.

Weiss, Timothy. "Paul Bowles as Orientalist: Toward a Nomad Discourse." *Journal of American Studies of Turkey* 7 (1998): 37–61.

Williams, Raymond. *Culture and Society, 1780–1950*. New York: Columbia University Press, 1983.

Wilson, Edmund. *Classics and Commercials: A Literary Chronicle of the Forties*. New York: Farrar, Straus and Company, 1950.

Wilson, Matthew. *Whiteness in the Novels of Charles W. Chesnutt*. Jackson: University Press of Mississippi, 2004.

Won-Shik, Choi. "West Goes East: Pearl Buck's *The Good Earth*." *Korea Magazine* 41.3 (Autumn 2001): 125–148.

Wright, Richard. *Black Boy: A Record of Childhood and Youth*. New York: Harper, 1945.

———. *Black Power: A Record of Reactions in a Land of Pathos*. Orig. 1954; New York: Harper Perennial, 1995.

———. *The Color Curtain: A Report on the Bandung Conference*. Orig. 1956; Jackson: University Press of Mississippi, 1995.

———. "How 'Bigger' Was Born." In *Native Son*, Richard Wright, pp. vii–xxxiv. Orig. 1940; New York: Harper Perennial, 2001.

———. "I Feel More at Home in France than Where I Was Born." In *Conversations with Richard Wright*, ed. Kenneth Kinnamon and Michel Fabre, trans. Michel Fabre, pp. 126–127. Jackson: University Press of Mississippi, 1993.

———. "Island of Hallucination." Undated, unpublished manuscript for a novel (1959). Richard Wright Papers, Yale Collection of American Literature, Beinecke Rare Books and Manuscript Library, Yale University.

———. "I Tried to Be a Communist." *Atlantic Monthly* 159 (August 1944): 61–70.

———. *The Long Dream*. Chatham, NY: Chatham Bookseller, 1958.

———. *Native Son*. Orig. 1940; New York: Harper Perennial, 2001.

———. *The Outsider*. Orig. 1953; New York: Harper Perennial, 2003.

———. *Pagan Spain*. Orig. 1957; Jackson: University Press of Mississippi, 1995.

———. *Uncle Tom's Children*. Orig. 1938; New York: Harper & Row, 1965.

———. *White Man Listen!* Orig. 1957; New York: Harper Perennial, 1995.

Yoshihara, Mari. *Embracing the East: White Women and American Orientalism*. Oxford and New York: Oxford University Press, 2003.

Zapf, Hubert. "Literary Ecology and the Ethics of Texts." *New Literary History* 39.4 (Fall 2008): 847–868.

Žižek, Slavoj. "Against Human Rights." *New Left Review* 34 (July–August 2005): 115–131.

Zunshine, Lisa. *Why We Read Fiction: Theory of Mind and the Novel*. Columbus: Ohio State University Press, 2006.

Lightning Source UK Ltd.
Milton Keynes UK
UKHW012002021021
391359UK00009B/441